THE COMMANDMENTS IN THE NEW TESTAMENT GOSPELS

A Commentary

WWJ—TUT—D?
WHAT WOULD JESUS TELL US TO DO?

Finding who we are under the Messiah, King, and Priest of Israel
Priests after Melchizedek

BEA BALDRIDGE

WESTBOW·
PRESS
A DIVISION OF THOMAS NELSON
& ZONDERVAN

All Scripture quotations, unless otherwise stated, are taken from the King James Version. I have changed the words thou, thy, and thine to you and yours throughout. I have removed the –eth and –est endings on certain words, changed shew to show, thee to you, and changed otherwise archaic spelling of words to modern English. Some sentences have been made clearer by translating them into modern English.

Scripture quotations marked NKJV, taken from the New King James Version. Copyright © 1979, 1980, 1982 by Thomas Nelson, Inc. Used by permission. All rights reserved.

Scripture quotations marked NIV, taken from the Holy Bible, NEW INTERNATIONAL VERSION®. Copyright © 1973, 1978, 1984 by Biblica, Inc. All rights reserved worldwide. Used by permission. NEW INTERNATIONAL VERSION® and NIV® are registered trademarks of Biblica, Inc. Use of either trademark for the offering of goods or services requires the prior written consent of Biblica US, Inc.

WestBow Press books may be ordered through booksellers or by contacting:

WestBow Press
A Division of Thomas Nelson & Zondervan
1663 Liberty Drive
Bloomington, IN 47403
www.westbowpress.com
1 (866) 928-1240

The web addresses (URLs) and web pages recommended throughout this book are solely offered as a resource to the reader. The citation of these web sites does not in any way imply an endorsement on the part of the author or the publisher, nor does the author or publisher vouch for their content for the life of the book.

As web addresses come and go, I have noted in the Notes and References the last time I accessed each web address, which was on October 31, 2014. If the link does not work, just search for the article under the author's name or the name of the article.

The views expressed in this work are solely those of the author and do not necessarily reflect the views of the publisher, and the publisher hereby disclaims any responsibility for them.

Any people depicted in stock imagery provided by Thinkstock are models, and such images are being used for illustrative purposes only. Certain stock imagery © Thinkstock.

ISBN: 978-1-4908-6447-1 (sc)
ISBN: 978-1-4908-6448-8 (hc)
ISBN: 978-1-4908-6446-4 (e)

Library of Congress Control Number: 2015901081

Printed in the United States of America.

WestBow Press rev. date: 1/29/2015

Dedications

This book is dedicated to my Lord and Savior, Jesus Christ, the Messiah, Yeshua HaMashiach. I thank him for saving me, keeping me, and giving me the knowledge and ability to write this book. I thank him for his trust in me, his love for me, and always being there for me. I look forward to his soon coming and living with him for eternity with all my loved ones.

Contents

Acknowledgements

First of all, I want to thank my dad, Arnim Lamb James, for being the example to me of Yeshua/Jesus in the home. He never preached a lot, never taught a lot verbally, but led the life. He would get upset if he heard someone misquote the Bible or preach a sermon that wasn't Biblical. The main thing he taught me was to never fall for any doctrine that wasn't in the Bible, to "study to show myself approved unto God." That advice has been my foundation to keep me from turning to any other doctrine but stick to the Scripturally sound doctrine that I was taught as a child by him. Church was the most important thing in his life and in ours. He made it a joy and privilege to serve the Lord and to fellowship with other believers in Jesus as Savior.

I want to thank my husband, my children, my children's spouses, and my grandchildren for their support through this endeavor, never doubting me, always encouraging. I thank my husband for always being there for me through the hard times and through the good times, never wavering, never doubting that I could write this book. My rock. My knight in shining armor.

How Do I Love You? (Sonnet 43)
Elizabeth Barrett Browning, 1806 – 1861

How do I love you? Let me count the ways.
I love you to the depth and breadth and height
My soul can reach, when feeling out of sight
For the ends of being and ideal grace.

I love you to the level of every day's
Most quiet need, by sun and candle–light.
I love you freely, as men strive for right.
I love you purely, as they turn from praise.
I love you with the passion put to use
In my old griefs, and with my childhood's faith.
I love you with a love I seemed to lose
With my lost saints. I love you with the breath,
Smiles, tears, of all my life; and, if God choose,
I shall but love you better after death.

I want to thank the many pastors and teachers I have had over my life that have brought me to where I am. As I've grown in the Word, you have all been a part of it.

I want to thank my friends, Bertha and Gilbert Pacheco, for their encouragement throughout the process of writing my book and for their input. You have been faithful friends and your support has meant the world to me.

I want to thank my friend, Gayle Mikovich, for always having faith in me and believing in me that I could write this book.

Introduction
The Journey

To give a little of my background, I was raised in a lumber mill town, Gilchrist, Oregon. It was an idyllic little town. Mr. Gilchrist came from Mississippi to build the town and the mill in 1938. He brought many men and their families with him. We were like one big family. Our family went to a Baptist Church in Crescent, about a mile down the road. At the age of eight, in a revival meeting on May 20, 1951, I went forward at the altar call and gave my heart to the Lord. It was my dad's birthday. I believe the evangelist was Blind Uncle Bob. He had a guide dog that would lead him in and then lie under the right front pew while Reverend Bob preached.

Our little church had revival meetings every summer. Some of the most interesting people crossed our paths. There was an evangelist called "Little George." He looked much like Jimmy Dickens, a famous country singer "back in the day." Little George had a huge 10-gallon hat, wore cowboy clothes, and had a guitar and sang. A guitar! In a Baptist church! Wow!

Then there were Maude, Clara, and Jane, three sisters that took turns preaching every night. And they sang. Boy, did they sing! One of them played the old upright piano. That poor little piano had never been played like that! She made it bounce around on the stage while they sang the house down. And boy, could they preach! Each one would try to out-preach the other every night. Happy times.

That little Baptist church was our life. Every Sunday morning, Sunday evening, Wednesday prayer meeting, and young people's meetings. I loved it. I loved the Lord. The night I got saved, they gave me a little red Book of John. I took it home and read it cover to cover. I felt it was speaking right to me. And it was. That is still my favorite book of the New Testament. I don't remember not being able to understand it at all. Some say nowadays that they can't understand the King James Version, but I've never had a problem understanding it. It was my love letter from the Father. I had always loved going to church, but that night when I was born again, accepted Jesus into my heart as my personal Savior, I loved it even more. That night I was changed. I knew I was a sinner and needed a Savior. That night is as real to me today as it was back then.

Growing up, I would see my dad read the Bible a lot. It was a part of our home and life. He would listen to the radio, various preachers, and get so upset if they taught anything not according to the Word. He always told us that if it's not in the Bible, it's not of God. I'm amazed now to think that with just a Bible that had no commentary, no Bible commentaries, no Strong's Concordance, no computer, how he knew the Bible so well. It is because of him that I knew we needed to study the Bible according to 2 Timothy 2:15:

> Study to show yourself approved unto God, a workman that needs not to be ashamed, rightly dividing the Word of truth.

I thank the Lord daily for my foundation biblically. My dad was a wonderful example to us of the Love of the Lord. We knew how much he loved the Lord because of the example he set.

That is my foundation. Knowing what I believed and not veering off the path I was taught, proving everything doctrinally with the Bible, and it was a solid foundational path. I am very blessed to have grown up in that environment. Since that time my husband and I have attended Baptist, Assembly of God, Christian and Missionary Alliance churches, and now we attend a Church of God Cleveland where we have the privilege of having a wonderful pastor and his wife who minister with their hearts to the people.

In about 1998, my husband and I began to study the Hebrew roots of the Scriptures. We have been on quite a journey since that time. I always go back to my roots and the doctrine I was taught and compare teachings with Scripture. I thank the Lord every day for that journey and what we have learned.

The curtain would open, and we would walk through it. So many things we learned along the way about the ways of the Lord. Along the way we would have warnings from the Holy Spirit if someone tried to teach us something that isn't scriptural. We would search it out and always come back to our foundational beliefs. There are many, many churches these days and they all have their Statement of Faith. Take a look at the one for your church and make sure it's biblically sound.

Remember that in order to know if something is biblically sound, you have to have read the Bible through. You have to know the real to recognize the counterfeit. It's not that you have to memorize the entire Word, although that would be great if we all could, but he promises to bring it to our minds.

> John 14:26: But the Comforter, which is the Holy Ghost, whom the Father will send in my name, he shall teach you all things, and bring all things to your remembrance, whatsoever I have said unto you.

After we got married, my husband got saved in "my" little Baptist Church. I am very blessed that he did. The Lord is the reason we have been married at this time for 55 years.

I first had a King James Version Bible that my sister, June, gave me when I was twelve. Many years later I got my first Bible that had commentary and got a Strong's Concordance. I still have it. It is gigantic and weighs about five pounds! As the years have gone by, I have had several Bibles, my favorite so far being the Thomas Nelson Study Bible that I have now. It is quite comprehensive. I like the New King James Version.

I have many "helps" at my fingertips besides the Thomas Nelson Study Bible. Now we have computers! I believe God the Father allowed men to invent them for believers in him to use. There's a lot of "stuff" you can get into that isn't good. However, as a believer, the computer has opened up a whole realm of Bible information that is at my disposal. One of the web sites I constantly use is called Blue Letter Bible. It is a free program on the internet and is fantastic.

Another tool I use is PC Bible by Bible Soft. It is a digital Bible program. I bought this program because it was the only one I could find at the time that was truly interlinear Hebrew and Greek and is linked to the Strong's Concordance numbers. I have it open when I am studying to check out words in Hebrew and Greek.

I also learned Hebrew a few years ago and now teach beginning and intermediate. I'm not to the point where I speak it very much, which wasn't my goal. My goal was to be able to read Hebrew and look up words and understand the true Hebrew meanings. I can read the Bible in Hebrew and recognize whether a word in English was translated correctly from the Hebrew. Hebrew words have several meanings. It is always the translator's choice of which one to use. I often say, "Why in the world did they translate that word that way?" The interpretation is chosen by the interpreter. This happens in Hebrew publications and English publications, and I'm sure other languages. It's good to know Hebrew well enough to recognize the deeper meaning of the words. I would encourage you to learn Hebrew and be able to read the Bible in its original language. It will open up a whole new world for you.

Over the years I have been a Sunday school teacher, Bible study teacher, Hebrew teacher, and have grown in the Word. I taught Sunday School 29 years, but not until I traveled to Israel in the year 2000 was the Word opened up to me like it was after I came back home. I walked where he walked, saw what he saw, and traveled to the places that were in the

Bible that I had only imagined before. Your whole perspective changes after you visit the place of the Book. I would encourage you to go to Israel at least once to have your eyes opened to the reality of what it really looks like. You can see how the places look that are in the Bible that you've only read about. I came back with a new zeal to study the Bible. As I read it now, it is like I am there and can see what it looked like in that place. Amazing! We have gone to Israel three times now and we would go again today if we could.

I now teach Hebrew in our home and at church and Bible classes to anyone that asks me to. I have been quite blessed in my life to have had the students I have had. When teaching, you have to stay ahead of your students, so that's one reason I like to keep teaching. It keeps me in the Word and up on the subjects. I've also had other offices in different churches and enjoyed that too. So that is my background.

About the same time that I went to Israel, I learned that we as Christians study differently than the Jews. In America, our mode of study is pretty much as the Greeks study. In studying the Word, we need to go back to the time the books were written and learn to whom they were written and what they meant at that time. Going back to the First Century and understanding their mindset and what was going on at that time politically and socially is the number one step in understanding the Christian Torah/New Testament. We need to understand the idioms that were used at that time and understand the audience Yeshua/Jesus was speaking to. They understood what he meant when he used these idioms. We have to learn to put the text back into the context the writers meant it to be.

An idiom is a combination of words that has a figurative meaning, due to its common usage. An idiom's figurative meaning is separate from the literal meaning or definition of the words of which it is made.

Suppose I asked you if you wanted to come over for "turkey day?" Wouldn't you know that that day is Thanksgiving? That is one of our American idioms.

The Heart of Wisdom web site has an excellent chart on the comparison of Greek versus Hebrew Education for children.

Here's an article by Robin Sampson from that web site:

Greek versus Hebrew Education
By Robin Sampson on April 05, 2010

"What we now consider 'The Church' is almost nothing like the Early New Testament Church. Think of an archeologist digging through layers to find out what life was like in ancient times.

Historians concur that the Greeks were destroyed by moral decay. Pursuing knowledge without God is a recipe for disaster. We simply cannot survive without clear moral direction. Look at the differences in education goals:

	Ancient Greek Education (as taught in Public Schools today)	Ancient Hebrew Education
Goal	Prepare individuals to serve the state.	Prepare individuals to serve God.
How Accomplished	1) Memorize the laws of Lycurgus, the Spartan lawgiver. 2) Memorize selections from Homer. 3) Develop physical excellence through games, exercises, and the pentathlon (running, jumping, throwing the discus, casting the javelin, and wrestling)	1) Transmit knowledge and skills from generation to generation. 2) Increase knowledge and skills. 3) Concretize cultural values into accepted behavior
	Teach students to trust the state.	Teach children to trust God in everything.
	Prepare for the state.	Prepare for eternity.
	Examine the world by classifying whole things into parts by removing them from the Creator. Redefine knowledge: Final reality is impersonal matter or energy, shaped into its present form by impersonal chance.	Look at God's world as a whole–interconnecting–revealing God in every area. The heavens declare the glory of God; and the firmaments show his handiwork (Psalm 19:1).
	Immerse students in literature written by ancient Greek philosophers.	Teach children to love learning so they will become self-motivated, lifelong learners.
	Focus on self-esteem, emotional adjustment, and external training of the body. Develop endurance, resourcefulness, and physical prowess.	Discover a child's God-given gifts and talents, and develop them to their fullest potential. Focus on spiritual training.
Result	Self-centered: "My will be done." Violence, corruption, pornography, racial tension, promiscuity, abortion, infanticide, etc.	God-centered: "Your will be done." Authority with responsibility. Literacy, strong family ties, love of learning, security, independent thinking, high morals and values.

Curriculum Subjects	Humanism Evolution Social Studies	Bible Creation Science "His Story" (true history) Character Self-government (internal obedience to God)
Curriculum Content	Trivium, the three stages: Grammar Logic (Dialectic) Rhetoric	The three main orders of study in ancient Israel consisted of: Religious education Occupational skills Military training with the basis of all knowledge being the fear of the Lord (Psalm 111:10; Proverbs 1:7).
Curriculum Text	Books by Homer, Aristotle, Virgil, Pliny, Cicero.	God's Word. Orthodox schools did not study subjects derived from Classical tradition.
Heroes	Homer, Plato, Socrates, Aristotle, Epicurus, Zeno	Abraham, Isaac, Jacob, Joshua, and David (Old Testament)
Philosophy	Lawlessness: To each his own. Look out for Number One. There are no absolutes.	Lawfulness. Love one another. The last shall be first. Deny yourself. Obey God's Commandments.
	That this is a rebellious people, lying children, children that will not hear the law of the Lord (Isaiah 30:9).	Submit yourselves to every ordinance of man for the Lord's sake: whether it be to the king, as supreme; or unto governors, as unto them that are sent by him for the punishment of evildoers, and for the praise of them that do well (1 Peter 2:13-14).

To understand the Early Church we must dig through layers of a mountain of man's influences, shoveling off and discarding man's traditions, theories, interpretations, and philosophies from Greek and Roman civilizations, Aristotle, Constantine, Marcion, etc., to be able to examine the Early Church.

During the Reformation, men such as Wycliffe and Calvin were digging in the right spot. They dug up and discarded many theological errors and found a view of God's plan of salvation by grace, but anti-Semitic layers remain and now there are new layers of tradition, interpretations, western thought (a return to the Greek and Roman philosophy), and conditioning that needs removal. Only then can we have a clear view of the Early Church.

Greek philosophy between Aristotle and Augustine is the foundation of Western thought (Aristotle tried to merge the Bible and Plato = Hellenistic Philosophy), which is the reason for so much Greek philosophy in the church."

Another great article on the subject of Greek versus Hebrew Education is by Tim Hegg of Torah Resource. It is done in two parts. (See reference page for link.)

We must first go back to the people of the Book to understand how to think Hebraically. Jesus taught Hebraically. Christianity is a root of the Jewish faith, so we must study the way HE taught.

How does all this fit into our study of the New Testament? It opens our eyes as to HOW to study and to focus on OUR story, the story from Genesis to the Book of Revelation, the story of the Messiah coming to earth to live and die for us, to be resurrected the third day that we may believe in him and be saved, that is told from the first verse in Genesis to the last verse in the Book of Revelation.

But what exactly are we supposed to do as Christians?

How are we supposed to live?

What are OUR commandments?

I hope to answer those questions in this book.

Preface

Covenants

I begin by using a term that helps me clear up the mindset of "Old Testament, New Testament." In the Hebrew publications, the Old Testament is simply called the Torah. That word means "instruction and teaching." It can refer to the entire Old Testament or the first five books of the Old Testament/Torah: Genesis, Exodus, Leviticus, Numbers, and Deuteronomy. This is what we call the Pentateuch.

I would like to call our New Testament the New Covenant, which in Hebrew is *Brit Chadashah* — our instruction and teaching — to instill a mindset that the New Testament was written to those under the New Covenant of Yeshua/Jesus. This covenant was written to those who receive Yeshua/Jesus into their hearts, believe he is the Messiah who came to save the world from their sins, believe he died on the cross and rose again the third day, and believe that if we believe in him, we will receive eternal life. 1 Corinthians 11:24–26 is my main verse to help us focus on the subject:

> And when he had given thanks, he broke it, and said, Take, eat: this is my body, which is broken for you: this do in remembrance of me. 25. After the same manner also he took the cup, when he had supped, saying, this cup is the New Testament (covenant) in my blood: this do you, as oft as you drink it, in remembrance of me. 26. For as often as you eat this bread, and drink this cup, you do show the Lord's death till he comes.

Also see the whole eleventh chapter of 1 Corinthians.

> *Diathēkē–Testament* from Strong's Concordance, #G1242:
> 1. A disposition, arrangement, of any sort, which one wishes
> to be valid, the last disposition which one makes of his earthly
> possessions after his death, a testament or will; 2. a compact, a
> covenant, a testament.

So he's speaking about his legal will!

Here are others:

> Matthew 26:28: For this is my blood of the New Testament
> (covenant), which is shed for many for the remission of sins. See
> Matthew 26:27–29 in context.

> Mark 14:24: And he said to them, "This is my blood of the
> New Testament (covenant), which is shed for many." See Mark
> 14:23–25 in context.

> Luke 22:20: Likewise he also took the cup after supper, saying,
> "This cup is the New Testament (covenant) in my blood, which
> is shed for you." See Luke 22:19–21 in context.

> Romans 11:27: For this is my covenant with them, when I take
> away their sins. See Romans 11:26–28 in context.

> Hebrews 8:9: "Not according to the covenant that I made with
> their fathers in the day when I took them by the hand to lead
> them out of the land of Egypt; because they did not continue
> in my covenant, and I disregarded them," says the Lord. See
> Hebrews 8:8 in context.

> Hebrews 8:10: "For this is the covenant that I will make with the
> house of Israel after those days," says the Lord: "I will put my
> laws in their mind and write them on their hearts; and I will be

their God, and they shall be my people." See Hebrews 8:9–11 in context.

Hebrews 10:16: "This is the covenant that I will make with them after those days," says the Lord: "I will put my laws into their hearts, and in their minds I will write them." See Hebrews 10:15–17 in context.

At the outset I want you to see what this book is about: Focusing on OUR covenant, written to us:

Hebrews 4:14: Seeing then that we have a great High Priest, that is passed into the heavens, Jesus the Son of God, let us hold fast our profession (or confession).

We have a High Priest! Do the above verses sound like the Mosaic covenant? Or the Adamic covenant? Or the Abrahamic covenant? Or the Noahide covenant? He says this is a New Covenant.

Hebrews 3:1: Wherefore, holy brethren, partakers of the heavenly calling, consider the Apostle and High Priest of our profession, Christ Jesus.

May I add, notice he is our Priest and King! The Levitical priesthood consisted of only priests, never a king. Here we find Yeshua/Jesus is both! His stepfather, Joseph, was from the tribe of Judah, so Yeshua/Jesus has the right to the throne as King of Israel. I believe he is from the tribe of Levi through his mother, Mary. (Please see her genealogy at Luke 3:23–38.) There is controversy concerning whether this is the genealogy of Joseph or Mary; but, John the Baptist's mother, Elizabeth, who was Mary's cousin, was from the tribe of Levi. (Luke 1:36.) IF it is true that it is Mary's genealogy, he had the lineage of Judah through his step-father, Joseph, and the lineage of Levi through his mother and is eligible to be king and priest. To the Israelites, the lineage of the child is from the mother.

So, that's why it's hard for the Jews to understand how you could be king and also be a priest. Either you were a priest or you were a king; never both except in the case of Melchizedek! After the Mosaic Law was written, all priests had to be from the tribe of Levi. The first king of Israel came from the tribe of Benjamin, King Saul, then from Judah through King David. We know our soon coming King, Yeshua/Jesus, is from the tribe of Judah.

To understand what this is all about — who we are — we need to go back to the covenant God entered into with Israel at Sinai.

> Deuteronomy 29:10,12,14,15: 10. You stand this day all of you before the Lord your God; your captains of your tribes, your elders, and your officers, with all the men of Israel, 12. that you should enter into covenant with the Lord your God, and into his oath, which the Lord your God makes with you this day: 14. Neither with you only do I make this covenant and this oath; 15. but with him that stands here with us this day before the Lord our God, and also with him that is not here with us this day:

This is an important key to understanding who we are. The first thing we need to do when reading the Bible is to ask who God is talking to.

Who was he talking to here? The Israelites who had come out of Egypt, plus the many that came out with them called "the stranger and the foreigner." In order to live with the Israelites, they had to enter into a covenant with the Israelites and vow to follow the True God and then they became part of the Nation of Israel. They were called "proselytes, sojourners in the land, converts." Those who fully converted were called "proselytes of righteousness."

See Exodus 20:10, 23:12; Exodus 12:19, 12:48; Deuteronomy 5:14, 16:11, 16:14.

The confusion comes where it says:

"But with him that stands here with us this day before the Lord our God, and also with him that is not here with us this day." Deuteronomy 29:15.

The ones who are "far off" are not Christians. He is talking about those Jews born over the centuries and those who have converted. We Gentiles were not given the Sinaitic covenant. We were not standing that day at Mt. Sinai and receiving the covenant. Think about it. If God is saying it *is* us, why did Yeshua/Jesus have to come and die on the cross for us? We could have just converted to Judaism!

Does that sound like part of the Sinaitic covenant? No. Gentiles are not part of that unless they convert to Judaism and become "Jews" by conversion.

God then says in Jeremiah after Israel broke the covenant given at Sinai (but he never broke it):

> Jeremiah 31:31-32: 31. Behold, the days come, says the Lord, that I will make a New Covenant with the house of Israel, and with the house of Judah: 32. Not according to the covenant that I made with their fathers in the day that I took them by the hand to bring them out of the land of Egypt; which my covenant they broke, although I was a husband unto them, says the Lord:

> Jeremiah 31:34: And they shall teach no more every man his neighbor, and every man his brother, saying, Know the Lord: for they shall all know me, from the least of them unto the greatest of them, says the Lord: for I will forgive their iniquity, and I will remember their sin no more.

But where do the Gentiles come in?

> Ephesians 2:11–13: 11. Wherefore remember, that you being in time past Gentiles in the flesh, who are called Uncircumcision by that which is called the Circumcision in the flesh made by hands; 12. That at that time you were without Christ, being

aliens from the commonwealth of Israel, and strangers from the covenants of promise, having no hope, and without God in the world: 13. But now in Christ Jesus you who sometimes were far off are made nigh by the blood of Christ.

There was no other way to God for us Gentiles. How could the whole plan be made any clearer? Paul is saying, "There was not a chance for you Gentiles to ever be able to come to God until Jesus came to make a way for you." By his blood he saved us.

Romans 1:16: For I am not ashamed of the gospel of Christ: for it is the power of God unto salvation to everyone that believes; to the Jew first, and also to the Greek.

Romans 2:10: But glory, honor, and peace, to every man that works good, to the Jew first, and also to the Gentile:

Why the Jew first? What did he promise in Jeremiah 31? What do we have to do to be part of the New Covenant, the Brit Chadashah?

I Corinthians 15:1–4: 1. Moreover, brethren, I declare unto you the gospel which I preached unto you, which also you have received, and wherein you stand; 2. By which also you are saved, if you keep in memory what I preached unto you, unless you have believed in vain. 3. For I delivered unto you first of all that which I also received, how that Christ died for our sins according to the Scriptures; 4. And that he was buried, and that he rose again the third day according to the Scriptures:

John 3:16–18: 16. For God so loved the world, that he gave his only begotten Son, that whosoever believes in him should not perish, but have everlasting life. 17. For God sent not his Son into the world to condemn the world; but that the world through him might be saved. 18. He that believes on him is not condemned: but he that believes not is condemned already, because he has not believed in the name of the only begotten Son of God.

What is the gospel? The good news that the Messiah has come, the Savior of the world.

Does any of this sound like the covenant given at Sinai? We are a part of the New Covenant. We do not become Jewish when we get saved. Being Jewish is a physical, separate entity, part of the DNA. Israel is a nation. We do not become part of that nation or people when we get saved.

It was about 15 years before any Gentiles got saved that we know of. Look at the story in Acts about Cornelius. In Acts 15, a decision was made about the Gentiles and what they would have to do in order to be able to have table fellowship with the Jewish Christians. These rules did not "save" them.

The first step in understanding the Bible is to understand who you are and who the Jews are. The second step is to study and understand the covenants, to learn what covenant you are under. When you get that sorted out, then you can begin to understand God and his plan for mankind.

Misquoting

Since the beginning of time, humans have been misquoting the words God really said. The first, of course, was Chava/Eve and the snake, Satan. They added to what Adam had told Chava that God had commanded them. Ever since that day, the human race has either added to, taken away, or given Scripture their own interpretation. We have many, many denominations of Christian churches because of this. One man's interpretation begats another one, and so on, until we interpret ourselves out of fellowship with one another. As Adam, we blame the other person, as he did Chava.

One of the biggest problems we have is that not many of us can read the original language the books of the Bible were written in. If we could, this would eliminate a huge amount of mistranslations. It is said some Hebrew words can have up to 10 meanings. How then does the translator decide which word to use? We wouldn't have to have translations if we would learn Hebrew and Greek. We have resources available to us to learn these languages. I'm learning Hebrew, but not fluent in it, nor am I to the point where I don't need these resources, but I'm striving towards that.

I do realize that it is still the choice of the translator. With tools like PC Bible, Logos, and Blue Letter Bible, we can get a much better idea of how and why it is translated as it is.

What Commandments?

How can we determine what commandments Yeshua the Messiah (Jesus the Christ) specifically told us to do? How are we supposed to live? Which commandments belong to us? How can we stop the confusion? I've seen friends over the years bounce back and forth between the testaments, quoting the Torah (The Old Testament) sometimes like it is our covenant, than saying we're not "under the law" heaven forbid. Or, are we lawless?

Do we follow the Ten Commandments? Ask almost any Christian and they will say "sure." Really? And, again, here's the big question we need to ask ourselves about any Scripture: Who was God talking to when he gave that Scripture? In the case of the Ten Commandments, the Israelite Nation. These, along with many other commandments, make up the 613 "laws" God gave the Israelite Nation. This word for *"law"* means *instruction*. It is the word Torah, Strong's Concordance #H8451. Christians shudder and run from anything called "law." This is a shame. Paul said in Galatians 3:24-25:

> 24. Wherefore the law was our schoolmaster to bring us unto Christ, that we might be justified by faith. 25: But after that faith is come, we are no longer under a schoolmaster.

Paidagōgos is the Greek word used here for *schoolmaster*. Strong's Concordance #G3807: A tutor, this is a guardian and guide of boys. Among the Greeks and the Romans the name was applied to trustworthy slaves who were charged with the duty of supervising the life and morals of boys belonging to the better class. The boys were not allowed so much as to step out of the house without them before arriving at the age of manhood.

Paul goes on to say here that there is neither Jew nor Greek, bond or free, male or female, for we are all one in Yeshua the Messiah.

So are we as Christians "under the law?" How can we know one way or another? And what does that mean? Remember, Torah means instruction and teaching. Again, are we lawless?

I had been praying for quite a while that the Lord would help me to help believers understand what our commandments are and what our doctrine should be. There are so many beliefs these days and more cropping up daily. So many roads traveled. So many at the crossroads wondering, "What am I supposed to do?" I believe I'm supposed to obey the Ten Commandments, but what about the other 603 in the Torah? That would certainly be putting me under the law wouldn't it?

I would try to explain to friends and people I met that we're not "under the law." We do not become a member of the physical Nation of Israel when we become believers in Yeshua as our Savior. The Bible says we become "new creatures." Did he ever promise PHYSICAL ISRAEL that? We aren't promised the physical Land of Israel. The Jews are. The physical Jews. The sons of Jacob. We don't physically get a blood transfusion and our blood does not change its DNA when we get saved. We remain the same physically. It is our soul that is transformed, renewed, born again, and become new creatures in Yeshua HaMashiach (Jesus the Messiah). There is major confusion about this, but it is so simple. Of course, the Jews that do accept Yeshua as their Messiah do become new creatures in him. They are still natural born Israelites physically. Their DNA does not change physically. Stern words from the Book of Revelation warn about saying you're a Jew and you're not:

Revelation 2:9: I know your works, and tribulation, and poverty, (but you art rich) and I know the blasphemy of them which say they are Jews, and are not, but are of the synagogue of Satan.

Revelation 3:9: Behold, I will make them of the synagogue of Satan, which say they are Jews, and are not, but do lie ; behold, I will make them to come and worship before your feet, and to know that I have loved you.

If you graft a wild olive into a regular olive tree, that branch still puts forth wild olives. Ask any orchard grower. You don't automatically become an olive just because you're grafted into an olive tree. You are part of the olive tree, but still a wild olive.

So what is the key to knowing without a doubt what our instructions are when becoming believers in Yeshua the Messiah?

One Friday I was praying and was impressed to sit down and read the entire Book of Hebrews straight through without stopping, without reading the commentary, without looking up words in the concordance. My husband had a men's breakfast the next day, early Saturday morning, and I got up and grabbed my Bible and read Hebrews straight through while he was gone to the meeting. I got so excited about what I read that I couldn't wait to share it with my husband when he came home. I asked him if he would allow me to read the Book of Hebrews out loud to him straight through without talking about it, commenting on it, or asking questions. He agreed. He got excited about what we were reading. It wasn't some strange interpretation. It was The New King James that we mainly use. It was like we had never read it before in our lives!

Hebrews is the only book in the New Covenant written directly to the "Hebrews," or Jews, or Israelites. It is said to have been written by Paul. I agree. However, in being grafted in, we, as Gentiles, need to see what Paul was saying to them.

In reading, I began to notice Paul saying in Hebrews, "You are a priest forever after the order of Melchizedec." Five times he says this. Four other times in Hebrews Melchizedec is also mentioned.

Hebrews 5:6: As he says also in another place, You are a priest forever after the order of Melchisedec. (See Psalms 110:4.)

Hebrews 5:10: Called of God a High Priest after the order of Melchisedec.

Hebrews 6:20: As he says also in another place, You are a priest forever after the order of Melchisedec.

Hebrews 7:1: For this Melchisedec, king of Salem, priest of the most high God, who met Abraham returning from the slaughter of the kings, and blessed him;

Hebrews 7:10: For he was yet in the loins of his father, when Melchisedec met him (speaking of Levi).

Hebrews 7:11: If therefore perfection were by the Levitical priesthood, (for under it the people received the law,) what further need was there that another priest should rise after the order of Melchisedec, and not be called after the order of Aaron?

Hebrews 7:15: And it is yet far more evident: for that after the similitude of Melchisedec there arises another priest,

Hebrews 7:17,21: 17. For he testified, you are a priest forever after the order of Melchisedec. 21. (For those priests were made without an oath; but this with an oath by him that said unto him, The Lord swore and will not repent, you are a priest forever after the order of Melchisedec:)

What? Why am I just now in my life noticing this? What is this "order of Melchizedec?"

I remembered the story of Abraham returning from the battle of the five kings and tithing to this person in Genesis and having communion with him. I checked it out. In the Torah, his name is Melchizedek with a Z. In the King James Version it is spelled Melchisedec. In the New King James Version it is Melchizedek. This "name" means *"King of Righteousness."* The word *"malchi"* means "king" in Hebrew. The word *"zedek"* means righteous. Some of the Jewish commentaries say they believe he was Shem. He lived in Jerusalem. Paul says Salem, which is one of the names for JeruSALEM, in Hebrew *shalom – peace*. I also believe he was physically Shem, but was a picture of "the order of Melchizedek" to come.

> Genesis 14:18-19: 18. And Melchizedek king of Salem brought forth bread and wine: and he was the priest of the Most High God. 19. And he blessed him, and said, blessed be Abram of the most high God, possessor of heaven and earth: 20. And blessed be the Most High God, which has delivered your enemies into your hand. And he gave him tithes of all.

> The word for *God Most High* here is *Elyon*, Strong's Concordance #H5945, which means "high, upper, highest, most high, a name of God, of rulers, either monarch or angel princes." The word *"Elyon"* is in the Torah 53 times. It is used for higher gate, higher court, etc., but used often also for *The Most High God*.

So Melchizedek was a priest of Elyon, The Most High God.

The only other place in the Torah that he is mentioned is in Psalms 110:4:

> The Lord has sworn, and will not repent, You are a priest forever after the order of Melchizedek.

Notice this Scripture says "forever." So this is an eternal priesthood. And in this context, Paul is talking about Yeshua. Hm–m. What have we missed? Did you ever hear a sermon on these Scriptures? Probably some of you have, but strangely, I don't remember ever hearing one until recently by Perry Stone. Nor do I remember ever discussing this with anyone.

I did find an item of information in the Dead Sea Scrolls about Melchizedek. This is in 11Q13, Column 2. "Your divine being is Melchizedek, who will deliver them from the power of Belial."

This certainly says that Melchizedek is divine and will deliver "them" from the power of Belial!

My book is about the Order of Melchizedek for the believers as laid out in the Book of Hebrews and the entire New Covenant. Our covenant. It is putting biblical facts together into our covenant under Jesus the Messiah, Yeshua HaMashiach, and what we are to do and how we are to act as believers.

So my search was on. We meet with a couple on Wednesday nights to study. I shared this with them. She was intrigued with "the order of," what is "the order?" Well, to the rest of us it was "the rules." If you join a club, such as the Elks, the Moose Club, etc., they have a book of rules. So what ARE the rules of this club of Melchizedek? And where do we find them? And what about the Scripture that says in Hebrews 7:3:

> "Without father, without mother, without descent, having neither beginning of days, nor end of life; but made like unto the Son of God; abides a priest continually."

Some Christian commentaries state that they believe Melchizedek is the pre-existent "Christ" as they put it. Of course, we believe the pre-existent Yeshua/Jesus was seen at different times in the Old Testament; for instance, by Abraham after his circumcision, and other places in the Torah. Abraham didn't seem the least bit surprised though, did he? And he seemed to be used to paying this guy Melchizedek his tithe. He had communion with him. Here we have the first picture in the Torah of the blood and body of the Messiah, the bread and the wine.

Never again in the Torah do we see the bread and the wine as communion mentioned except in the sacrifices done under the Mosaic covenant. We see it mentioned three times again in the New Covenant:

Matthew 26:26: And as they were eating, Jesus took bread, and blessed it, and broke it, and gave it to the disciples, and said, Take, eat; this is my body.

Mark 14:22: And as they did eat, Jesus took bread, and blessed, and broke it, and gave to them, and said, Take, eat: this is my body.

1 Corinthians 11:24: And when he had given thanks, he broke it, and said, Take, eat: this is my body, which is broken for you: this do in remembrance of me.

So I began searching commentaries on the Book of Hebrews. Books are my life, so I have many. There was nothing different in any of them, even the Jewish ones. I searched online. There are many articles about Melchizedek, but nothing to explain this "order" and who he was. I prayed and prayed and asked the Lord to give me the answer we needed. There was a key here I was missing.

Finally, a couple days later, one of my favorite authors of all time came to mind. Arthur Pink! I have loved his books for years. He is one of the biggest reasons I love to study types and shadows in the Scriptures. He lived from 1886 to 1952. I have many of his books, but didn't know if he had even written one on the Book of Hebrews. His books are all available online now in the public domain. I went to one of the web sites that have his books and voila! The Book of Hebrews! I copied and pasted the chapters on Melchizedek to my word processor. I found the exact answer I had been searching for. The answer is so simple that many of us have missed it. Many of us have bounced back and forth between the Torah, quoting the Ten Commandments, quoting other Scripture as if written to us. (All Scripture is ordained of God, but we must differentiate between whether it is written TO us or FOR us, for our insight into God's heart.) Confusion has reigned.

In Arthur Pink's thirtieth chapter of his book on Hebrews he says,

> "And here men that die receive tithes; but there he of whom
> it is witnessed that he lives" (Hebrews 7:8). Here the apostle
> advances a further argument to support his demonstration
> of the inferiority of the Aaronic order of priesthood to the
> Melchizedekean: the "here" referring to the former, the
> "there" to the latter as stated in Genesis 14. The point singled
> out for notice is that, the Levitical order of office was but
> temporary, not so of that priest who blest Abraham. "The type
> is described as having no end; the order of priesthood which it
> represents is therefore eternal." (Calvin) The Scripture makes
> no mention of the death of Melchizedek when it relates that
> tithes were paid to him; so the authority of his priesthood
> is limited to no time, but on the contrary there is given an
> intimation of perpetuity."

The Key

Here's the key: It is not about the <u>man</u>, it is about the <u>priesthood</u>. The
man is not eternal, but it is the <u>priesthood</u> that is eternal:

> Hebrews 7:3: Without father, without mother, without descent,
> having neither beginning of days, nor end of life; but made like
> unto the Son of God; abides a priest continually.

I've been confused over that verse my whole life, and, like I said, would
skip right over it, not knowing where to get information about this. Most
of us say, "Oh, well, I don't know what it means," and go our merry way.
We have been missing the KEY to the New Covenant. We are not part
of the old covenant. That was given to the <u>Israelite Nation</u>. We are never
promised their promises. We are part of the New Man, a new creation, a
royal priesthood. This answers so many questions that we all have had
about who we are. It is such a relief to me to find out exactly who we
are and to help people realize what commandments we are to follow and
where we fit in the big scheme of things.

My husband and I read the weekly Parashah, or portion, of Scripture from the Torah every week (we call it the Pentateuch) that most Jewish people follow. All the portions are named for one of the Hebrew beginning words of the first sentence; for instance, Genesis/Bereishit 1:1–6:8 is named Bereishit, In the Beginning, the first portion that is read after the New Year. The whole book of Genesis in Hebrew is named Bereishit.

After I discovered the information about the priesthood not being about the man, but about the priesthood, we read Parashah Emor, Leviticus 21:1–24: Emor means "and he said." In chapter 21, it is talking about the kohanim/priests, giving them instructions. The Hebrew/English Bible we use has a lot of commentary. In the commentary to 21:4, it is talking about contamination from a dead person that is allowed/disallowed for priests/kohanim. The Great Kohen, or high priest, has to be stricter than the regular kohen.

"The reason for this difference is that a kohen's holy status is not earned; since it comes to him only by birth, he honors his family by participating in their burial. A Kohen Gadol, however, must be personally worthy of his exalted status, and a nazir (nazarite) accepts his holy status upon himself voluntarily. The family tragedy, therefore, may not interfere with their required ritual purity. (R' Avraham of Sochatchov.)

I was shocked. Here was confirmation to my revelation about Melchizedek. It's not the man who is holy, it's the priesthood.

For a long time, I have wanted to write a book on The Commandments of Yeshua. I have tried to help people see that the Ten Commandments and the other 603 Commandments in the Torah were given to the Israelite Nation at Sinai when they said "I do" at the mountain. That was their covenantal contract as the chosen nation of God.

When we said "I do" to Yeshua, we came under this eternal priesthood, without beginning or end, having neither father or mother, having neither beginning of days nor end of life through Abraham. Our priest was, is, and is to come. This priesthood existed before the earthly Melchizedek and exists today in our High Priest, Yeshua HaMashiach, Jesus the Messiah. We will live and reign with him for eternity. The New Covenant is our covenantal contract as the new believers in Yeshua the Mashiach/Jesus our Savior.

> Revelation 5:10: And has made us unto our God kings and priests: and we shall reign on the earth.

> Revelation 22:5: And there shall be no night there; and they need no candle, neither light of the sun; for the Lord God gives them light: and they shall reign forever and ever.

Arthur Pink points out in Chapter 30 of his book on Hebrews:

> "In Hebrews 2:17, the apostle announced that the Lord Jesus is "a merciful and faithful High Priest in things pertaining to God", while in Hebrews 3:1 he calls on those who are partakers of the heavenly calling to "Consider the Apostle and High Priest of our profession". Having shown in Hebrews chapters three and four the superiority of Christianity's Apostle over Judaism's, viz. Moses, whose work was completed by Joshua, Paul then declared that "We have a great High Priest, that is passed through the heavens, Jesus the Son of God", an High Priest who can be touched with the feeling of our infirmities, seeing that he also was tempted in all points like us (in his spirit, his soul, and his body), sin excepted; for which reason we are bidden to "Come boldly unto the throne of grace, that we may obtain mercy, and find grace to help in time of need." (Hebrews 4:14–16).

> In the opening verses of Hebrews 5 we are shown how Christ fulfilled the Aaronic type, and how that he possessed every necessary perfection to qualify him for filling the sacerdotal (*relating to or characteristic of a priest or the priesthood*) office, see articles 19 to 21. But while the Holy Spirit there shows how

Christ provided the substance of what was foreshadowed by the Levitical priests, he is also particular to exhibit how that Christ excelled them at every point. Finally, he declares that the Lord Jesus was, "Called of God a High Priest after the order of Melchizedek" (verse 10). We have previously called attention to it, but as this detail is so important and so little understood, we repeat: it is highly essential to observe that Christ is not there said to be "High Priest of the order of Melchizedek", but "after the order of", etc. The difference between the two expressions is real and radical: "of" would have limited His priesthood to that particular order; "after" simply shows that there is a resemblance between them, as there also was between Aaron's and Christ's.

At Hebrews 5:11 the apostle declared, 'Of whom we have many things to say and hard to be uttered, seeing you are dull of hearing.' The difficulty lay in the strong disinclination of man to relinquish that which has long been cherished, which nowhere appears more evident than in connection with religious things."

I would suggest that in order to get greater insight into this subject that you read Arthur Pink's book on the Book of Hebrews. He is pretty adamant about saying that the covenant with the children of Israel has been done away with, which I don't agree with, God never did away with any of his covenants, another story, but overall his commentary can be very informative and show us pictures/symbols in the Bible of Yeshua/Jesus.

So I come to this point of knowing who we are and to the subject: The order of Melchizedek, or, as Arthur Pink says, "After the order of Melchizedek." What is this order and where do we find it? Well, of course, in our covenant writings of our High Priest/King, Yeshua/Jesus. The New Covenant, Brit Chadashah. Most of us know a lot about what Yeshua/Jesus said during his time here on earth, but do we really understand that this is our order/rules written by him for us? There are many places on the internet where you can find lists of his commandments, or you already know most of them from reading the Bible, but I would like to take the time to break them down for us. In breaking them down, you need to know something about Temple language and how to tie it into some of the commandments he and the writers of the New Covenant wrote. A good part of the entire Bible is related to Temple language. I was told one time that it is about 80 percent. I don't know, but I know there are a lot of pictures or types in the Old and New Testaments concerning the Temple.

In the next chapter, we will begin with the Book of Matthew and research the first leg of our journey. From there we will go on to the rest of the gospels in the New Covenant and see what we come up with. The Jews have 613 commandments to obey. It may surprise you to find out how many we have in the New Covenant. In any case, THESE are OUR commandments! Our order. Our Torah/instructions. Our covenantal contract.

How many covenants are there? The Edenic covenant, The Adamic covenant, The Noahic covenant, The Abrahamic covenant, The Sinaitic covenant or Mosaic covenant, The Davidic covenant, and the New Covenant. God never reneged on any of his covenants. But which covenant are we under? The New Covenant. The Brit Chadashah.

Commandments in the Book of Matthew

The commandment number is listed to the left of the commandment verses. I have included pertinent other verses to give the context of the commandment.

The first thing we need to do when reading the Christian Torah is remember who Yeshua/Jesus was speaking to throughout the gospels. The people he was talking to in the gospels were Jews who knew the Torah/Old Testament. He spoke with many idioms and key words that we have lost the meaning of along the way after the Gentile Christians got separated from the Jewish believers under Constantine. There are only a couple of places where he spoke to Gentiles in the gospels.

There were no Gentile believers in Yeshua/Jesus that we know of until Cornelius and his family in the Book of Acts, Chapter 10. (See the chapter on Melchizedek.) He was a Roman Centurion. There were some Gentiles called "God-fearers" that were sympathizers to the Jewish faith. They believed in God, Yahweh, Elohim, but did not convert to Judaism. They went to the Jewish synagogues and many of the God-fearers gave to support the synagogues. We have to read the New Covenant with that mindset. WHO was being spoken to? We need to do this with the whole Bible when we're reading it. Then we have to ask ourselves, "What is this verse, chapter, book saying to me, a Gentile believer in the Jewish Messiah?"

In this book, I endeavor to make us aware of what exactly Yeshua/Jesus was saying to us from a Hebraic context and what it means also in the

Jewish context of the time, in that culture, and what the events were that were going on at that time. What did that have to do with what was being said, such as "who was in political power?"

The people of Israel were under Roman jurisdiction at the time the New Covenant was written. What did that have to do with anything? Granted, they had a lot more freedom than when Antiochus IV Epiphanes ruled from 175 BC until his death in 164 BC. (Chanukah) So here we are in about 33 AD in the gospels. We need to pay attention to what the people would be hearing with their First Century Hebrew Ears and put things into that context.

Definitions

Torah: Instruction, teaching. The first five books of the Bible: Genesis, Exodus, Leviticus, Numbers, and Deuteronomy. This is also said of the entire Old Testament.

Christian: One who professes belief in the life, death, resurrection, and the teachings of Jesus the Jewish Messiah and enters into the New Covenant with him. They were first called "Christians" in Antioch, Acts 11:26. They were followers of Yeshua/Jesus.

New Covenant: Often called "New Testament." In Hebrew, "Brit Chadashah." Instruction and teaching for the followers of Yeshua (Jewish Name)/Jesus.

There is a commandment given in Matthew Chapter One specifically to Joseph:

Matthew 1:21: And she shall bring forth a son, and you shall call his name JESUS: for he shall save his people from their sins.

The word for salvation in Hebrew is Yeshua.

We aren't told much about Joseph. There is a lot of speculation about him. We know for certain he was obedient to the Scriptures. We know he was a righteous man. We know the Creator of the Universe entrusted the care of his son to him.

The Bible says he was a "carpenter." Matthew 13:35. In the Old Testament, Isaiah 41:7, the word for *carpenter*, Strong's Concordance #H2796, can be craftsman, artisan, engraver, artificer.

In the New Testament/Covenant, Mark 6:3 says Yeshua/Jesus was a carpenter. Strong's Concordance #G5045, *tekton*. "A worker in wood, a carpenter, joiner, builder, a ship's carpenter or builder, any craftsman or workman, the art of poetry, maker of songs, an author."

Another meaning is iron-worker or smith and a stone-worker or mason. It is also suggested that the term in the Talmud, *"carpenter,"* can signify a very learned man. The New Testament description of Joseph as a carpenter could indicate that he was considered wise and literate in the Torah. In later Talmudic texts, the term "craftsman" is used as a metaphor for a skilled handler of the Word of God.

So here we have speculation on just what kind of carpenter Yeshua/Jesus and his father were. There certainly wasn't much wood in that area. Everything was built out of stone. His father may have been a Torah scholar that taught others. That would make sense for God the Father to put his son in a house that taught Torah. The Living Torah living in that house.

I believe that they were stone masons. It is speculated that he and his father, and probably his brothers, worked in Sepphoris, Tzippori in Hebrew, six miles from Nazareth. They have excavated a beautiful synagogue there with amazing mosaic tile work. It is famous for the beautiful woman in mosaic tile referred to as *the Mona Lisa of the Galilee*. During Yeshua's/Jesus youth it is said Sepphoris underwent the largest restoration project of his time.

The first commandment given to all in Matthew:

1.   Matthew 3:1-2

1. In those days came John the Baptist, preaching in the wilderness of Judaea, 2. And saying, Repent you: for the Kingdom of heaven is at hand.
Mark 1:3–8, Joshua 14:10, Daniel 2:44, Malachi 4:5-6.

Daniel 2:44-45 details that Kingdom:

44. And in the days of these kings shall the God of heaven set up a Kingdom, which shall never be destroyed: and the Kingdom shall not be left to other people, but it shall break in pieces and consume all these kingdoms, and it shall stand for ever. 45. Forasmuch as you saw that the stone was cut out of the mountain without hands, and that it brake in pieces the iron, the brass, the clay, the silver, and the gold; the great God has made known to the king what shall come to pass hereafter: and the dream is certain, and the interpretation thereof sure.

Malachi 4:5-6 prophesies about John the Baptist, the forerunner of the Messiah. Also see: Matthew 11:9-10, Verse 10 quotes Malachi 4:5-6. (Kingdom of heaven: Matthew 10:7, also Mark 1:3-8.) Isaiah 40:3, the prophecy of John the Baptist. Luke 1:76: Zacharias' prayer about his son, John the Baptist.

This is the first commandment in the New Covenant and it is from John the Baptist. The prophecy about John (Yochanan in Hebrew) is from Isaiah 40:3:

The voice of him that cries in the wilderness, Prepare you the way of the LORD, make straight in the desert a highway for our God. See also Luke 1:76.

And saying, "Repent you: for the Kingdom of heaven is at hand."

As mentioned above, I have used a Strong's Concordance for many, many years. It lists every word in the Bible and gives the Hebrew meaning if it's in the Torah/Old Testament or the Greek meaning if it's in the New Covenant. It is a great study tool. Nowadays, we have the internet and can easily find the meanings of these words with programs such as Blue Letter Bible and software, such as my PC Bible. These are wonderful resources for study. You can find a digital Strong's Concordance just by typing in the words, "Strong's Concordance." I always use the lexicon on the Blue Letter Bible web site.

Our word study for "*repent*" in the New Covenant is from *Blueletterbible.org*:

> Strong's Concordance #G3340: (Greek) (*metanoeo*), repent:
> 1) to change one's mind, i.e. to repent. 2) to change one's mind
> for better, heartily to amend with abhorrence of one's past sins.

We have to exhibit a change of attitude in our life, a change of thinking. In Hebrew, "shuva," a turning.

In order for us to understand our Torah, The Christian Torah, the New Covenant, we need to go back to our roots and understand from a Hebraic viewpoint what the New Covenant is talking about. As I said in the last chapter, much of the Bible is in Temple language. This is one of those places.

John the Baptist was out on the banks of the Jordan preaching repentance.

> In Hebrew, Strong's Concordance #H7725, *teshuv, teshuvah*, repentance, which means "to turn back, return." In the lexicon: "To be converted, as a sinner. To return and do." Another word for repent is *nacham*, #H5162: "To be sorry, console oneself, repent, regret, comfort, be comforted."

Sometimes we as Christians think we understand repentance. We think that after asking God to forgive us for our sins and ask Yeshua/Jesus into our heart, that that's all there is to it. We then just coast on into heaven. Salvation through repentance and accepting Yeshua/Jesus as our Savior is the point of being "born again." You are saved at the point you accept salvation. However, let us take a look at what the depth of searching the soul in doing repentance brings out.

Let me say here that I believe it is not our "works" that save us, but once we are saved, we have the Key of Salvation in our pocket, then there are the "works" James talks about. These are not done to earn our salvation, but these are what our rewards are going to be based on. We're not working for "points," but as this book tries to point out, our journey doesn't stop at accepting Yeshua/Jesus into our hearts. If you accept him on your deathbed, you're saved for all eternity, but if you're still alive and saved, then there are certain commandments and instructions we are given, certain rules of the Order of Melchizedek to follow. These, again, do not save you. If you get saved and go no further in your Christian life as far as "works," I believe you're still saved. Only God knows our hearts.

> James 2:14-26: 14. What does it profit, my brethren, if someone says he has faith but does not have works? Can faith save him? 15. If a brother or sister is naked and destitute of daily food, 16. and one of you says to them, "Depart in peace, be warmed and filled," but you do not give them the things which are needed for the body, what does it profit? 17. Thus also faith by itself, if it does not have works, is dead.

> 18. But someone will say, "You have faith, and I have works." Show me your faith without your works, and I will show you my faith by my works. 19. You believe that there is one God. You do well. Even the demons believe and tremble! 20. But do you want to know, O foolish man, that faith without works is dead? 21. Was not Abraham our father justified by works when he offered Isaac his son on the altar? 22. Do you see that faith was working together with his works, and by works faith was made perfect? 23. And the Scripture was fulfilled which says, "Abraham believed God, and it was accounted to him for righteousness." And he was called the friend of God. 24. You see then that a man is justified by works, and not by faith only.

25. Likewise, was not Rahab the harlot also justified by works when she received the messengers and sent them out another way? 26. For as the body without the spirit is dead, so faith without works is dead also.

There is one of the Lord's Festivals called Yom Kippur. It is also called the Day of Atonement, the holiest day of the year for the Jewish people. It is found in Leviticus 16 and Leviticus 23. This is the second festival of the Jewish Civil Year. The Jewish people are supposed to fast and pray that day. They have serious and moving services in the synagogues.

Yom Kippur is a picture of what Yeshua/Jesus did for us with his atoning blood. He is the once and for all sacrifice to save us from our sins. The debt was paid.

As believers in Yeshua/Jesus, on this day we reflect on the fact that he was born as a baby and placed in a manger, lived, died for us, and rose again, and removed the weight of sin and guilt that we had in our lives. We acknowledge that we were sinners and desperately in need of a Savior. We thank him for His Grace and Mercy on our lives, that he paid the ultimate so that we could be free.

As above, there is a Hebrew word for repentance, *teshuv*. I want you to grasp the depth that forgiveness brings to our lives. From our Jewish brethren we need to see just how important it is to acknowledge what Yeshua/Jesus did for us on the cross in his suffering and in his resurrection. This is shown throughout the ceremonies of the Jewish Festivals.

Pursuing works of <u>chesed</u> (kindness) and truth (not for salvation, but as actions showing our belief.)

James 2:18: Yes, a man may say, You have faith, and I have works: show me your faith without your works, and I will show you my faith by my works.

Not that we "earn" our salvation, but if we love him, we will work for him, show him we love him. He used Abraham for an example. Abraham's "works" were that he believed.

> James 2:23: And the Scripture was fulfilled which says, Abraham believed God, and it was imputed unto him for righteousness: and he was called the Friend of God.

He also proved his faith by taking Isaac to sacrifice him. We need to see the depth of the connection between what we call "sacrifices" and what this word really means, which is "drawing near," korban. God doesn't require the Jewish people to bring korban anymore because they don't have a Temple, but picture this: I'm a Jewish man in First Century Israel. I have broken one of the laws or I just want to bring a Thanksgiving offering, a "peace" offering. Depending on what it was, there is a certain korban/sacrifice/drawing-near offering I need to bring in order to receive forgiveness. I go to Jerusalem to the Temple. I bring my sacrifice. I go through the Court of the Women, through the Nicanor gates, to the Northern side of the altar. I have to slay my offering or the priest does, which could be a bull, goat, lamb, or pigeon. If I'm poor, I can only afford wheat flour, oil, and frankincense. If I'm very rich, I bring a bull. A goat or lamb is for the middle class. A pigeon is for a poor person. I have to place my two hands on the head of the animal and press down and recite the "vidui."

The vidui is a prayer of repentance, a way of saying I'm sorry for committing this sin against God or against mankind. If I have sinned against a person, I need to go to that person first and ask forgiveness. Remember what Yeshua/Jesus said in Matthew 5:23-24:

> 23. Therefore if you bring your gift to the altar, and there remember that your brother has ought against you; 24. Leave there your gift before the altar, and go your way; first be reconciled to your brother, and then come and offer your gift.

He was talking about the altar at the Temple. There was not and is not today an altar in the synagogues.

The people brought their perfect gifts, or offerings, to the Temple in Jerusalem in the Second Century and in Solomon's time. They were a physical offering to show an inward devotion. Sacrifice is the word used in our English Bibles, in Hebrew *Korban*, "to draw near."

I perform the "vidui." The confession, transferring my sins to the animal. I then personally have to slit the throat of the animal if it's a bull, lamb, or goat. If it's a pigeon, the priest cuts its throat with his thumb fingernail. A priest is standing there with a pitcher with a pointed bottom so it can't be set down lest the blood congeal. He goes and throws it around the bottom of the altar. I have to hang it up, skin it, cut it up in pieces, and wash it. I have to personally hand it to the priest to offer on the altar. How close do I have to get in order to hand this to the priest? Pretty close. Korban. To draw near. Do you see the point now?

The whole process of confession and repentance brings me closer and closer to God. The priest, the representative of God, then takes the offering up on the altar and completely burns it if it is an olah, a burnt sacrifice, or burns part of it, etc., depending on what I have brought the offering for. The offerings are always salted, plus the ramp up the altar. The salting of the sacrifices and ramp represents the salt covenant. The salt covenant entails another study.

If, when we accept Yeshua/Jesus as our Savior and ask him into our hearts, we do not sincerely regret our sins or acknowledge them, we need to pray again. I remember as an eight-year-old girl how I felt that night on the front pew of our little Baptist Church. I knew I was a sinner and needed a Savior. I remember to this day how the weight of sin was heavy on my heart and how I felt when I accepted him into my heart. What joy.

We need to forsake all sin in our lives and never sin again. Well, with us humans, is that possible? As much as we are able, we can. If we are truly repentant, we will recognize sin in our lives. Of course, what does John say about that?

I John 1:8-9: 8. If we say that we have no sin, we deceive ourselves, and the truth is not in us. 9. If we confess our sins, he is faithful and just to forgive us our sins, and to cleanse us from all unrighteousness.

If we have truly repented and accepted him as our Savior, we will worry if we think we have committed a sin and will willingly repent of it in order to be in a right relationship with him.

One of the signs of our being "saved" is that we will be humble. Sometimes it takes a while to accept servanthood, but Yeshua/Jesus says to be a servant to all.

We act different.

We read the Word and learn it. We begin to recognize more what sin is. In the Old Testament/Torah are the moral laws for humanity. In the New Testament/Christian Torah, Yeshua/Jesus expounds on those and tells us how he wants us to live.

We pray and repent daily and thank him for bringing us to salvation.

We teach others not to sin. We teach our children, family, or friends, not shaking our fingers in their faces and yelling, but lovingly explaining how God expects us to live and how to recognize when our behavior goes against his Word.

Do you begin to see what Yeshua/Jesus did for us? He covered it all. He is THE final sacrifice. His blood given for salvation for us once and for all!

So there's a lot more to this repentance business than we may have thought. It's a daily, ongoing thing. We don't just say the sinner's prayer and go on with our lives. That is just the key that opens the door. We form a relationship with the Creator, and the only way to approach him is to come in repentance in order to "draw near" to him, "korban." The Apostle Paul said, "I die daily." This means we need to come before the

Lord every day and confess our sins and ask him to reveal anything that is in our life that shouldn't be. We need to "draw near" to him daily.

We need to be in the Word daily and studying. We need to go to church, fellowship with other believers, and grow in him.

If we're in a right relationship with a loved one, don't we feel really bad if we've hurt them or done something that comes between us? More so with Yeshua/Jesus, our Savior.

This is speaking here of John the Baptist/Immerser:

> Matthew 3:5: Then went out to him Jerusalem, and all Judaea, and all the region round about Jordan.

Also see Mark 1:5.

This is information we need to learn. As you recall from the story of his birth in Luke chapter 1, John the Baptist was born to Zechariah and Elizabeth. It is said by some that Luke was Greek; however, Luke is one of the most Hebraic books in the New Covenant. (If he was Greek and got saved, why was such a big deal made over Cornelius in the Book of Acts?) In verses 1:1-4, he is speaking to a Greek speaker, Theophilus. No one knows who this is, but the word means "friend of God." Then from verse 5 on it has quite a lot of Temple language. In Hebrew, the word "and" is used a lot. If you look at the first five books of the Hebrew Bible, you can turn the pages and see the letter vav as the beginning letter on almost every page, the sixth letter of the Hebrew aleph-bet, which looks like a stick with a hook: ו. This is very Hebraic. It means "and" when used as a prefix. It shows a connection with the last sentence. In his narrative of the conception of John the Baptist, notice all the "ands" in English in Luke 1.

The story goes that Zacharias was a priest after the order of Abijah. The Levites had 24 courses/divisions wherein they served in the Temple each year at a certain time. 1 Chronicles 24 tells us about the courses. Abijah is mentioned in verse 10. He was of the eighth course. Also see Nehemiah 12:4.

So Luke tells us that Zacharias was serving at the time designated for him. The Jews keep a list still to this day. They know when these courses served. In studying Temple protocol, when a priest went to serve in the temple, he was there for eight days, from one Sabbath to the next Sabbath. They also all served at the three Pilgrimage Festivals: Passover, Shavuot/Pentecost, and Sukkot/Tabernacles.

Early in the morning before sunrise, they all came out to the Temple floor and got in a circle after they ate pancakes. The high priest would think of a number for each duty for the day, then count off as they all held up their hands, raising a certain number of fingers as they wished. The high priest would count off until he reached the number he had thought of for that duty and that priest would have that duty for the day.

There were many duties. When it came to the counting of fingers to light the incense on the table of incense in the Holy Place, only those priests who had never done this in their entire life were eligible. We know on this day Zacharias was chosen and had never done this duty before.

Where is this rule found?

> From Jacob Neusner's, *The Mishnah*, page 869, tractate Kedoshim/ Holy Things: Tamid 5:2: The superintendent said to them, "Those who are new to the preparation of the incense, come and cast lots."

However, when the Jewish people returned from exile, Ezra tells us only four of the twenty-four courses returned with him.

Alfred Edersheim says in his book, *The Temple: Its Ministry and Services*, about this subject:

> The institution of David and of Solomon continued till the Babylonish captivity. Thence, however, only four out of the twenty-four courses returned: those of Jedaiah, Immer, Pashur, and Harim (Ezra 2:36–39), the course of Jedaiah being placed first because it was of the high-priest's family, 'of the house of

Jeshua,' 'the son of Jozadak' (Ezra 3:2; Haggai 1:1; 1 Chronicles 6:15). To restore the original number, each of these four families were directed to draw five lots for those which had not returned, so as to form once more twenty-four courses, which were to bear the ancient names. Thus, for example, Zacharias, the father of John the Baptist, did not really belong to the family of Abijah (1 Chronicles 24:10), which had not returned from Babylon, but to the 'course of Abia,' which had been formed out of some other family, and only bore the ancient name (Luke 1:5). Like the priests, the Levites had at the time of King David been arranged into twenty-four 'courses,' which were to act as 'priest's' assistants' (1 Chronicles 23:4,28), as 'singers and musicians' (1 Chronicles 25:6), as 'gate-keepers and guards' (1 Chronicles 26:6 and following), and as 'officers and judges.' Of these various classes, that of the 'priest's assistants' was by far the most numerous, and to them the charge of the Temple had been committed in subordination to the priests."

However, to return to our story, this was Zacharias' day. Here he was in old age and had never been honored with this duty, but today he won the lot/lottery (that is what it was called). He was chosen. What does this mean? During the week that the priests served in the Temple, there was an order. To be chosen to light the incense was a huge honor. What a day this turned out to be!

Luke tells us that Zacharias' wife, Elizabeth, was of the daughters of Aaron, which means she was also a Levite. Luke says they had no child for she was barren and "they were both well advanced in years." He tells us that all the people were praying outside "at the hour of incense." Then an angel of the Lord appeared to him (Zacharias), standing on the right side of the altar of incense. And when Zacharias saw him, "he was troubled and fear fell upon him." The angel told him to not be afraid, that he and Elizabeth will bear a son and that he should call his name John. (Yochanan in Hebrew.) So Zacharias kind of doubts, "How shall I know this? For I am an old man and my wife is well advanced in years." So the angel tells him he won't be able to speak until the child is born.

John is born on what is thought to be the day of Passover, Nisan 14, according to the calendar of the courses/divisions of the priesthood. They would still have kept the same schedule at that time. Six months after John is born, Yeshua/Jesus is born, we believe on the first day of the festival of Sukkot, Tishrei 15, about our September/October, with the picture in this feast of "God tabernacling among us." There is a slaughter of the innocents and there is nothing more about John until we see him on the banks of the Jordan baptizing.

It is speculated that John too would have been in danger as he was only six months old or so. It is speculated that his mother, Elizabeth, took him to Qumran to the Essenes to hide him. This is just speculation. There is no proof text here. Zacharias is never mentioned again. It is thought that John may have been raised by the Essenes or in the Qumran region. (He certainly doesn't have their doctrine however.) Just interesting speculation.

So we find him on the banks of the Jordan preaching repentance. He is a Levite. Why isn't he in the Temple serving with the rest of the Levites? Because of the illegal priesthood. He is serving the people down along the Jordan River. The people that are coming to him also do not agree with the illegal priesthood who are serving in the Temple at this time. This is the month of Elul, about our month of August. It is the month before Rosh HaShanah, the lunar New Year on the first day of the month of Tishrei on the Jewish calendar.

The custom was to totally repent of every sin you've ever committed during the month of Elul. Every day the father of the house or leader is to get up in the morning and blow the shofar, calling the family to repentance. You pray sincerely and deeply during that time, asking God to reveal any sin in your life you haven't acknowledged and then you repent of it. You try to make amends with people you have wronged or who have wronged you. You "draw near" to God for the entire month leading up to the New Year.

If the people had been going to the Temple, they would have gone through a ritual bath called a *mikveh*, wherein John is called the "baptizer." There have been many of these excavated around the Temple below the Southern steps and elsewhere in Israel. The people would have to go through these in order to be able to go into the Temple and to prepare for the festival coming up, Rosh HaShanah. This is a ritual bath, not for physical cleansing of the body, but as a prerequisite for purification on entering the Temple. The people coming to John were being "baptized" for repentance in the Jordan River. They were going through the mikveh, the ritual bath, for which the Jordan River qualifies.

This would be the last day of the month of Elul before the first day of Tishrei, the Jewish New Year. They had come to Jerusalem for Rosh HaShanah, the Jewish New Year, but would not go to the Temple. Instead, they went out in the wilderness to John.

They didn't baptize people manually. The people baptized themselves, or put themselves through the mikveh. They would go down in the water in a squatting position and come up three times. There were prayers and blessings they would say. John would be the witness. For the women, they would have a woman witness, further downstream, of course, or upstream. This was a sign of teshuvah, turning away from sin and turning to God, becoming closer to him. This is what it means when it says John was baptizing to repentance. He said, "Teshuv!" Turn! Repent! He was being the witness. He would have been the witness to Yeshua/Jesus going through the mikveh.

About the illegal priesthood: Here's the point. It is said that the time of the first and second centuries were quite a turbulent time. During that turbulence, the Romans were in power in Israel. The priesthood that served in the Temple, of course, were Levites. The high priesthood office was supposed to be handed down by lineage.

(See the Wikipedia article on the priestly divisions.)

When the Romans came into power, they were paid by the highest bidder for the office of high priest. The high priest was supposed to follow a succession. It was supposed to be from one of the sons of

Aaron, then through his son Eleazar, and then on down the line from Zadok. However, when the Romans came in, as above, it was given to the highest bidder. The Temple high priest took in a lot of money. It is said to be in the millions each year. Remember when Yeshua came in and ran the money changers out? That is because this illegal priesthood of Annas and Caiaphas were charging exorbitant prices for everything. That Annas and Caiaphas were in power because they paid the most for the office is the reason John the Baptist would not serve in the Temple at that time. Annas and Caiaphas were not in line for chief priest. That is why instead of going to the Temple and going through the mikvehs, "all" of Judea and Samaria came to John to go through the mikveh, the Jordan River, for repentance in preparation for the Jewish New Year, Rosh HaShanah. That is why the Essenes, Levitical priests, were at Qumran instead of serving in the Temple, which was a political mess.

Allen Ross in his series on *The Religious World of Jesus* says about this time:

> "The priesthood traced its lineage from Aaron through his son Eleazar to Zadok; the other son was Ithamar. The line of the high priests was in the Zadokite family until the time of Antiochus IV Epiphanes, when Onias III had to flee for his life. Until that time, the office had a life-long tenure; but afterward the high priests were appointed and deposed at the will of the ruler, whether Seleucid, Roman, or Herodian.

> The Hasmoneans were priests, but not of the line from Zadok. They first obtained the office of the high priest from the Seleucids, but then simply took the office upon ascending the throne. Their control ended when Herod eliminated every male in the Hasmonean line.

> During the Roman period there were 28 high priests. Herod appointed seven of them himself. So there were always several ex-high priests around, and they still retained their titles and

their influence. But Herod and his successors controlled the office. There were only a few families of the nobility from which the high priests could be chosen, but it may be that any member of these families could use the title. Jeremias suggests that anyone above the rank of an ordinary priest could be called one of the "chief priests." In the Gospel accounts, the two best-known high priests are Caiaphas (who ruled from 18–36 AD), who presided over the group that turned Jesus over to Pilate for crucifixion, and Annas (who ruled from 6–15 AD), his father-in-law, who first examined Jesus."

See also the Wikipedia article on Caiaphas.

I said all that to say this:

You notice verse five says it was in the days of Herod (the Great), the king of Judea? In those days, the Romans ruled the country. Herod the Great was appointed by the Roman emperor. He reigned from 37 BC to 4 BC over Judea, Samaria, Galilee, and much of Perea and Syria. It is thought the events of Luke 1:5–25 probably occurred around 6 BC. The entire kingship and priesthood serving in the Temple were corrupt. The Herods were not even Jewish and not in line to the throne. They were from Idumea, or Edom, and were descendants of Esau, Israel's arch enemy. Think of that. The king of Israel at this time was from Esau! He had a huge hand in the crucifixion of Yeshua/Jesus! The arch enemy, Amalek, rearing his ugly head.

Levitical priests like John and the Essenes refused to serve in the Temple under this illegal priesthood, so they went out to other places and served. They were said by some to be the true priests, descended from Zadok. There were a lot of the priests that did stay and serve in the Temple during this time. The ones that stayed went along to get along. In charge of the Temple at that time were the Sadducees, a sect of Judaism.

Nevertheless, here is Yochanan (John) the Immerser, out along the Jordan, "baptizing for repentance of sins." Why did Yeshua/Jesus have to "repent?" Or did he? He who had no sin. Because in order to fit the qualifications to be the Messiah of the Jewish people, the job description we might say, as the Jewish Messiah, he had to obey every single jot and tittle of the commandments, every ritual, every "law," or he would be rejected by the people. He had to go through the mikveh before Rosh HaShanah to fulfill the laws concerning this. If he had not, he would not be considered at all as their Messiah.

The word used in the Torah for repent is *teshuvah*, which comes from the word for "turn." See above.

As John Parsons says on his web site, *Hebrew4Christians, concer*ning repentance:

> In Modern Hebrew, *teshuvah* means an "answer" to a shelah, or a question. God's love for us is the question, and our teshuvah – our turning of the heart toward him – is the answer. Teshuvah is one of the great gifts God gives each of us – the ability to turn back to him and seek healing for our brokenness.

So we see as believers how important it is to repent every day and ask the Lord to reveal to us any sin we've committed that we didn't realize we were doing, anyone we've hurt, any sin of omission. King David said, "Early will I seek you" in Psalms 63. There are many Scriptures about repentance. We need to repent and draw near to him (korban) and not have any sin between us and him. If we want a closer walk with him, we need to "draw near."

So here we have the first and most important commandment, "Repent, for the Kingdom of God is at hand." As you see, this story from a Hebraic perspective carries with it the whole history of the Jewish people and how important it was for them to keep their commandments. The Jewish people and how they obey the Scriptures should be a testimony to us of how important it is for us to keep that relationship open between us and God. The first step is salvation. Then we start our walk with him and follow his Word.

2.   Matthew 3:8

Bring forth therefore fruits meet for repentance.

"Bring forth" is a picture or example of the festival of First Fruits. This commandment is also from John the Baptist. What are the "fruits" worthy of repentance? We need to put this back in context. He was talking to the Pharisees and Sadducees. The next verses are:

3.   Matthew 3:9–12

9. And think not to say within yourselves, we have Abraham to [our] father: for I say unto you, that God is able of these stones to raise up children unto Abraham. 10. And now also the ax is laid unto the root of the trees: therefore every tree which brings not forth good fruit is cut down, and cast into the fire. 11. I indeed baptize you with water unto repentance: but he that comes after me is mightier than I, whose shoes I am not worthy to bear: he shall baptize you with the Holy Spirit and [with] fire: 12. Whose fan [is] in his hand, and he will thoroughly purge his floor, and gather his wheat into the garner. He will burn up the chaff with unquenchable fire.
John 8:33, Matthew 7:19, Luke 3:16, Acts 2:3–4, Malachi 3:3.

Matthew 3:7: But when he saw many of the Pharisees and Sadducees come to his baptism, he said unto them, O generation of vipers, who has warned you to flee from the wrath to come?

Even though they thought they were so free of sin and holy, John tells them that just because they have Abraham for their father, that doesn't free them from repentance. Just because they were Israelites by lineage, that didn't give them a free ticket to heaven. They couldn't just sit back and coast into heaven by their DNA. None of us are free from sinning. We need to recognize that and be careful to repent daily.

What is our fruit?

Galatians 5:22–26: 22. But the fruit of the Spirit is love, joy, peace, longsuffering, gentleness, goodness, faith, 23. meekness, temperance: against such there is no law. 24. And they that are Christ's have crucified the flesh with the affections and lusts. 25. If we live in the Spirit, let us also walk in the Spirit. 26. Let us not be desirous of vain glory, provoking one another, envying one another.

Ephesians 5:8–10: 8. For you were sometimes darkness, but now are you light in the Lord: walk as children of light: 9. (For the fruit of the Spirit is in all goodness and righteousness and truth;) 10. Proving what is acceptable unto the Lord.

It is said that "bringing forth fruit" in a Hebraic context means more than simply doing good deeds. Bringing forth fruit also refers to having spiritual insight and teachings. In other words, being so knowledgeable of the Word that when asked a question on it, you can answer.

Yeshua/Jesus says in another place what is most important:

Matthew 6:19-20: 19. Lay not up for yourselves treasures upon earth, where moth and rust does corrupt, and where thieves break through and steal: 20. But lay up for yourselves treasures in heaven, where neither moth nor rust does corrupt, and where thieves do not break through nor steal:
Proverbs 23:4, Matthew 19:21.

Luke 12:33: Sell that you have, and give alms; provide yourselves bags which wax not old, a treasure in the heavens that fails not, where no thief approaches, neither moth corrupts.
Matthew 19:21, Luke 11:41, Matthew 6:20.

The temptation of the Messiah in Matthew doesn't contain commandments specifically to us, but I wanted to include this as an example of how to properly discern the Word.

4.   Matthew 4:4

But he answered and said, It is written, man shall not live by bread alone, but by every word that proceeds out of the mouth of God.
Deuteronomy 8:3.

Jesus said this to Satan, quoting Deuteronomy 8:3. How much more should we answer with the Word when tempted or in a trial? He set the example for us. He gave us the power to rebuke the enemy, but we also need to quote Scripture, the Word, to the enemy, not to think we're strong in ourselves. He is our Teacher. Listen to him.

5.   Matthew 4:7

But he answered and said, It is written, Man shall not live by bread alone, but by every word that proceeds out of the mouth of God.
Deuteronomy 6:16.

Again, here we have Yeshua/Jesus using the Word to defeat the enemy. Don't tempt the Lord at all. Famously, there is a group of people who are known as "snake handlers." They take the Scripture in Mark 16:18:

They shall take up serpents; and if they drink any deadly thing, it shall not hurt them; they shall lay hands on the sick, and they shall recover.

That is, IF you pick up a serpent accidentally, not deliberately, or drinking a cup of arsenic accidentally. For example, Paul in Acts 28:3–6: 3:

And when Paul had gathered a bundle of sticks, and laid them on the fire, a viper came out of the heat, and fastened on his hand. 4. And when the barbarians saw the venomous beast hang on his hand, they said among themselves, No doubt this man is a murderer, whom, though he has escaped the sea, yet vengeance suffers not to live. 5. And he shook off the beast into the fire, and felt no harm. 6. Howbeit they looked when he should have swollen, or fallen down dead suddenly: but after they had looked a great while, and saw no harm come to him, they changed their minds, and said that he was a god.

Ha! Wouldn't you like to have been there? Well, maybe not, but you get my point. Trusting that He WILL protect us from these things and many more is the point. Not deliberately "tempting God."

6.   Matthew 4:8–10

8. Again, the devil took him up into an exceeding high mountain, and showed him all the kingdoms of the world, and the glory of them; 9. And says unto him, All these things will I give you, if you will fall down and worship me. 10. Then says Jesus unto him, get you hence, Satan: for it is written, You shall worship the Lord your God, and him only shall you serve.
Deuteronomy 6:13 and 10:20.

7.   Matthew 4:17

From that time Jesus began to preach, and to say, Repent: for the Kingdom of heaven is at hand (or "near").
Mark 1:14–15, Matthew 3:2 and 10:7.

So here is our third "repent" in Matthew! Yeshua's admonition is exactly the same as John's!

"From that time" occurs twice in the Book of Matthew. The other time is Matthew 16:21. When studying Hebrew, any time there is a repeat of a verse, you need to pay attention and study out why and what it means. In our verse here, it marks the beginning of his ministry. Chapter 16 verse 21 is looking towards his crucifixion and resurrection.

8.   Matthew 4:19

And he said unto them, Follow me, and I will make you fishers
of men.
Luke 5:10.

What did he mean to "follow" him? Did they have to traipse after him
day and night and go everywhere he went and do everything he did? No.
He was speaking to Peter and Andrew here. This alludes to Jeremiah
16:16:

Behold, I will send for many fishers, says the Lord, and they
shall fish them; and after will I send for many hunters, and they
shall hunt them from every mountain, and from every hill, and
out of the holes of the rocks.
See also Ezekiel 49:10.

Of course, the disciples, knowing the Scriptures, would recognize
this right away, the link. The time had come. The disciples went out
afterwards and preached the gospel. At first, it was only to the Jewish
people. About 15 years later God spoke to Peter and showed him the
non-kosher animals dropped down in a sheet, which stood for Gentiles,
and he went to the house of Cornelius and was stunned to find a whole
houseful of Gentiles worshipping THE God! Amazing story.

The story in Acts chapter ten doesn't say Peter could eat pork or shellfish.
Acts chapter ten is not about kosher law, but about the Gentiles being
grafted in at this time to the root. The Jewish people consider us pigs!
I have read that a wait of approximately 15 years before a Gentile came
in was to get the church established. Cornelius had been a God-fearer.
(See introduction to Matthew.) There were many in that day. Until this
time, the disciples had only gone to the Jews. Yeshua/Jesus went also
to the Samaritan woman.

Acts 10:22: And they said, Cornelius the centurion, a just man,
and one that fears God, and of good report among all the nation

of the Jews, was warned from God by an holy angel to send for you into his house, and to hear words of you.

(Some speculate this may have even been the centurion whose daughter was healed by Jesus, but there's no real proof. Makes a nice story.)

However, this is a fantastic story. I pray you will read the whole thing, Acts the tenth chapter.

As above, a God-fearer was a Gentile who wanted to learn about the God of Abraham, Isaac, and Jacob. They attended synagogue, gave their monetary support to the synagogue, but did not convert to Judaism. As we see above, Cornelius was a man that "feared God." A God-fearer. The "nation of the Jews" thought highly of him. They obviously knew him. It says he was a "just man."

> *Just*, Strong's Concordance #G1342, *dikaios*, means "*righteous.*" It means "observing divine laws."

Obviously, to me, he had already been going to the synagogue and learned the laws.

> This word also means *virtuous, innocent, guiltless, faultless.* Used of him whose way of thinking, feeling, and acting is wholly conformed to the will of God, and who therefore needs no rectification in the heart or life.

This same word is used for Joseph, the husband of Mary. Matthew 1:19. It is also used for John the Baptist's parents in Luke 1:6, although the King James Version uses "righteous" here. It is the same word, Strong's Concordance #G1342. It is used 81 times in the New Testament.

So when Peter came to him, he was already a believer in the True God. He was close enough to God to hear the Holy Spirit speak to his heart and to see and hear an angel!

Jeremiah 16:15-16 is one of the most fascinating Scriptures in the Bible to me.

Are you a fisher or a hunter? What is your calling? He said he would make them "fishers of men." What does that mean? We are to "fish and hunt" amongst the people of the world to preach the gospel to them. Remember the parable of Yeshua/Jesus and how the disciples had been fishing all night and had caught nothing?

> John 21:6: And he said unto them, Cast the net on the right side of the ship, and you shall find. They cast therefore, and now they were not able to draw it for the multitude of fishes.

They obeyed him and verse 11 tells us they brought up 153 fish. If you're fishing for men and aren't catching anything, move on. Also, the net represents the Word of God. Sometimes we don't use the right bait! We need to minister to people where they are and use the bait that they can understand in their language, in their customs, in their understanding. The sea is the world. The fish are the rescued people of all nations.

The same situation happened when they began to follow Yeshua/Jesus at the first. Luke 5:1-11. A miraculous catch of fish. Simon Peter, James, and John forsook all and followed him after this.

In our story of the 153 fish, this is after his resurrection. Now here they all were, discouraged. Simon Peter said, "I'm going fishing." The other ones said, "We're also going with you."

Now they're at the Sea of Galilee, going back to their livelihood. John 21:4 tells us the disciples didn't know it was Jesus standing on the shore. Only when they caught the 153 and brought them to shore, John said to Peter, "It is him." Peter girded himself and jumped into the water. Jesus cooked them bread and fish and they were all astonished.

Here he was, performing the same miracle that started their discipleship. Reminding them of who he was. Oh, how he loved them. How he loves you and I even when we have doubt. He comes along and causes something to happen in our lives to show us he's still Lord. He causes something in our lives to remind us of all the times he was there.

As an aside, why 153? This is just some extra information for you.

In the first century, they were on a three-year cycle of reading the Torah, which was divided into 153 portions.

The number 153 is the triangular of the numbers 1–17. If you add all the numbers from 1 to 17, you get 153.

John tells the story of the 5 loaves and 12 baskets left over, adding up to 17.

Seventeen is the age of Joseph at the time he was sold into slavery.

Jacob lived in Egypt 17 years.

The Book of Acts lists 17 nations present at Pentecost.

Seventeen seems to be the number of the nations. Seventy also represents the nations.

$10 \times 7 = 70$.

$10 + 7 = 17$.

The number 153 is the sum of the cubes of its own digits. $1 \times 1 \times 1 + 5 \times 5 \times 5 + 3+3+3 = 153$.

You can study more about this on your own. It is quite interesting.

The verse before this one in Jeremiah is verse 15:

> But, The Lord lives, that brought up the children of Israel from the land of the north, and from all the lands where he had driven

them: and I will bring them again into their land that I gave unto their fathers.

So the Lord has also been a Fisher and Hunter to bring the people of Israel back to their land, searching them out among the nations and causing them to have a desire to return. The promise to come back to the land is being fulfilled in our eyes today in Israel.

"Follow me" he says. "I will make you fishers of men." To follow someone is to watch their life, listen and learn what they teach, do what they say, be a talmid/disciple/student. From the dictionary search for "disciple:" "One who embraces and assists in spreading the teachings of another. An active adherent, as of a movement or philosophy."

> The "hunter" part of our verse in Jeremiah in verse 16 says: "and afterwards, I shall send for many hunters, and they will hunt for them from every mountain and every hill, and from the clefts of the rocks."

This reminds me of the parable Jesus told about the people invited to the wedding.

> Luke 14:16–24: 16. Then said he unto him, a certain man made a great supper, and bade many: 17. And sent his servant at suppertime to say to them that were bidden, come; for all things are now ready. 18. And they all with one consent began to make excuse. The first said unto him, I have bought a piece of ground, and I must needs go and see it: I pray you have me excused. 19. And another said, I have bought five yoke of oxen, and I go to prove them: I pray you have me excused. 20. And another said, I have married a wife, and therefore I cannot come. 21. So that servant came, and showed his Lord these things. Then the master of the house being angry said to his servant, Go out quickly into the streets and lanes of the city, and bring in hither the poor, and the maimed, and the halt, and the blind. 22. And the servant said, Lord, it is done as you have commanded, and yet there is room. 23. And the Lord said unto the

servant, Go out into the highways and hedges, and compel them to come in, that my house may be filled. 24. For I say unto you, None of those men who were bidden shall taste of my supper.

See, it's not our job to force them to believe, but it IS our job to tell them. Follow him. Use his examples. Be a fisher AND a hunter.

Matthew Five: This chapter begins the Sermon on the Mount as we call it. First he gave the Beatitudes, the "blessed are" verses, Chapter 5:3–11. Then he says:

9.   Matthew 5:12

33. Rejoice, and be exceeding glad: for great is your reward in heaven: for so persecuted they the prophets who were before you. I Peter 4:13–14, Acts 7:52.

When we're persecuted, don't we feel sorry for ourselves usually? Our Master here says, "Rejoice! AND be exceeding glad!" Seems impossible, doesn't it? But when we are in the midst of that persecution, look up! For your redemption draws near! Remember how HE suffered and the prophets of old, and our brothers and sisters in Yeshua/Jesus who are suffering now and have suffered in the past. If we suffer for HIS sake, how blessed are we? What an honor to be counted his FRIEND.

10.   Matthew 5:13–16

13. You are the salt of the earth: but if the salt has lost its savor, wherewith shall it be salted? It is thenceforth good for nothing, but to be cast out, and to be trodden under foot of men. 14. You are the light of the world. A city that is set on a hill cannot be hid. 15. Neither do men light a candle, and put it under a bushel, but on a candlestick; and it gives light unto all that are in the house. 16. Let your light so shine before men, that they may see your good works, and glorify your Father who is in heaven. I Peter 2:12, John 15:8.

Leviticus 2:13: Neither shall you suffer the salt of the covenant of your God to be lacking.

Numbers 18:19: It is a covenant of salt forever.

You'll notice that all the sacrifices were salted. The ramp up to the altar was covered with salt to prevent slipping.

In the Talmud, Bereshith, Section 1, Page 241b: Salt was to be used because it softens bitterness, and so mankind cannot do without it. Salt is the covenant upon which the world is established: hence it is called "the covenant of your God."

I'd recommend you study the salt covenant. A book I'd recommend is The Salt Covenant by H. Clay Trumbull, now in the public domain.

Verse 14: We used to sing a song in Sunday School: "This little light of mine, I'm gonna let it shine." Is our light shining today? Or do we hide it under a bushel? Doing good works and giving our Father in heaven the glory is what it's all about. Causing others to glorify him is awesome. People in the world can tell if you're a Christian or not. Think of the times you've been at the grocery store or somewhere and you're just drawn to a certain person. You say a little something to them, they say a little something back, and the Holy Spirit in you greets the Holy Spirit in them and you're off! Just like Mary and Elizabeth.

The world sees that too, but their reaction is usually different. They automatically are put off at once or drawn to us. They never think why, but it is the Holy Spirit in us that they are either condemned by or drawn to.

Paul says in 1 Corinthians 15:31: I affirm, by the boasting in you which I have in Christ Jesus our Lord, I die daily.

We need to die daily to self or else we start being offended by others. Taking off "self" hurts.

1 Corinthians 6:19-20: 19. What? Know you not that your body is the temple of the Holy Spirit which is in you, which you have of God, and you are not your own? 20. For you are bought with a price: therefore glorify God in your body, and in your spirit, which are God's.

It takes growing in Yeshua/Jesus, reading the Word, and praying daily to be able to put self aside for the sake of the Messiah. Sometimes we bounce back into our "self" mode and then we have to get alone with him and repent and try harder to put ourselves aside for his sake.

At the beginning of Matthew, I asked you to remember who Yeshua/ Jesus was talking to: The Israelites. They understood immediately when he spoke of salt and light. They understood they were sent as a "Light to the Nations" and were to keep that in mind at all times.

God's Plan in a nutshell is given in Isaiah:

Isaiah 42:6-7: 6. I, the Lord, have called you in righteousness, and will hold your hand, and will keep you, and give you for a covenant of the people, for a light of the Gentiles; 7. to open the blind eyes, to bring out the prisoners from the prison, and them that sit in darkness out of the prison house.

Then in Isaiah 49:6 he gives the plan. He is speaking to Israel:

And he said, It is a light thing that you should be my servant to raise up the tribes of Jacob, and to restore the preserved of Israel: I will also give you for a light to the Gentiles, that you may be my salvation unto the end of the earth.

This is quoted in Acts 13:47: NKJV:

For so the Lord has commanded us: "I have set you as a light to the Gentiles, that you should be for salvation to the ends of the earth."

Keep in mind that the word "salvation" here in Hebrew is Yeshua.

What he was saying here was, paraphrasing, "It would be an easy thing for me to send the Messiah to the twelve tribes and that they would recognize him." They were looking for him! (See Daniel's prophecy.) They were expecting him! He says he would also give them for a "light to the Gentiles" that they should be his salvation to the ends of the earth.

However, a lot of the Jews couldn't accept the fact that Yeshua/Jesus was the Messiah, as in John 1:10-11. They were expecting the Messiah to come and take over the world as king and live and reign for eternity at that time. Even Yeshua's cousin, John, sent word to him:

> Luke 7:20: When the men were come unto him, they said, John the Baptist hath sent us unto you, saying, "Are you he that should come? Or look we for another?"

Messiah ben Yosef-Joseph was understood from Isaiah 53 about the suffering servant, but some didn't hold to this belief. They believed, and still do, that this pertains to the Nation of Israel. Their eyes were blinded to the fact that his first coming was as Messiah ben Yosef, son of Joseph, lowly, and riding on a donkey, a sign of a servant, Zechariah 9:9, and his second coming would be as Messiah ben David, riding on a white horse, Conquering King, conquering the world!

There are four "Servant Songs" in the book of Isaiah: 42:1-4; 49:1-6; 50:4-9; and 52:13–53:12, although the "servant" theme is throughout Isaiah chapters 40–53. Most of them pertain to the Servant of God, the Messiah. Some of them also pertain to the nation of Israel.

The Jewish people can act out the implements of the Passover, each one pointing to Yeshua/Jesus, and still not see that he is the Messiah. They can celebrate all the Festivals of the Lord that tell God's Plan for the world and not recognize him. Amazing! But many are being saved and many are teaching us the deeper meaning of the Scriptures. And when he comes back as King of Kings and Lord of Lords, they will recognize him and realize he WAS and IS the Messiah!

So the people that Yeshua/Jesus was talking to in all the gospels were Jewish people except for a couple of places where he speaks to Gentiles.

See John Parson's article on this subject on the Hebrew4Christians web site.

> Acts 13:42: And when the Jews were gone out of the synagogue, the Gentiles begged that these words might be preached to them the next Sabbath.

Who was speaking and who was he speaking to? Paul was speaking to the Gentiles in the synagogue in Antioch.

This was an outstanding sermon by Paul. And then what happened? You see, it wasn't just "any" Jews that came to listen to that sermon. In verse 15, we see it was the "rulers of the synagogue" who invited Paul to speak.

> Acts 13:43–52: 43. Now when the congregation was broken up, many of the Jews and religious proselytes followed Paul and Barnabas: who, speaking to them, persuaded them to continue in the grace of God. 44. And the next Sabbath day came almost the whole city together to hear the Word of God. 45. But when the Jews saw the multitudes, they were filled with envy, and spoke against those things which were spoken by Paul, contradicting and blaspheming. 46. Then Paul and Barnabas waxed bold, and said, It was necessary that the Word of God should first have been spoken to you: but seeing you put it from you, and judge yourselves unworthy of everlasting life, lo, we turn to the Gentiles. 47. For so has the Lord commanded us, saying, I have set you to be a light of the Gentiles, that you should be for salvation unto the ends of the earth. 48. And when the Gentiles heard this, they were glad, and glorified the word of the Lord:

and as many as were ordained to eternal life believed. 49. And the word of the Lord was published throughout all the region. 50. But the Jews stirred up the devout and honorable women, and the chief men of the city, and raised persecution against Paul and Barnabas, and expelled them out of their coasts. 51. But they shook off the dust of their feet against them, and came unto Iconium. 52. And the disciples were filled with joy, and with the Holy Spirit.

Paul is quoting Isaiah again here in verse 47.

Notice: Verse 13:43: It isn't talking about proselytes to Christianity. It is talking about proselytes to Judaism, from Strong's Concordance #G4339. *Prosēlytos.* A newcomer, a stranger, an alien, a proselyte, one who has come over from a Gentile religion to Judaism.

By the way, the Greek word there for *congregation* is *synagogue.* Strong's Concordance #4864.

So we see here what happened. The rulers of the synagogue saw the multitudes (of Gentiles) and were filled with jealousy and opposed Paul and Barnabas. Then Paul quotes our Isaiah verse and the Gentiles are glad. Then the rulers of the synagogue stirred up people to persecute Paul and Barnabas and run them out of town, but Paul and Barnabas obeyed what Yeshua said and shook off the dust from their feet and left. Here they were persecuted and what happened? They were filled with JOY and with the HOLY SPIRIT!!! What a day.

Remember in places where it might say "the Jews," to always check because it's probably a group of certain Jews, not ALL Jews, as in the Pharisees who opposed Yeshua. It was not ALL Pharisees. Here in these verses it is the "rulers of the synagogue." This would be like our elders of our churches. There would be a president, then a ruling body. A ruler is mentioned in Mark 5:22, Luke 8:41, Jairus, and again mentioned in Matthew 9:18, but not by name.

11.　　Matthew 5:17–19

17. Think not that I am come to destroy the law, or the prophets: I am not come to destroy, but to fulfil. 18. For verily I say unto you, Till heaven and earth pass, one jot or one tittle shall in no wise pass from the law, till all be fulfilled. 19. Whosoever therefore shall break one of these least commandments, and shall teach men so, he shall be called the least in the Kingdom of heaven: but whosoever shall do and teach them, the same shall be called great in the Kingdom of heaven.
Romans 10:4, Luke 16:17.

Jesus definitely tells the Pharisees that he DID NOT come to destroy the Torah. God forbid! He IS the Torah! The walking, breathing, speaking WORD of God.

Romans 10:4: For Christ [is] the end of the law for righteousness to everyone who believes.

One of the definitions for the word *"end"* here is Thayer's Greek Lexicon: *Telos*: Termination, the limit at which a thing ceases to be; always of the end of some act or state, but not of the end of a period of time. The word can also can mean *"goal."*

There is such confusion over these verses. Here's a proof text for proving that "the law" is not destroyed. Heaven forbid! If the Torah was destroyed, we would not be here. Paul says:

Galatians 3:16–29: 16. Now to Abraham and his seed were the promises made. He says not, and to seeds, as of many; but as of one, and to your seed, which is Christ. 17. And this I say, that the covenant, that was confirmed before of God in Christ, the law, which was four hundred and thirty years after, cannot disannul, that it should make the promise of none effect. 18. For if the inheritance be of the law, it is no more of promise: but God gave it to Abraham by promise. 19. Wherefore then serves the law?

It was added because of transgressions, till the seed should come to whom the promise was made; and it was ordained by angels in the hand of a mediator. 20. Now a mediator is not a mediator of one, but God is one. 21. Is the law then against the promises of God? God forbid: for if there had been a law given which could have given life, verily righteousness should have been by the law. 22. But the Scripture has concluded all under sin, that the promise by faith of Jesus Christ might be given to them that believe. 23. But before faith came, we were kept under the law, shut up unto the faith which should afterwards be revealed. 24. Wherefore the law was our schoolmaster to bring us unto Christ, that we might be justified by faith. 25. But after that faith is come, we are no longer under a schoolmaster. 26. For you are all the children of God by faith in Christ Jesus. 27. For as many of you as have been baptized into Christ have put on Christ. 28. There is neither Jew nor Greek, there is neither bond nor free, there is neither male nor female: for you are all one in Christ Jesus. 29. And if you be Christ's, then are you Abraham's seed, and heirs according to the promise.

And who was Abraham? A descendent of Shem, who was the picture of the king/priest here on earth, Melchizedek! We as believers in Yeshua/Jesus are of Abraham's seed. We are not "under the law," or the covenant given to the Jewish people at Sinai, but are under the New Covenant, The New Order of Melchizedek! But the Torah/Instructions are for our moral compass and we need to study it. If we throw the Torah out as having no effect today, we miss learning about the Heart of God! Write this down and put it in your Bible to remember:

The whole Bible was written FOR us, but the whole Bible was not written TO us.

Remember the part about being our tutor or schoolmaster. The Torah is our teacher!

In other words, the whole point of this book: We are not under the Mosaic covenant given to the Jews at Sinai. We are under the New

Covenant paid for by Yeshua/Jesus dying on the cross for our sins and creating a Way to God for the Gentiles. And Malchi–Zedek, King of Righteousness/Priest of the Most High God, is our leader, who is Yeshua! King Yeshua! OUR High Priest. There had not been a king who was also a high priest since Melchizedek.

We most certainly need to study Torah. It is the history of the world! You're coming in on half the story if you don't study the Torah. As someone said, "The New Testament is the Old Testament revealed." What I interpret this as saying is the plan of salvation is in the Torah, but hidden! In the New Covenant the plan is revealed! The Old and New go together! The Old Testament/Torah is our mirror. It is our moral compass. It is the revealing of God the Father's heart. If you don't study the Torah, you can't see clearly what Yeshua/Jesus the Messiah came to do. He didn't "destroy" anything, but came to give us a New Covenant. He never reneged on any of his covenants.

If I ask my son to do the dishes and later say, "Did you fulfill my request?" That doesn't mean he destroyed the dishes! He DID the dishes. Yeshua fulfilled the covenant of Moses by paying for every sacrifice, offering, and commandment in the Torah! He paid the debt! Once and for all he paid for every one of us to become Sons of God.

So the next time someone tells you that the Old Testament has been done away with, say, "Think not." It's a commandment.

12.   Matthew 5:21-22

21. You have heard that it was said by them of old time, You shall not kill; and whosoever shall kill shall be in danger of the judgment: 22. But I say unto you that whosoever is angry with his brother without a cause shall be in danger of the judgment: and whosoever shall say to his brother, Raca, shall be in danger of the council: (*Sanhedrin, the ruling authority*) but whosoever shall say, You fool, (*or "empty head"*) shall be in danger of hellfire.

In verse 21, Yeshua/Jesus gives the sixth commandment, "You shall not kill," or murder in some translations. Exodus 20:13 and Deuteronomy 5:17.

Verse 22: I John 3:15, James 3:6 about the tongue. In Romans 13:9 Paul gives six of the Ten Commandments. Luke 18:20, Mark 10:19, James 2:11.

The rabbis say that ruining a person's reputation is equal to murder.

Proverbs 11:13: A talebearer reveals secrets: but he that is of a faithful spirit conceals the matter.

"Lashon hara" means "evil speaking" in Hebrew. We are not to gossip about a person even if we know the matter is true. In our English speech, we often hear people being called stupid or a fool. Here Yeshua says not to do that! We get in habits of speech sometimes that are quite hard to break, but if you think, "What I say about this person may bring this onto his head," then maybe we'll all try harder to say good things about people, even if we think they don't deserve it. Bless people instead of cursing them!

James 3:10-11: 10. Out of the same mouth proceeds blessing and cursing. My brethren, these things ought not so to be. 11. Does a fountain send forth at the same place sweet water and bitter?

The Babylonian Talmud, Bava Mezia 58b says: One who shames the face of his fellow, it is as if he has murdered him.

There is a Japanese doctor, Dr. Masaru Emoto, who did an experiment on plants and water and the effect of different sounds and music on them. From his web site:

"Through the 1990's, Dr. Masaru Emoto performed a series of experiments observing the physical effect of words, prayers, music and environment on the crystalline structure of water.

Emoto hired photographers to take pictures of water after being exposed to the different variables and subsequently frozen so that they would form crystalline structures. The results were nothing short of remarkable."

Amazing research! Think how much more of an effect our words, our music, our prayers, and our environment have on human beings! It takes a lot of effort to break habits we get into, but the next time we think of calling somebody a bad name, think of this: It's the same as committing murder in God's eyes.

13.   Matthew 5:23-24

Therefore if you bring your gift to the altar, and there remember that your brother has something against you; 24. leave there your gift before the altar, and go your way; first be reconciled to your brother, and then come and offer your gift.
Matthew 8:4, Job 42:8.

It's a matter of the condition of the heart. If you have enmity between you and your brother or sister, you cannot come to God with a clear conscience with an offering.

There is a story about Norman Vincent Peale when he was a boy. He found a large cigar and hurried off to a secluded spot to try it out. He didn't like it, but he felt grown up, at least till he saw his father coming. Hoping to distract his father, he pointed to a billboard advertising a circus. "Can I go?" he begged. "Can I go to the circus when it comes to town? Please, dad?" "Son," his father said, "one of the first lessons you need to learn about life is this: never make a petition while at the same time trying to hide a smoldering disobedience behind your back."

God sees our hearts and wants us to come before him with nothing between him and us or a brother or sister. Repent! Turn! Teshuv! Sure it's hard to go to a person and ask forgiveness. Funny thing is, he says if your brother has something against you! We would think it would be the other way around! But no, we have to humble ourselves and go to that person and try to get things straightened out between us. If that person refuses to listen and won't forgive you, then you've done what you're commanded to do and then you can come before God with your offering, drawing near to him.

14. Matthew 5:25-26

25. Agree with your adversary quickly, while you are in the way with him; lest at any time the adversary deliver you to the judge, and the judge deliver you to the officer, and you be cast into prison. 26. Verily I say unto you, you shall by no means come out thence, till you have paid the uttermost farthing. (Love your enemies, seek peace with all men.)
Luke 12:58–59.

Hebrews 12:14: Follow peace with all men, and holiness, without which no man shall see the Lord:

Agree, isthi from the Greek, Strong's Concordance #G2468: It can mean "be you, give yourself wholly to," and combined with G2132: *eunoeō,* "To wish one well, to be well disposed, of a peaceable spirit."

Bible translators sometimes have a difficult time deciding on what Greek or Hebrew word to use. Here we have a difficult verse with a difficult translation. So which word would you have applied to this verse other than agree? Maybe "be well minded towards your adversary?" Or "be good to your enemy?" Maybe, "be well to your adversary?" Then there's, "know your adversary." In the word for "adversary," the Strong's Concordance says this could be an opponent in a lawsuit, especially Satan (Satan is not his name, it is a description and means adversary, one who withstands).

What did Yeshua do when confronted by Satan? Quoted Scripture to him.

I believe after looking at all the words this word "agree" can be translated into, he's telling us to treat them kindly, be as nice as you can be, and take them to arbitration and try to settle before you go to court. Even though we have the Holy Spirit living in us, our "evil inclination" as the Jews call it, our "selves" we call it, our flesh, rises up sometimes and wants to really hurt someone. It is hard because of the unfairness of it all, but, what would Yeshua do? I am far from thinking the word should be translated "agree." Very far. I would probably use "reconcile." Try to reconcile with your enemy before he takes you to court. Come to an agreement, which is different than "agree." Arbitration. It's a good thing.

Don't agree with something that is wrong, not biblical, and a downright lie. But try to stay in the spirit through this thing, have friends and your pastor pray, and trust that the Lord will take care of it for you. What if you lose? That is so hard. You know he's wrong, everyone knows he's wrong, but he wins. This is where testing comes in. I could tell you about instances in mine and my husband's lives where people have lied about us or done us wrong and it seems like they're getting away with it and then the Lord brings something into their life that has shown us he's in charge. It is very fearful sometimes to see the hand of the Lord defending you. So, stay in the spirit, trust him no matter what. Don't make friends with the adversary. Don't trust him. Trust the Lord.

On the other hand, Paul in Chapter 6 of First Corinthians talks about how to deal with a brother over a matter of law. The verse above is talking about our "enemy."

15.   Matthew 5:27

You have heard that it was said by them of old time, you shall not commit adultery:

Another of the Ten Commandments, quoting from Exodus 20:14, Deuteronomy 5:18, and Matthew 19:18.

Our secular society is all about promoting illicit sex. A lot of the advertisements on television are sensual, enticing us to buy, buy, buy! Making the product desirable to us. A lot of the music our children, teens, and adults are listening to is despicable. A lot of parents don't check out what words are being pounded into their children's ears. Our children are becoming numb to hearing illicit sex sung about, murder, beating women, etc. We're to be the watchmen over our children and screen everything that comes into our homes to keep them clean minded and free from the assault of the world on them. Maybe we can't screen what they hear or see while out of our homes, but while in our homes we can teach them about the effects of these things on people's lives. Looking on a woman (or man) with lust is "the thing." It's exalted in movies, songs, television, and books. The Bible says that in the last days good will be called evil and evil good. Teach your children and others about what the Bible says about living a life that is approved of by the Father.

One year our daughter Sherrie and son Jim went to our church's junior high camp. The leader was quite enthusiastic and a good youth leader, so much so that when they came home from that camp they were so "on fire" for the Lord that they wanted to tear through our house and get rid of "every evil thing." Well, they had to stop short because there wasn't anything. I think they found a pack of playing cards. Ha! But their enthusiasm was a joy to see. They learned at that camp to recognize things that shouldn't be in our homes or lives and in a way that they WANTED to please the Lord and get rid of anything that was between the Lord and them. That's the way we should all be — wanting to be pleasing to the Lord in everything in our lives. Don't go along just to get along. Follow the Word and listen to the leading of the Holy Spirit. Don't ignore the promptings of the Holy Spirit. It may cost you a friend or two, but better that than to cost you the displeasure of the Lord.

16.   Matthew 5:29-30

29. And if your right eye offend you, pluck it out, and cast it from you: for it is profitable for you that one of your members should perish, and not that your whole body should be cast into hell.

30. And if your right hand offend you, cut it off, and cast it from you: for it is profitable for you that one of your members should perish, and not that your whole body should be cast into hell. Mark 9:43, Colossians 3:5.

Proverbs 23:2: And put a knife to your throat, if you be a man given to appetite.

This is an exaggeration like we as parents sometimes do. It is called hyperbole. Also, the Pharisees were known for "building fences" around the commandments in order to keep them "religiously." Yeshua is stressing here to be careful to be watchful of sin in your life.

Babylonian Talmud, Kallah, Chapter 1: One who gazes lustfully upon the small finger of a married woman, it is as if he has committed adultery with her.

Babylonian Talmud, Niddah 13b: Better that one's belly burst than one should go down to the pit of destruction.

17.   Matthew 5:31-32

31. It has been said, Whosoever shall put away his wife, let him give her a writing of divorcement: 32. But I say unto you, That whosoever shall put away his wife, saving for the cause of fornication, causes her to commit adultery: and whosoever shall marry her that is divorced commits adultery.
See Luke 16:18. Also see Matthew 19:3–12.

This is a controversial and hard subject. Here, again, from Luke:

Luke 16:18: Whosoever puts away his wife, and marries another, commits adultery: and whosoever marries her that is put away from her husband commits adultery.

My friend, Sam Peak of Biblical Faith Ministries explains it this way:

"The first part of this verse (a) translates back into the Hebrew perfectly. The second part (b) does not." He explains that in part A, there is a "vav of purpose." Vav is the sixth letter of the Hebrew aleph-bet. It can stand for *and, but, or, so, then, because, therefore, namely, since, while, on the contrary*, etc. This vav tells us the purpose of what is going on. The vav used in this verse means *"in order to"* marry another. Whoever divorces his wife *"in order to marry another"* commits adultery. He explains that this could also mean *"Whoever divorces her husband."* In the Jewish law, a man can divorce his wife over any petty thing, like burning the toast. Here in our example, a wife could deliberately burn the toast, etc., *"in order to marry another."*

Part B of our verse, Luke 16:18b: "If the husband has set her up, she is free from this obligation not to marry and may marry. This is committing fraud."

The Delitzsch Hebrew Gospels, a Hebrew/English translation, in the footnotes for Luke 16:18 says, Or, "sends away his wife in order to marry."

In other words, he causes his wife to commit adultery or she causes her husband to commit adultery.

In Mark 10:1–12 we see this same question from one of the Pharisees:

1. And he arose from thence, and came into the region of Judaea by the farther side of Jordan. Again the people came to him. As was his custom, he taught them. 2. Some Pharisees came and tested him, asking, "Is it lawful for a man to put away his wife?" Yeshua tells them: 5. "For the hardness of your heart he wrote you this precept. 6. But from the beginning of the creation God made them male and female. 7. For this cause shall a man leave his father and mother, and cleave to his wife; 8. And they twain shall be one flesh: so then they are no more twain, but one flesh. 9. What therefore God has joined together, let not man put

asunder. 10. And in the house his disciples asked him again of the same matter. 11. And he said unto them, Whosoever shall put away his wife, and marry another, commits adultery against her. 12. And if a woman shall put away her husband, and be married to another, she commits adultery."

If you are a believer and have divorced your spouse and have remarried, don't let Satan condemn you. That's his job. Just ask the Lord to forgive you, repent of any sin you may have committed causing this divorce, then go on with your life. No one among us can cast the first stone, I guarantee it! If you haven't remarried and your ex-spouse hasn't remarried, don't even think of remarrying him or her.

Malachi 2:14: NIV: You ask, "Why?" It is because the Lord is the witness between you and the wife of your youth. You have been unfaithful to her, though she is your partner, the wife of your marriage covenant.

If you are married, you are bound before God in that relationship. If you are being abused, your spouse has broken your covenant. You are not expected to stay in that marriage. If he or she is committing adultery, you have a legal right to divorce.

The discussion continues in the next two verses:

Malachi 2:15-16: NIV: 15. Has not the one God made you? You belong to him in body and spirit. And what does the one God seek? Godly offspring. So be on your guard, and do not be unfaithful to the wife of your youth. 16. "The man who hates and divorces his wife," says the Lord, the God of Israel, "does violence to the one he should protect," says the Lord Almighty. So be on your guard, and do not be unfaithful.

To sum up, there are only three things that biblically release a marriage partner from a marriage: (1) the death of one marriage partner; (2) breaking the covenant through sexual unfaithfulness or acts that would void the contract, such as abuse; and (3) the desertion and divorce by an unbelieving marriage partner as told in the Christian Torah. That is the plain teaching of Scripture.

> Deuteronomy 24:4: Her former husband, who sent her away, may not take her again to be his wife, after that she is defiled; for that is abomination before the Lord: and you shall not cause the land to sin, which the Lord your God gives you for an inheritance.

Here we have what the Torah says about remarrying an ex–spouse. Although this is in the Sinaitic Covenant, the principle seems to me to be also pertaining to us as believers. It says if you're married and divorce your wife, don't take her back if she has been with another man. I'd say vice versa. That is considered "defiled." If we don't take this principle as pertaining to us, it opens the door for a lot of defilement in the church. It defiles the home, the children, and our families. God looks at the union of a husband and wife as sacred, a gift given to them. If we neglect that gift and take it as just a suggestion, it opens up a lot of excuses for sin in our lives. The bottom line is, how much do we want to live for the Lord? How much of our lives do we give to him? All, half, two-thirds? If we truly say that we accept Yeshua/Jesus as our personal Savior and are spirit filled, we need to give him ALL our lives and give up any wants in our life that aren't pleasing to him.

You have to work out your salvation in this one. Many people are married to someone they thought they loved and after a while realize they don't love them and want out. I'm the merciful person. I would tell you "leave him." But I'm sure not God. Pray a lot, talk to your pastor or a counselor, and then you decide which road to take.

To you who are not married, heed this. Make sure you love that person and are compatible and want to spend the rest of your life with them. Don't rush into it. Spend a couple years getting to know them, then weigh the pros and cons and see what you believe you can live with and what you can't. If you know there's one thing that's going to drive you crazy for the next 50 to 70 years of marriage, don't marry him. Both of you go to a believing marriage counselor before you marry. Many churches require it now and have some excellent counselors. If you don't click with the first counselor, ask for another one. But be sure you are going into this marriage with eyes way wide open.

If a little voice whispers in the back of your mind some doubts, heed it. Don't marry him or her if there are any doubts at all. Write these doubts down. Write the pros down. Compare them. Make yourself look at the reality of it all. Don't lie to yourself and think you can change him or her or that you can live with this one thing. Get it out in the open. Pray a lot.

18.   Matthew 5:33–37

33. Again, you have heard that it has been said by them of old time, You shall not swear falsely, but shall perform unto the Lord your oaths: 34. But I say unto you, Swear not at all; neither by heaven; for it is God's throne: 35. Nor by the earth; for it is his footstool: neither by Jerusalem; for it is the city of the great King. 36. Neither shall you swear by your head, because you cannot make one hair white or black. 37. But let your 'yes' mean 'yes' and your 'no' mean 'no,' for whatsoever is more than these comes of evil.
Matthew 23:16–22, Leviticus 19:12, Deuteronomy 23:23, James 5:12, Isaiah 66:1. Matthew 5:35, Colossians 4:6.

Don't make an oath or a vow you cannot keep. This does not forbid official oaths.

From the Babylonian Talmud, Bava Batra 49b: A righteous yes is a Yes; a righteous no is No.

"Don't swear." How many times do we hear, "I swear to God?" What? Just say yes or no? Or anything else is from the evil one? Or we hear, "I swear!"

You aren't to make an oath or vow in God's Name or in the Name of Yeshua/Jesus. Don't make promises to God because you might regret it. This is legally binding, so be careful. To show how serious this was, remember the story of Jephthah in Judges 11? Such a sad story, but this is an example that when you take an oath to God, you cannot renege on it without consequences.

> Judges 11:30–40: 30. And Jephthah vowed a vow unto the Lord, and said, If you shall without fail deliver the children of Ammon into mine hands, 31. then it shall be, that whatsoever comes forth of the doors of my house to meet me, when I return in peace from the children of Ammon, shall surely be the Lord's, and I will offer it up for a burnt offering. 32. So Jephthah passed over unto the children of Ammon to fight against them; and the Lord delivered them into his hands. 33. And he smote them from Aroer, even till you come to Minnith, even twenty cities, and unto the plain of the vineyards, with a very great slaughter. Thus the children of Ammon were subdued before the children of Israel. 34. And Jephthah came to Mizpeh unto his house, and, behold, his daughter came out to meet him with timbrels and with dances: and she was his only child; beside her he had neither son nor daughter. 35. And it came to pass, when he saw her, that he rent his clothes, and said, Alas, my daughter! You have brought me very low, and you are one of them that trouble me: for I have opened my mouth unto the Lord, and I cannot go back. 36. And she said unto him, My father, if you have opened your mouth unto the Lord, do to me according to that which has proceeded out of your mouth; forasmuch as the Lord has taken vengeance for you of your enemies, even of the children of Ammon. 37. And she said unto her father, Let this thing be done for me: let me alone two months, that I may go up and down upon the mountains, and bewail my virginity, I and my fellows. 38. And he said, Go. And he sent her away for two months: and she went with her companions, and bewailed her virginity upon the mountains. 39. And it came to pass at the end of two months, that she returned unto her father, who did with

her according to his vow which he had vowed: and she knew no man. And it was a custom in Israel, 40. that the daughters of Israel went yearly to lament the daughter of Jephthah the Gileadite four days in a year.

Be careful what you vow. Think about the consequences. Rather say, "If I can, I will," or, "If the Lord wills, I will."

Laws of non-retaliation:

19.   Matthew 5:39–42

39. But I say unto you, That you resist not evil: but whosoever shall smite you on your right cheek, turn to him the other also. 40. And if any man will sue you at the law, and take away your coat, let him have your cloak also. 41. And whosoever shall compel you to go a mile, go with him two. 42. Give to him that asks you, and from him that would borrow of you turn not you away.

I Corinthians chapter 6 goes into detail about this subject. This is also in the Beatitudes message and the subject is "go the second mile."

Here we have another hyperbolic teaching. He's speaking about what our attitude should be towards others. Remember, he was slapped and he had his cloak removed.

I Thessalonians 5:15: See that none render evil for evil unto any man; but ever follow that which is good, both among yourselves, and to all men.

To slap someone on the right cheek, if you're right handed, this means you give them a backhanded slap. How did he respond? With subjection. However, this was for the sake of his goal, to be sacrificed for us. If someone is robbing us, we are to defend ourselves. If we are being persecuted for the Gospel's sake, imitate him.

Verse 40: People usually only had two garments. This means if someone sues you and wins, he gets your coat. He says to give them your cloak also. This means you're left naked; in other words, you've given everything.

5:41: "Compels" is a technical term that refers to the law of impressment. "The act or policy of seizing people or property for public service or use." The Roman government could press anyone into its service to carry a load as far as one mile. Matthew records a Roman officer doing this to Simon of Cyrene in 27:32.

I don't think many of us if slapped on one cheek would gladly say, "Hit me here too!" I don't think many of us, if sued, would happily turn over his coat, let alone his cloak! None of us lose easily. That "dying to self" issue is hard to swallow if either of these happen. Let's check this out.

I was wondering if that word was really "evil" in verse 39.

The word "evil" in Greek is *ponēros,* Strong's Concordance #G4190: 1. Full of labors, annoyances, hardships. A. Pressed and harassed by labors. B. Bringing toils, annoyances, perils; of a time full of peril to Christian faith and steadfastness; causing pain and trouble. 2. Bad, of a bad nature or condition. A. In a physical sense: Diseased or blind. B. In an ethical sense: Evil, wicked, bad.

From a derivative of Strong's Concordance #G4192; hurtful, i.e. evil (properly, in effect or influence, and thus differing from Strong's Concordance #G2556, which refers rather to essential character, as well as from Strong's Concordance #G4550, which indicates degeneracy from original virtue); figuratively, calamitous; also (passively) ill, i.e. diseased; but especially (morally) culpable, i.e. derelict, vicious, facinorous; neuter (singular) mischief, malice, or (plural) guilt; masculine (singular) the devil, or (plural) sinners:

Used as: KJV – bad, evil, grievous, harm, lewd, malicious, wicked (–ness). See also Strong's Concordance #G4191.

Uh–hem. Well? Looks like to me it was hard for the translators to define this word. It's hard for us too. So all these years we've read, "But I tell you not to resist an evil person" meant to let them do what they will with you? Well, none of us have really <u>thought</u> that and we certainly haven't acted it out. So, how would you interpret this word? The Lord sure doesn't mean "stand there and take it" as elsewhere in Scripture he tells us to protect ourselves and our households. Yet now comes the big picture: What did the Lord do when arrested and taken before the accusers? Sure, Peter cut off a guy's ear, what we might do, but the Lord rebuked him. Yeshua/Jesus went meekly and took everything they dished out for our sakes. He certainly did not retaliate.

I think he's speaking to those that are going to go through hardships in the coming years. In 70 AD, the Romans destroyed the Temple and killed many of the Jewish people. Those left fled to other countries, which is one reason Christianity was spread throughout the world. In the holocaust, look at the stories of the Jewish people. Some of them did resist, but many did not. We have to use our judgment on this. Self-defense is part of the morality of the Scripture. The Jewish tendency I've noted throughout the years is to try to avoid it.

Look at King David. He tried his best to stay away from King Saul and others that were trying to kill him. I would say about this verse to "avoid" evil at all costs, stay out of danger as much as you can, do not provoke evil people to beat you up or kill you. If you are attacked or threatened and your life is in danger, protect yourself.

In some translations it says, "Resist the evil ONE," as Yeshua/Jesus did during the temptation.

Verse 42 was a Roman law.

20.   Matthew 5:43–48

43. You have heard that it has been said, You shall love your neighbor, and hate your enemy. 44. But I say unto you, Love your enemies, bless them that curse you, do good to them that hate you, and pray for them which despitefully use you, and persecute you; 45. That you may be the children of your Father which is in heaven: for he makes his sun to rise on the evil and on the good, and sends rain on the just and on the unjust. 46. For if you love them which love you, what reward have you? Do not even the publicans the same? 47. And if you salute your brethren only, what do you more than others? Do not even the publicans so? 48. Be you therefore perfect, even as your Father which is in heaven is perfect.

Leviticus 19:18 (love your neighbor as yourself). Luke 6:27, Romans 12:20–21, Acts 7:60 (the ultimate love sacrifice), I Peter 2:21, I Corinthians 4:12, I Peter 3:9, Colossians 1:28, 4:12, and Ephesians 5:1.

Here in a nutshell we have the Christian life. We have an understanding about why evil people prosper. We have our precious Lord telling us that it's easy to love our loved ones; the true test is loving those that are really hard to love; the unsaved, the downtrodden, the homeless, the orphan, the unlovely. If you wave and speak and love only those in your "circle," big deal! And here he says, "Be perfect, just as your Father in heaven is perfect." Wow. Me perfect? Do you really know me Lord? There's no way I can be anywhere near perfect. This makes me laugh. And cry. I wish I could be perfect like you Lord. But you have made me perfect in your eyes through your blood you shed for me on Calvary.

Let's take a look at a couple of people in the Torah that God called "perfect." This first one might surprise you as in Christian thinking, his name means in the English lexicons: *"traitor, deceiver, heel holder, supplanter."* But God calls him "perfect." (This might spur you on to learn Hebrew so you can see for yourselves what the Scripture really says.)

Genesis 25:23–28: 23. And the Lord said unto her, Two nations are in your womb, and two manner of people shall be separated from your bowels; and the one people shall be stronger than the other people; and the elder shall serve the younger. 24. And when her days to be delivered were fulfilled, behold, there were twins in her womb. 25. And the first came out red, all over like a hairy garment; and they called his name Esau. 26. And after that came his brother out, and his hand took hold on Esau's heel; and his name was called Jacob: and Isaac was threescore years old when she bare them. 27. And the boys grew: and Esau was a cunning hunter, a man of the field; and Jacob was a plain man, dwelling in tents. 28. And Isaac loved Esau, because he did eat of his venison: but Rebekah loved Jacob.

The word used to describe Esau is that he was *"a skillful hunter, a man of the field."* Another description of him is in Genesis 16:12: He shall be a wild man; his hand [shall be] against every man, and every man's hand against him. And he shall dwell in the presence of all his brethren.

The word used there for *"wild"* is actually *wild ass: Pere`* in Hebrew, Strong's Concordance #H6501. He will be a "wild ass of a man." We see this scenario being played out in the Middle East today with those coming against Israel being the descendants of Esau and Ishmael. The lexicon says *"so called for its running (the wild ass)."*

The word used in the Strong's Concordance to describe Jacob here is *"mild."* In other translations it is used as a "plain man, quiet man, peaceful man." The actual word in Hebrew is *"tam, perfect."*

From *BlueLetterBible.org* lexicon for "perfect:" Strong's Concordance #8535: *Tam.*

> 1) perfect, complete
> a) complete, perfect

1) one who lacks nothing in physical strength, beauty, etc
   b) sound, wholesome
1) an ordinary, quiet sort of person
   c) complete, morally innocent, having integrity
1) one who is morally and ethically pure

This is how God sees Jacob. So where in Christianity did we come up with the idea that Jacob is a deceiver? True, the name Jacob means: "heel holder" or "supplanter." He certainly did grab hold of his brother's heel when he was coming out of the womb. So why does God call him "perfect?" Have we been given the wrong slant on this man? Has that one thing colored our idea of the Jewish people too much? And if we see now that GOD calls him perfect, shouldn't we take a closer look?

Here Jeremiah explains why we might have believed lies.

> Jeremiah 16:19: "O Lord, my strength, and my fortress, and my refuge in the day of affliction, the Gentiles shall come unto you from the ends of the earth, and shall say, surely our fathers have inherited lies, vanity, and [things] wherein [there is] no profit."

So what do we do? First, you can learn Hebrew or use study material to help you glean out the true meaning of words, or find someone who knows these things. The People of the Book. Find a Jewish believer to study with or someone who knows the Torah. Check out more than one commentary, letting at least one of those be a Jewish one. Look at different translations of the Bible.

Here it is prophesied in Zechariah about the end times:

> Zechariah 8:23: Thus says the Lord of hosts; In those days [it shall come to pass], that ten men shall take hold out of all languages of the nations, even shall take hold of the skirt of him that is a Jew, saying, We will go with you: for we have heard [that] God [is] with you.

In other words, we, the goy, or Gentiles, will seek out a Jewish believer or a rabbi and learn what they know. We'll ask them to teach us. They are the People of the Book and know things we don't. We see that happening right now with the advent of the "Messianic Movement" in about 1960.

When Constantine came in and persecuted the Jews and loved the Gentile Christians, the Jewish believers were dispersed to other lands; thus, the distribution of the gospel to the world! But the Gentile Christians were left to fend for themselves as far as learning the Bible. We've done a pretty good job, but there are a few things that need to be explained. Who better to teach us than a Jewish man or woman that was raised learning the Word, the Torah (teaching), in the Hebrew Language since the day they were born? They've explained to us many things. They shiver in their boots when we call Jacob "the deceiver" because they look at the big picture of what God thought of him, a perfect man.

As we know, many of the interpretations have been done by men that hated Jews. They are men that think the church replaced Israel. This is called "replacement theology." Certainly, if you read the Word, you can see there is a time coming where Israel will be restored as a nation. Israel became a nation in 1948. The slant here in our verse was put on the meaning of Jacob's name in those translations and commentaries. If we stand back and look at the big picture, we see what the outcome was of Jacob and his mother deceiving Isaac.

We are not going into an in-depth commentary here on the story of why Rebecca did what she did and what would have been the outcome had she not. We only have to see the prophecy given to Rebecca by the Lord that Esau would serve Jacob. Did she tell Isaac what the Lord had told her? I wonder if Isaac discerned it himself. We see later that Jacob received the duty to carry on the Abrahamic covenant, that Isaac did bless him with that. Was Rebecca wrong in what she did? Was Jacob wrong in obeying her? That's not for us to judge, but God knew her heart and the reason. We as mothers try to run ahead of the Lord concerning our children sometimes and work things out for their good instead of trusting and turning it over to him.

IF Esau had been given the duty of carrying on the Abrahamic covenant, where would the Jews be today? We see what Esau's descendants turned into while looking at the Middle East today and the enemies surrounding Israel. Would there have even been an Israel? In the end, God's will was done in that Isaac became the father of Jacob who had twelve sons that did carry out the blessing. Of course, we know God worked it out.

Back to our verse that God called Jacob a *"perfect man."* We look at Jacob's life and sometimes it didn't look so perfect, but he obeyed God and worshipped him.

Does God look at us and call us perfect? In Luke 1:5-6, Luke talks about Zacharias and Elizabeth as being "righteous, walking in all the commandments and ordinances of the Lord, blameless."

> Luke 1:5–6: 5. There was in the days of Herod, the King of Judaea, a certain priest named Zacharias, of the course of Abia: and his wife [was] of the daughters of Aaron, and her name [was] Elisabeth. 6. And they were both righteous before God, walking in all the commandments and ordinances of the Lord blameless.

They were called "righteous" and "blameless."

> In the Greek dictionary, it explains the word *"blameless"* as "blameless, deserving no censure, free from fault or defect." The lexicon also says "in which nothing is lacking."

This does not mean that they were without sin as our "sin nature" is always there. The Jews call it our "evil inclination." Like Adam and Chava (Eve's real name), they had a choice. Adam and Chava chose evil and Zacharias and Elizabeth chose good. They "walked in all the commandments and ordinances of the Lord, blameless." They kept and obeyed the 613 commandments given to the Jews at Sinai. Abraham kept the commandments that were given to him. Jacob kept the Word as given to him at that point from Shem and Abraham. He obeyed God. If he had not, there would be no Jewish nation.

The second man in the Torah called *"perfect"* was Job:

> Job 1:1: There was a man in the land of Uz, whose name [was] Job; and that man was perfect and upright, and one that feared God, and eschewed evil.

He didn't seem so perfect sometimes though, did he? The story of Job is fascinating. We should read it carefully as it is also a picture of ourselves and gives us an insight into how things work in the heavenlies. It opens a door for us to see "the other side."

It is said in the Jewish commentaries that this was on Rosh HaShanah, the Jewish New Year on the civil calendar, the first month, Tishrei 1. It is said that every Jewish new year, Rosh HaShanah, the books are opened, the gates are opened, and we are judged, but ten days later on Yom Kippur, the books are closed, the gate is closed, and the judging is final for the year.

Satan (the adversary) came before God with the other "sons of God." (Job 1:5) God asks him, "Where are you coming from?" Satan answers, "From going to and fro in the earth and from walking up and down in it." Then God says something so absolutely awesome. Pay attention. Herein the insight:

> Job 1:8–12: 8. And the Lord said unto Satan, Have you considered my servant Job, that [there is] none like him in the earth, a perfect and an upright man, one that fears God, and shuns evil? 9. Then Satan answered the Lord, and said, does Job fear God for nothing? 10. Have not you made a hedge about him, and about his house, and about all that he has on every side? You have blessed the work of his hands, and his substance is increased in the land. 11. But put forth your hand now, and touch all that he has, and he will curse you to your face. 12. And the Lord said unto Satan, Behold, all that he has [is] in your power; only upon the man himself put not forth your hand. So Satan went forth from the presence of the Lord.

Wow! What insight into how things operate. "Have you considered my servant, Job?" Does the Lord say this to Satan about us? You see here how the Lord gives the leeway to Satan. Satan can't just do to you whatever he wants or he'd kill you, destroy your family, etc.; but God knows how much testing you can take and allows only that. You see also Satan says, "Have you not made a hedge around him, around his household, and around all that he has on every side?" There you go. We all, believers in Yeshua/Jesus, have a hedge built around us. Does he not give us a guardian angel?

> Psalm 91:11: For he will command his angels concerning you to guard you in all your ways.

See the story of Peter in Acts 12. The Word says an angel was sent to rescue him.

> Acts 12:11: And when Peter was come to himself, he said, Now I know of a surety, that the Lord has sent his angel, and has delivered me out of the hand of Herod, and from all the expectation of the people of the Jews.

And in Acts 12:15 the group says, "You are mad." But the girl constantly affirmed that it was even so. Then said they, "It is his angel."

And, most importantly, our Savior says,

> "See that you despise not one of these little ones: for I say to you, that their angels in heaven always see the face of my Father who is in heaven." Matthew 18:10.

There are many other examples of this in the Scriptures that you can find.

I have seen my angel. We lived in a house that had a fireplace and a gas heater on the same wall in the living room. At night we used the heater and during the day when my husband and kids were at work and school I heated the house with the fireplace. I started getting severe headaches, so severe I couldn't even see. I thought I was dying of a brain tumor. They got worse and worse and I prayed and asked the Lord to help me many times and had my husband and children pray for me.

One night I woke up to see a transparent, beautiful being standing at the foot of my bed and he was communicating with me by mental telepathy. You've seen pictures of the aurora borealis? Those were the transparent colors he was wearing. He was saying, "You're dying. You're dying." Somehow he impressed on me to call the gas repairman. The next day I called the repairman and when he examined the heater, he said, "Lady, by all rights, you should be dead. The fireplace is sucking pure carbon dioxide into this room constantly."

Many times my husband and I have been saved while driving on the highways, many that we probably don't even know about. One time we came around a corner on a steep mountain road where the drop off on our side was many feet down. A pickup towing a trailer was coming around the corner the other direction, half over on our side. We both screamed, "Jesus!" and the trailer went right through our car. We both looked at each other in disbelief and my husband had a hard time concentrating on driving! Wow. He is God and he is alive today. He says to call on him in our day of trouble. I bet the guy in the pickup had a little bit of a heart attack!

Many more stories I could tell you, but I just want to say to you to believe in him, trust in him, and call on him. He's right there! He looks at you believers in him as TAM, a perfect person under the blood of Yeshua. Imagine that. Do you think our loving heavenly Father would command us to be perfect if he thought we couldn't? But we become perfect through Yeshua HaMashiach, Jesus the Messiah, when we accept him into our hearts and lives. Nothing we can do can earn us that perfection. It is a free gift.

1 John 3:1-2: 1. Behold, what manner of love the Father has bestowed upon us, that we should be called the sons of God: therefore the world knows us not, because it knew him not.

2. Beloved, now are we the sons of God, and it does not yet appear what we shall be: but we know that, when he shall appear, we shall be like him; for we shall see him as he is.

In the Babylonian Talmud, Yoma 23a, Gitin 36b, Shabbat 88b: They who are insulted but insult not back; who hear themselves reproached but answer not; who serve out of love and rejoice in their affliction — of them it is written in Scripture: They that love God are as the going forth of the sun in its might."

Wow, people! That's you and I!

21.   Matthew 6:1–4

1. Take heed that you do not your alms before men, to be seen of them: otherwise you have no reward of your Father which is in heaven. 2. Therefore when you do [your] alms, do not sound a trumpet before you, as the hypocrites do in the synagogues and in the streets, that they may have glory of men. Verily I say unto you, They have their reward. 3. But when you do alms, let not your left hand know what your right hand does: 4. That your alms may be in secret: and your Father which sees in secret himself shall reward you openly.
Romans 12:8, Luke 14:12–14.

Notice he says, "When." When you do a charitable deed. So that means you should do it, right?

Don't brag about how much you give for charity. Don't even let your left hand know what your right hand gave.

Notice this isn't talking about tithing. This is talking about giving to charity.

Sounding the trumpet is a Hebrew idiom I am told. When people gave money for charity at the Temple, they put it in a box designated for that purpose. The top of the box was shaped like a wide trumpet. It was made out of metal. Some of the people that wanted everyone to know they were giving would be sure that their money made a great noise while going down the "trumpet" to the box where it was collected. They made sure to have lots of coins. Therefore, "sounding the trumpet."

The Pharisees were often guilty of not following their own teachings:

Babylonian Talmud, Berachot 17b: Don't do good deeds to be noticed.

Babylonian Talmud, Bava Batra 9b: He who gives alms in secret is greater than Moses.

Babylonian Talmud, Bava Batra 10b: The greatest form of charity is when you give and do not know to whom you give, and the recipient takes and does not know from whom he takes.

Awesome. True charity.

22.   Matthew 6:5–8

6. And when you pray, you shall not be as the hypocrites [are]: for they love to pray standing in the synagogues and in the corners of the streets, that they may be seen of men. Verily I say unto you, They have their reward. 6. But you, when you pray, enter into your closet, and when you have shut your door, pray to your Father which is in secret; and your Father which sees in secret shall reward you openly. 7. But when you pray, use not vain repetitions, as the heathen [do]: for they think that they shall be heard for their much speaking. 8. Don't be like them: for your Father knows what things you have need of, before you ask him.
Ecclesiastes 5:2, I Kings 18:26, Romans 8:26–27.

I like the verse in Ecclesiastes 5:2:

Do not be rash with your mouth, and let not your heart utter anything hastily before God. For God is in heaven and you on earth; therefore, let your words be few.

In other words, pray from the heart to the Father. Pray with a sincere heart.

Babylonian Talmud, Berachot 55a: One who prays too intensely and too lengthily brings on himself heartache.

23.   Matthew 6:9–13

9. After this manner therefore pray you: Our Father which art in heaven, Hallowed be your name. 10. Your Kingdom come. Your will be done in earth, as [it is] in heaven. 11. Give us this day our daily bread. 12. And forgive us our debts, as we forgive our debtors. 13. And lead us not into temptation, but deliver us from evil: For yours is the Kingdom, and the power, and the glory, forever. Amen.

This prayer Yeshua taught his disciples has been taught many times over the last 2000 years. So many good points I have seen made. The one I like best is that it is akin to the Aveinu prayer prayed by the Jews. Our Father. Av is father and the nu ending makes it our. You see in the above teaching, he said not to pray repetitively, so he's not teaching us here to quote these exact words, but he's teaching us the pattern of prayer. The tavneet.

Verse 9: First of all, we recognize that God is in heaven and he is holy and his name is holy. This pertains to the first commandment in the 10 Commandments.

Exodus 20:3: You shall have no other Gods before me.

You begin your prayer with this acknowledgement. A lot of Jewish prayers begin with, "Blessed are you O Lord our God, King of the universe." Then you state "who created," and say what he created, like bread or fruit, etc. But you always acknowledge him as King.

You acknowledge he is Holy. "Holy is your Name."

Verse 10: Secondly, you acknowledge that his kingdom will come and his will WILL be done in earth as it is in heaven. If he is a king, he has to have a Kingdom. If he's YOUR king, you acknowledge that.

Verse 11: Thirdly, you acknowledge that he is the supplier of all sustenance in your life. Daily bread speaks of the manna in the wilderness. We need to acknowledge that just like that manna in the desert, he also gives us our daily needs. Manna is a picture of the sustenance of his Word also. Physical and spiritual.

> From Jerome's commentary on Matthew 6:11: "In the gospel, which is named according to the Hebrews, instead of supersubstantial bread I found mahar (מהר), which means "of tomorrow," so that the sense would be: Our bread for tomorrow, that is, the future [bread] give us this day."

Verse 12: Fourthly, forgive us our debts as we forgive our debtors. Remember the parable of the rich man that owed a lot of money to someone and a poor person owed him a little amount? He could not forgive that poor person, but wanted his debtor to forgive him.

Verse 13: Fifthly, lead us not into temptation, but deliver us from evil. This reaches clear back to Adam and Chava in the garden. If they had only prayed this prayer that day and acknowledged that God was in control, maybe they wouldn't have fallen. We need to pray this every morning for ourselves and our family.

I was reading a book by Rabbi Avraham Sutton, *Spiritual Technology* On page 41, chapter three, he says,

> "We can now render, "The tree of knowing good and evil" as "the tree of JOINING (my emphasis) good and evil." He explains that the problem is that good and evil were intermingled with each other. "When this occurs, the lines between them become

blurred. We lose our ability to distinguish between them. There is nothing farther away from true knowledge than this. For here, instead of good (goodness) being connected to truth and holiness, it becomes connected to evil, giving it existence and power."

In the Book of Leviticus we read about mixture in chapter 19:19. God hates mixture in our lives. It is a complicated subject for Christians as we aren't usually taught about this. We're taught for sure to stay away from sin and to guard our hearts and don't smoke, don't chew, and don't go with the girls that do, but understanding what God says about mixture is foreign to most of us.

> Leviticus 19:19: You shall keep my statutes. You shall not let your cattle breed with another kind: you shall not sow your field with mingled seed: neither shall a garment mingled of linen and woolen come upon you.
> Also see Deuteronomy 22:9–11.

What does this have to do with us? And what do the three things have to do with each other?

We can understand number one and maybe number two, but what difference was it if they wore a garment that was interwoven with linen and wool? What is the spiritual implication of that?

I was studying this and I prayed and asked the Lord to help me understand. The Jews say this verse is a "chok," pronounced "hoke," or a commandment that has no explanation, they're just commanded to obey it. I wouldn't take no for an answer, so I e-mailed Rabbi Sutton and asked him. He wrote me back and suggested I read about this in the Rabbi Hirsch Chumash. Chumash in Hebrew means five and is the five books of what we call the "Pentateuch." Behold, I had my Leviticus Chumash lying right there on the coffee table. Rabbi Hirsch is one of the most famous rabbis to the Jewish people. His commentaries are in-depth and thorough.

I picked it up and found Leviticus 19:19. I was in for quite a trip. I won't go into the long details of it all. The meaning of not wearing linen and wool together is not simple, but I'll just try to explain to you the bottom line. This law is called "shatnez" in Hebrew.

From page 634 in The Hirsch Chumash on Vayikra/Leviticus: "Wool and linen are the materials specifically suited for man's clothing. They are related to the very essence of man – and this provides us with the key to their meaning. An analysis of this meaning reveals the following: The separation of these materials in clothing is a direct and positive expression of man's ultimate purpose, and invests clothing with the character of human clothing.

We explained in our commentary of the law of not eating meat with dairy in Exodus 23:19 that the human body – like the animal organism – contains two elements: the vegetative (nourishment and reproduction) and the animal (perception and motion). But man differs from the animal in the relation of these two elements to each other: In the animal, the animal element serves the vegetative element. That is to say, perfection, sensation, and motion serve the physical drives for nourishment and reproduction. Man, however, has a different purpose. His task is to subordinate within himself the vegetative element to the animal element, and the animal element to the human element; he is to subordinate his lower faculties to his intelligent and free-willed spirit. Through the spirit, also the animal and the vegetative are to be subordinated to God, and to his Holy Will. Man is like a pyramid pointing upward to God, whereas the animal is like a closed circuit. In the animal, the animal and vegetative forces are closely intertwined."

Therefore, linen comes from a plant, the flax plant. It stands for our vegetative element. Wool comes from an animal, a sheep. It stands for our animal element. We would think that the animal was the lower element because of the fact that we're always talking about our "animal nature," but in this case, it is the higher element.

I heard this saying one time. It has variously been attributed to being an old Indian saying: "Inside of me there are two dogs. One of the dogs is mean and evil. The other dog is good. The mean dog fights the good dog, all of the time." When asked which dog wins, he reflected for a moment and replied, "The one I feed the most."

In view of this description, if your focus is mostly on what you wear, what you eat, etc., then you are feeding the vegetative element. The physical element is number one in your life. If you subdue that element with the desire to raise yourself above the vegetative element by perception and motion, moving yourself away from the materialistic being your main focus, this is having the willpower to make the eternal our main focus. We are putting the spiritual element first in our life.

Remember in the story of Cain and Abel that Cain brought a vegetable offering and Abel brought an animal offering. In this instance, it must be a blood offering. God rejected Cain's offering because there was no blood in his offering and blood atones.

This is like the two sons of Aaron, Nadab and Abihu, who took "strange fire" before the Lord. Their hearts may have been right, but they were in disobedience concerning what God had asked.

The same with Cain. He knew that God required animal sacrifice with blood. His heart may have been right, but he was in disobedience to what God had asked. He killed his brother in a rage over being rejected by God. This is the same as people in the world who act like they're doing everything right, giving to charities, working to help people in all kinds of organizations, etc., but it is the blood that God requires of us to be acceptable in his sight. The blood of Yeshua HaMashiach, Jesus the Messiah, is the only thing that takes away our sin and makes us acceptable before him.

We all need to do acts of kindness, give to charities, and help people, but these are not what save us. Only the blood of Yeshua can do that.

Let us "draw near," which the Hebrew word is "korban," which we translate "sacrifice," to him. Only through the blood can we draw near to him. Let us put the spiritual, the animal element of perfection, sensation, and motion, first. The vegetative element is to support that element in us, make us able to draw near to him so he can perfect our spirits.

> Revelation 19:8: And to her was granted that she should be arrayed in fine linen, clean and white: for the fine linen is the righteousness of saints.

The linen garment is what the Levitical priests wore. We see at the end of the book that that is what we will be wearing. "Fine linen is the righteousness of saints." So at the end we see linen does have a part in bringing it all together. Fine linen, clean and bright, representative of what he is clothing us with, righteousness.

Also see Matthew 6:19–34 below.

From *Yashanet.com's* study on Matthew:

> The verses commonly known as, the "Lord's Prayer," can be paralleled to concepts found in other Jewish sources. It is a combination of ideas already familiar to his audience:

Our Father which art in heaven, Hallowed be thy name.	Our Father who art in heaven (Babylonian Talmud; Yoma 85b, Sotah 49b, Avot 5:20; Vayikra Rabbah ch 32.)
Thy Kingdom come,	May God's kingdom be established during the days of your life. (Kaddish prayer)
Thy will be done in earth, as it is in heaven. Give us this day our daily bread.	Do thy will above and give comfort to those below, and to everyone his need. (Babylonian Talmud, Berachot 29b)
And forgive us our debts, as we forgive our debtors.	One who is merciful toward others, God will be merciful toward them. (Babylonian Talmud, Shabat 151b)

And lead us not into temptation, but deliver us from evil:	Bring me not into temptation, and lead me away from iniquity ... and save me from the evil one. (Babylonian Talmud, Berachot 80b)
For thine is the Kingdom, and the power, and the glory, forever. Amen.	For Thine, O Lord, is the greatness and the power and the glory and the victory and the majesty (Tenakh, 1 Chronicles 29:10)

From John Parson of *Hebrew4Christians.org* (see above) on the portion reading for the week of July 20, 2013:

"Our Torah portion for this week begins, "And I pleaded with the Lord at that time, to say..." (Deuteronomy 3:23), which implies that we must first pray in order to be able to pray, that is, we make ourselves ready to pray by finding the inner freedom and grace to groan before the Lord. If you can't find the words to pray, then plead with the Lord and ask for the Holy Spirit to groan on your behalf (Romans 8:26). "Ask, and it will be given to you; seek, and you will find; knock, and it will be opened to you" (Matthew. 7:7). "O Lord, open my lips, and my mouth will show forth your praise." (Psalm 51:15)."

24.   Matthew 6:14-15

14. For if you forgive men their trespasses, your heavenly Father will also forgive you: 15. But if you forgive not men their trespasses, neither will your Father forgive your trespasses. See Mark 11:25, Matthew 18:35.

Wow! This sometimes takes a lot of prayer. Sometimes the other person never repents for something he's done to you. Nevertheless, you have to forgive him, and only through the power of the Holy Spirit can you do this, and then you can expect the Lord to forgive you for trespasses you have committed against him.

Babylonian Talmud, Rosh HaShanah 17a: Only if you forgive others will God forgive you.

Babylonian Talmud, Shabat 151b: One who is merciful toward others, God will be merciful toward him.

25.   Matthew 6:16–18

16. Moreover when you fast, be not, as the hypocrites, of a sad countenance: for they disfigure their faces, that they may appear unto men to fast. Verily I say unto you, They have their reward. 17. But you, when you fast, anoint your head, and wash your face; 18. That you appear not unto men to fast, but unto your Father which is in secret: and your Father, which sees in secret, shall reward you openly. See Isaiah 58:3–7.

This is pretty self-explanatory. He does not say IF you fast, he says WHEN you fast. Fasting is a powerful tool used along with fervent prayer. Fasting connects you to the person or thing you're praying for and changes their heart or changes the situation. If you say, "I can't fast," just try one or two meals at first. Did you see where Yeshua says the Father is? "In the secret place."

The word used here for "*secret*" is "*kryptos*" in Greek, Strong's Concordance #G2927: "Hidden, concealed, secret."

Here Yeshua tells us the Father is hidden, concealed, in a secret place. How exciting for us that we will someday see that secret place and be with the Father. However, today God hides. What helps us to learn the heart of the Father? Prayer, fasting, Bible study. Yeshua/Jesus promised to send the Holy Spirit to reveal all things. If we pray, he will.

By the way, you see in Isaiah the word "afflict?" That means to fast. How do we know this? From my friend, Joseph Good of Hatikva Ministries:

Afflicting the soul is a requirement on Yom Kippur. This is equated with fasting. How do we know this? Tractate Yoma lays out that afflicting the soul is equal to fasting because of a reference in Devarim (Deuteronomy) 8:16 "Who has fed you in the wilderness with manna, which your fathers knew not, in order to afflict you." I would also reference Yeshiyahu 58 (Isaiah) that begins with a reference to Rosh HaShanah and the blowing of the shofar to show the people their transgressions. Further on, in verses 5–8, it says, "Is it such a fast that I have chosen, a day for a man to afflict his soul?" The verse from the Tanach (the Old Testament) corroborates what the Talmud teaches.

26.   Matthew 6:19–24

19. Lay not up for yourselves treasures upon earth, where moth and rust does corrupt, and where thieves break through and steal: 20. But lay up for yourselves treasures in heaven, where neither moth nor rust does corrupt, and where thieves do not break through nor steal: 21. For where your treasure is, there will your heart be also. 22. The light of the body is the eye: if therefore your eye be single, your whole body shall be full of light. 23. But if your eye be evil, your whole body shall be full of darkness. If therefore the light that is in you is darkness, how great [is] that darkness! 24. No man can serve two masters: for either he will hate the one, and love the other; or else he will hold to the one, and despise the other. You cannot serve God and money.

Verse 23 speaks of the good eye or bad eye. In context, if your eye is "evil," this is speaking of being stingy. This is a Hebrew idiom, meaning you are stingy with your giving. You don't open your heart to those in need. You don't give to causes. You're stingy with giving to your family. I know a stingy person and it is not a pleasant sight. It affects everyone around you. You have no compassion on others. I've noticed also that stingy people are always unhappy.

What does the Bible say about this:

1 John 3:17: But whoso has this world's good, and sees his brother have need, and shuts up his bowels [of compassion] from him, how dwells the love of God in him?

If you have this problem, it can only be changed by the Holy Spirit and your will to want to change. If you pray fervently and ask the Lord to forgive you for being stingy and diligently seek him, he will help you to change. After all, didn't your Lord Yeshua/Jesus give EVERYTHING for you?

Babylonian Talmud, Sotah 48b: He who has what to eat today, and says, "What shall I eat on the morrow?" has little faith.

Babylonian Talmud, Berachot 9b: Each day has enough of its own troubles.

27.   Matthew 6:25–27

25. Therefore I say unto you, Take no thought for your life, what you shall eat, or what you shall drink; nor yet for your body, what you shall put on. Is not the life more than meat, and the body than raiment? 26. Behold the fowls of the air: for they sow not, neither do they reap, nor gather into barns; yet your heavenly Father feeds them. Are you not much better than they? 27. Which of you by taking thought can add one cubit unto his stature?

28.   Matthew 6: 28

And why take you thought for raiment? Consider the lilies of the field, how they grow; they toil not, neither do they spin:

29.   Matthew 6:31–34

31. Therefore take no thought, saying, What shall we eat? or, What shall we drink? or, Wherewithal shall we be clothed? 32. (For after all these things do the Gentiles seek:) for your heavenly Father knows that you have need of all these things. 33. But seek you first the Kingdom of God, and his righteousness; and all these things shall be added unto you. 34. Take therefore no thought for the morrow: for the morrow shall take thought for the things of itself. Sufficient unto the day is the evil thereof.

This goes back to our commentary on the Lord's Prayer and the physical and spiritual elements. This is a beautiful discourse by our Messiah on what matters in this world, on trusting. It's really difficult as human beings not to worry, but here he commands us not to. If you catch yourself worrying, go away to your secret place and seek him and ask him to comfort you and help you to trust. Get into the Word and read encouraging passages with a promise, play Christian/Messianic music. Read books on faith. Sing. And trust him. Seek the one thing that matters in this life and the next, putting him first in our lives.

30.   Matthew 7:1–4

1. Judge not, that you be not judged. 2. For with what judgment you judge, you shall be judged: and with what measure you mete, it shall be measured to you again. 3. And why behold you the mote that is in your brother's eye, but consider not the beam that is in your own eye? 4. Or how wilt you say to your brother, Let me pull out the mote out of your eye; and, behold, a beam [is] in your own eye?
Romans 14:3, Luke 6:38, Luke 6:41.

31.   Matthew 7:5

You hypocrite, first cast out the beam out of your own eye; and then shall you see clearly to cast out the mote out of your brother's eye.
James 1:23–25. (Be doers of the Word and not hearers only.)
Romans 2:21–23. James 2:1-4.

James in chapter two is speaking of partiality. We're all partial to certain others, aren't we? But should we hold that person as above others?

There was a story going around Facebook about a man that was taking over a church as pastor one Sunday. No one had met him, only the elders. Church started and in came this bum dressed in rags, unshaven, hair askew. He walked around asking for change and food. Everyone in the church shunned him. No one spoke to him. People walked way around him. He sat down on the front pew and the usher asked him to sit in the back. The singing started, the announcements were given, and then an elder got up to the pulpit to introduce their new pastor.

The people all started clapping and looking around for him. Up came the bum! Everyone gasped! The new pastor, dressed in rags, unshaven, hair askew, said, "Then the King will say to those on his right, 'Come, you who are blessed by my Father; take your inheritance, the Kingdom prepared for you since the creation of the world. For I was hungry and you gave me something to eat, I was thirsty and you gave me something to drink, I was a stranger and you invited me in, I needed clothes and you clothed me, I was sick and you looked after me, I was in prison and you came to visit me.' Then the righteous will answer him, 'Lord, when did we see you hungry and feed you, or thirsty and give you something to drink? When did we see you a stranger and invite you in, or needing clothes and clothe you? When did we see you sick or in prison and go to visit you?' The King will reply, 'Truly I tell you, whatever you did for one of the least of these brothers and sisters of mine, you did for me.'" (Matthew 25:34–46)

After he recited this, he looked towards the congregation and told them all what he had experienced that morning. Many began to cry and many heads were bowed in shame. He then said, "Today I see a gathering of people, not a church of Jesus Christ. The world has enough people, but not enough disciples. When will YOU decide to become disciples?" He then dismissed service until next week. Being a Christian is more than something you claim. It's something you live by and share with others.

An article on *examiner.com* says, "This tale is also one that is extremely similar to something that happened in the opening of an 1897 novel from Charles Monroe Sheldon called "In His Steps: What Would Jesus Do?" The tale was also one that was a social psychology experiment at Princeton University in 1970. Again, the story of Pastor Jeremiah Steepek is one that is heartwarming and one that merits much thought. It's true in some regard, but not entirely as it is being made out to be as it makes the Internet rounds."

So the story is a made-up one, but it makes us think deeper about our attitude, doesn't it? We should all be more kind to those that we think are below us and remember that they're also the creation of God and need our kindness, compassion, and respect.

Babylonian Talmud, Avot 2:14: Do not judge your fellow until you have been in his place.

Babylonian Talmud, Avot 4:10: Do not be a judge of others, for there is no judge but the one (God).

Babylonian Talmud, Mishnah Sotah 1:7: By a person's standard of measure, is he, too, measured.

Babylonian Talmud, Shabat 127b: How you judge others, does God judge you.

Babylonian Talmud, Er'chin 16b: Rabbi Tarfon said, "I wonder if there be anyone in this era who will allow himself to be reproved. If someone says to another, 'Cast out the speck that is in your eye!' he will retort, 'Cast out first the beam that is in your own eye!'"

Babylonian Talmud, Kidushin 70a: He who condemns others, sees in them his own faults.

Babylonian Talmud, Bava Mezia 59a: Do not rebuke your fellow with your own blemish.

Pretty clear. How often do we judge someone by what we THINK we see? Put yourself in other people's place. If you haven't walked in their shoes, you have no right to judge them. Our Master says, "Don't judge." But love. Love that person and put yourself last. Pray about the "logs" in our own eyes. What others see in us. And love. Love covers a multitude of faults. If you can help that person, do it lovingly and not judgingly or acting superiorly.

32.   Matthew 7:6

Do not give what is holy to the dogs; nor cast your pearls before swine, lest they trample them under their feet, and turn and tear you in pieces.
See Proverbs 9:7–8, Matthew 15:14, 2 Corinthians 6:14–18.

That which is holy is the Torah.

Babylonian Talmud, Ket. 111a: R. Levi said: "God made Israel swear that they should not reveal the [Messianic] end, and should not reveal the secrets of [of the Torah] to the idolaters."

You might be surprised to learn that the dogs and pigs to the Jews are the Gentiles! They have to be careful whom they come into contact with concerning uncleanness. All the purity laws to them are so important. If they came into contact with a Gentile that was contaminated, they would have to go to the mikveh (ritual bath) for cleansing. There are rituals attached to all types of uncleanness. Swine, of course, are the most unclean. The swine is a non-kosher animal. They could not eat it. But what is casting our "pearls" before them?

The Lexicon word for "*pearls:*"

"A proverb, a word of great value." From Thayer's Greek Lexicon: "To thrust the most sacred and precious teachings of the gospel upon the most wicked and abandoned men (incompetent as they are, through their hostility to the gospel, to receive them), and thus to profane them." Strong's Concordance #G3135.

In other words, telling unbelievers scriptural things they aren't ready for or want to believe. They will make a mockery of it.

Carey Kinsolving from his *Kids Talk about God* web site says,

> "Jesus spoke of religious leaders who were offended by what he said: 'Let them alone. They are blind leaders of the blind. And if the blind leads the blind, both will fall into the ditch.' (Matthew 15:14). Don't waste your time preaching to those who are obviously hardened and scornful. Think about this: The pearl of great value in the gospel of Matthew is the messianic King and Kingdom foretold by the ancient prophets. Memorize this truth: 'Again, the Kingdom of heaven is like a merchant seeking beautiful pearls, who, when he had found one pearl of great price, went and sold all that he had and bought it.' (Matthew 13:45-46). Ask this question: Then and now, some see Jesus Christ as the promised messiah and trust him as their Savior, while others mock and scornfully reject him. Which will you do?"

By the way, the word for pearl in Greek is *margarites*. So if your name is Pearl, it is *Margarita* in Greek.

33.   Matthew 7:7–12

7. Ask, and it shall be given you; seek, and you shall find; knock, and it shall be opened unto you: 8. For every one that asks receives; and he that seeks finds; and to him that knocks it shall be opened. 9. Or what man is there of you, whom if his son ask bread, will he give him a stone? 10. Or if he ask a fish, will he give him a serpent? 11. If you then, being evil, know how to give good gifts unto your children, how much more shall your Father which is in heaven give good things to them that ask him? 12. Therefore all things whatsoever you would that men should do to you, do you even so to them: for this is the law and the prophets.
Luke 11:9–13, Mark 11:24, Proverbs 8:17, Luke 11:11, Luke 6:31–36, James 1:17–21 (every good gift).

Notice he says, "For this IS the Law and the prophets?" Not was.

Romans 2:13: For not the hearers of the law are just before God, but the doers of the law will be justified.

James 1:22: But be doers of the Word, and not hearers only, deceiving your own selves.

From Yashanet: The prime example of what we are to pray for was given to us by Yeshua. He prayed for us to become one (a unity – Hebrew: *echad)* with the Father, as he is *echad* with the Father: Ask for what? Money, fame or happiness? No, the spiritual man seeks spiritual things in the form of the truth and blessings of the Torah.

James 1:17–21: 17. Every good gift and every perfect gift is from above, and comes down from the Father of lights, with whom is no variableness, neither shadow of turning. 18. Of his own will he brought us forth with the word of truth, that we should be a kind of firstfruits of his creatures. 19. Wherefore, my beloved brethren, let every man be swift to hear, slow to speak, slow to wrath: 20. For the wrath of man works not the righteousness of God. 21. Wherefore lay apart all filthiness and superfluity of naughtiness, and receive with meekness the engrafted word, which is able to save your souls.

Swift to hear.

Slow to speak.

Slow to wrath.

The entire chapter of John 17 is absolutely beautiful. Here is the Heart of our Savior. This is how he feels about us:

John 17:9–26: 9. I pray for them: I pray not for the world, but for them which you have given me; for they are yours. 10. And all mine are yours, and yours are mine; and I am glorified in them. 11. And now I am no more in the world, but these are in the world, and I come to you. Holy Father, keep through your own name those whom you have given me that they may be one, as we [are]. 12. While I was with them in the world, I kept them in your name: those that you gave me I have kept, and none of them is lost, but the son of perdition; that the Scripture might be fulfilled. 13. And now come I to you; and these things I speak in the world, that they might have my joy fulfilled in themselves. 14. I have given them your word; and the world has hated them, because they are not of the world, even as I am not of the world. 15. I pray not that you should take them out of the world, but that you should keep them from the evil. 16. They are not of the world, even as I am not of the world. 17. Sanctify them through your truth: your word is truth. 18. As you have sent me into the world, even so have I also sent them into the world. 19. And for their sakes I sanctify myself, that they also might be sanctified through the truth. 20. Neither pray I for these alone, but for them also which shall believe on me through their word; 21. That they all may be one; as you, Father, are in me, and I in you, that they also may be one in us: that the world may believe that you have sent me. 22. And the glory which you gave me I have given them; that they may be one, even as we are one: 23. I in them, and you in me, that they may be made perfect in one; and that the world may know that you have sent me, and have loved them, as you have loved me. 24. Father, I will that they also, whom you have given me, be with me where I am; that they may behold my glory, which you have given me: for you loved me before the foundation of the world. 25. O righteous Father, the world has not known you: but I have known you, and these have known that you have sent me. 26. And I have declared unto them your name, and will declare [it]: that the love wherewith you have loved me may be in them, and I in them.

What do we have to do first? ASK.

The brother of Yeshua/Jesus, James/Yacov (Jacob), the fiery preacher, gives us the answer. He says in James 4:1–3:

1. From where do wars and fighting come from among you? Do they not come from your lusts that war in your members?
2. You lust, and have not: you kill, and desire to have, and cannot obtain: you fight and war, yet you have not, because you ask not.
3. You ask, and receive not, because you ask amiss, that you may consume [it] upon your lusts.

Ouch! So be aware that you may not get that Mercedes Benz you've been asking for. "Pray and God will supply your needs according to his riches in Glory." He will supply your needs. My needs. Where do we mess up in this aspect? By praying foolishly. He's aware of your need before you ask. He just wants you to ASK. We teach our children before they can walk, "Do you want a cookie?" Or something. And they point. When they can talk a little we teach them to say, "please" and "thank you." We are acting in the same way God acts. We want our children to be aware of where everything comes from and to be grateful. Nothing is earned or given to us because we deserve it. Grace. It's all about grace. God's mercy on us.

Also, we do a lot of "presuming." We used to say jokingly, "You pack, I'll pray," about a move. You know that leads to disaster. You get to where you think God wants you and find out he's still back where you were, waiting. ASK the Lord for his provision and leading in situations.

The best thing to ask for is to understand his Word. He will open it to you in ways you never dreamed. ASK every morning, "Lord, what do YOU want me to study today." Then watch. You opened the door a crack, he will give you more information than you ever dreamed. Sometimes I think I'll study one thing, and he changes it to what HE wants me to study. He supplies abundantly teachers, preachers, commentary, articles, books, songs, and people who come into my life. I absolutely do marvel at his abundant grace and mercy to me.

From The Gospel According to the Hebrews, translation by Clement of Alexandria, Miscellanies 5:14:

> For those things can be the same as these: He who seeks shall not cease until he finds, and finding he shall marvel, and having marveled he shall reign, and having reigned he shall rest.

The next thing is to seek. Seek out the answers in his Word, in prayer, in Godly counsel. Yeshua/Jesus said,

> 2 Corinthians 13:1: "In the mouth of two or three witnesses every matter will be established."
> Deuteronomy 17:6, 19:15.

In other words, don't act by one word or confirmation alone. Ask the Lord to confirm it with another word or action by two or three witnesses.

In Matthew 7:12, Yeshua is saying the same as Hillel, the grandfather of Gamliel, who taught Paul, but in reverse logic:

> Therefore all things whatsoever ye would that men should do to you, do even so to them: for this is the law and the prophets.

> Babylonian Talmud, Shabat 31a: What is hateful to you, do it not unto others — this is the entire Torah, and the rest is commentary.

34.   Matthew 7:13-14

13. Enter you in at the strait gate: for wide is the gate, and broad is the way, that leads to destruction, and many there be which go in by it: 14. Because strait is the gate, and narrow is the way, which leads unto life, and few there be that find it.
Luke 13:24.

The "narrow gate" is salvation. Making a decision to believe that Yeshua/ Jesus is the Son of God, he is the Messiah, that he came and lived and died for you, that he rose again the third day, and is in heaven preparing a place for you. Think of when you accepted Yeshua/Jesus into your heart. You asked him to come into your life and save you. You may have struggled mightily with this over a period of time. You may have been a child, as I was, but I knew I was a sinner and needed a Savior. When you and I walked through that narrow gate, we were reborn. We became new creatures in the Messiah. We entered at that moment into the Kingdom Yeshua/Jesus was always talking about.

Many have struggled with walking through this narrow gate and have never said, "Yes," to God. They think they have too much to lose. They think God will ask them to do something they don't want to do. But when you say, "Yes," and you walk through that gate, it is a powerful life changer. You have started on a journey, a walk that carries you towards knowing your creator, knowing what life is all about. Through that gate you learn that God the Father absolutely loves and adores you; so much, in fact, that he sent his only son to die for you that you may have eternal life with him. He was then resurrected and sent His Holy Spirit to live in you to teach you, lead you, guide you, and warn you.

But the wide gate is broad and leads to destruction. There are many who go in by it. It may seem like a good life you're living right now, but eternity waits. There's coming a day for all of us when we have to face the Judge to answer for the choice we made. I pray that if you haven't made the choice to accept Yeshua/Jesus as your Savior that you will bow your head right now and ask him to come into your heart, to save you, and start you on a marvelous walk with him.

35.   Matthew 7:15-16

15. Beware of false prophets, which come to you in sheep's clothing, but inwardly they are ravening wolves. 16. You shall know them by their fruits. Do men gather grapes of thorns, or figs of thistles? Jeremiah 23:16–17, Micah 3:5.

I could probably write another book on this subject. Just today I watched a program on television that I hardly ever watch, but just "happened" to turn to it. There was a very sad, pitiful woman on that had followed a man who led a cult. Of course, she didn't know it was a cult. She said she knew the Bible and believed in Jesus. This man beat all of his followers, drank, did drugs, made them commit crimes for him, and yet they stayed with him. Why? He said he was Jesus. The man had died by the time she was on the show. She had married another man, but she had not let go of the leader of the cult. She had kept everything concerning him in a box. She wept and wept and wept over this. She said it even haunted her concerning "what if" he had been Jesus.

Friend, let me tell you where this woman and hundreds like her go wrong. They do not know the Word of God. They do not really know him. My favorite verse to point to this is 2 Timothy 2:15:

> Study to show yourself approved unto God, a workman that does not need to be ashamed, rightly dividing the word of truth.

If this woman had been a diligent student of God's Word, this guy never would have gotten the first date with her. Deception is like a whirlpool that sucks you down and down and down until you're enveloped in it. If you would just study the Word and find out the truth, you could not fall into deception because the Holy Spirit would warn you. You might fall for a while, but suddenly the truth will be revealed to you and you can repent and get back on the right road.

It is our responsibility as believers to "rightly divide the word of truth." This means knowing the Bible, everything that is in it, doing word studies, having a great study Bible, having resources at hand to make sure this verse really says what is written in this particular translation, having tools to study the Hebrew and Greek, having someone you can trust to go to when you need further insight on a subject, having a daily study time, prayer time, and praise time. You are responsible and no one else for working out your salvation. In order to understand the New Covenant, you must know the Torah/Old

Testament. If you fall into deception, it's your fault because you didn't take the responsibility to study the real and when the counterfeit comes along, you fall for it.

We've all heard the story of how the FBI trains their people to recognize counterfeit money. They never look at a counterfeit bill. They study the real until they see it in their dreams. That's how we should study God's Word. Then we will recognize the false.

Job 11:4: For you have said, my doctrine [is] pure, and I am clean in your eyes.

Proverbs 4:2: For I give you good doctrine: Do not forsake my law.

John 7:17: If any man will do his will, he shall know of the doctrine, whether it be of God, or [whether] I speak of myself.

In other words, always check out a church's doctrine. Get their statement of faith. Keep your ears perked up and be in touch with the Holy Spirit to listen for anything that isn't in the Bible and is being taught. It's up to you. No one else can do this for you. Study.

Other "doctrine" verses from the NKJV:

John 7:17: If anyone wills to do his will, he shall know concerning the doctrine, whether it is from God or [whether] I speak on my own [authority].

Romans 16:17: Now I urge you, brethren, note those who cause divisions and offenses, contrary to the doctrine which you learned, and avoid them.

Ephesians 4:14: That we should no longer be children, tossed to and fro and carried about with every wind of doctrine, by the trickery of men, in the cunning craftiness of deceitful plotting,

1 Timothy 1:10: For fornicators, for sodomites, for kidnappers, for liars, for perjurers, and if there is any other thing that is contrary to sound doctrine,

1 Timothy 4:6: If you instruct the brethren in these things, you will be a good minister of Jesus Christ, nourished in the words of faith and of the good doctrine which you have carefully followed.

1 Timothy 4:13: Till I come, give attention to reading, to exhortation, to doctrine.

1 Timothy 4:16: Take heed to yourself and to the doctrine. Continue in them, for in doing this you will save both yourself and those who hear you.

1 Timothy 6:3: If anyone teaches otherwise and does not consent to wholesome words, [even] the words of our Lord Jesus Christ, and to the doctrine which accords with Godliness,

2 Timothy 3:10: But you have carefully followed my doctrine, manner of life, purpose, faith, longsuffering, love, perseverance,

2 Timothy 3:14–17: 14. But you must continue in the things which you have learned and been assured of, knowing from whom you have learned [them], 15. and that from childhood you have known the Holy Scriptures, which are able to make you wise for salvation through faith which is in Christ Jesus. 16. All Scripture [is] given by inspiration of God, and [is] profitable for doctrine, for reproof, for correction, for instruction in righteousness, 17. that the man of God may be complete, thoroughly equipped for every good work.

Paul told Timothy to continue in the things he had learned. He was speaking of the Old Testament, the Torah. There was no written New Covenant at that time. Reading the Old Testament acquaints you with the moral code for living so that when you read the words of Yeshua/Jesus it is familiar to you and not something foreign. He said the words of the Torah will make you wise "for salvation." Timothy's mother was Jewish.

Remember Yeshua/Jesus said:

Hebrews 10:7: NKJV: Then I said, 'Behold, I have come—In the scroll of the book it is written of me—To do your will, O God.'

Psalms 40:7: NKJV: Then I said, "Behold, I come; in the scroll of the book [it is] written of me.

Reading the Old Testament reveals the Messiah to us and teaches us what to look for in the New Covenant.

"Rightly dividing the word of Truth" goes back to the covenant between the parts in Genesis 15 where God cut a covenant with Abraham. God didn't tell Abraham to just throw some animal parts around on the ground, but lay them down like he told him to in an orderly fashion. That is the way we need to study God's Word. In an orderly fashion, correctly interpreting a passage.

You have to study the Word according to application and agreement with Scripture. You can't just come up with your own interpretation using one Scripture, like "Judas went out and hanged himself, do you likewise." There are methods to studying the Word, too long to go into here, but look up some methods from reliable sources and learn how to and how not to "divide the word of Truth." Use commentaries and word helps. Be a sincere student of the Word.

36.   Matthew 8:21-22

21. And another of his disciples said unto him, Lord, suffer me first to go and bury my father. 22. But Jesus said unto him, Follow me; and let the dead bury their dead.
Luke 9:59–60, I Kings 19:20.

Was Yeshua/Jesus being cruel? No. In the Jewish customs, a dead person has to be buried the day they die and before the sun goes down. Obviously, this man's father wasn't dead! For one thing, the disciple wouldn't have been out of the house yet. Once a loved one is buried, they have to "sit sheva," which means they sit in mourning for seven days.

"Bury the father" is a Hebrew idiom meaning, "Let me take care of my father."

Don't make excuses when God calls you to do a certain task. You'll regret it later. This is from experience.

37.   Matthew 9:10–13

10. And it came to pass, as Jesus sat at meat in the house, behold, many publicans and sinners came and sat down with him and his disciples. 11. And when the Pharisees saw [it], they said unto his disciples, why does your Master eat with publicans and sinners? 12. But when Jesus heard [that], he said unto them, they that are whole need not a physician, but they that are sick. 13. But go you and learn what [that] means, I will have mercy, and not sacrifice: for I am not come to call the righteous, but sinners to repentance.
Matthew 11:19, Hosea 6:6, 1 Timothy 1:15.

Isaiah 64:6: But we are all as an unclean [thing], and all our righteous acts [are] as filthy rags; and we all do fade as a leaf; and our iniquities, like the wind, have taken us away.

The word here for "filthy" speaks of menstrual rags, Strong's Concordance #H5708, *iddah*.

The word *niddah* is from this, which describes a woman during menstruation and the laws concerning this. It takes up an entire chapter in the Talmud. This is also referred to as "family purity." The word "*iddah*" is only used here in Isaiah 64:6. The word "niddah" appears

25 times. It is used as "uncleanness." The Torah in Leviticus and Numbers sets out the laws concerning this. Niddah means "moved." Zechariah 13:1 speaks of a fountain opened up for the house of David and the inhabitants of Jerusalem for sin and "uncleanness." Who is this fountain? Of course, Yeshua/Jesus.

This is where the red tent teaching comes from. The menstruating woman had to be "set apart" from the rest of the family. Think about it. For one week out of every month you got a vacation. Books to read. Catch up on your favorite television series. Eat what you want, do what you want. Get up in the morning when you want. Go to bed at night when you want. What a deal!

"Unclean thing" is Strong's Concordance #H2931, *tame'*, or tamei. Unclean, impure, defiled, polluted. Ritually impure.

Think of how God looks at sin according to this verse in Isaiah. We usually don't like to think of the extent of the world's sin, but it is described here as the worst thing imaginable. Yeshua/Jesus died to save the world and rectify the world back to the Father. We were all "niddah and tamei," set apart from God, unclean, impure, and defiled. The depth of this is impossible for us to comprehend. He paid the debt that mankind owed God.

The Pharisees were not bad people. They were the scholarly elite! However, Yeshua/Jesus chided them often for teaching the people things that are not in the Torah. These are called "fences." In order not to break a law in the least, they added to the commandment and expounded on it. Then Yeshua says that they themselves don't do these things. Hypocrites! He said they were as much in need of a physician as the common man. They were so stuck on "the letter of the law" that they forgot the heart of the law, the reasons for the do's and don'ts. They needed their hearts to be changed and that came about only by salvation through Yeshua HaMashiach, Jesus the Messiah.

Go and learn. Study it out. So let's do that.

First of all, let us get this clear: It was not "all" the Pharisees that followed him around judging him. Many of the Pharisees came to believe he was the Messiah. Paul was a Pharisee. However, checking him out was their job. They were the keepers of the law and protectors of the law (Torah) of that day. They were in charge of teaching the people, along with another sect called the Sadducees. They had schools of learning. It would be, as I explained above, to know the Word. They knew every "jot and tittle" of the Torah/Old Testament. They wanted to be sure this rabbi did not teach false doctrine. A lot of Christians condemn them, but they were the elite keepers of the Torah in that day, the guardians to make sure that no false doctrine was taught by any of the rabbis.

> Hosea 6:6: For I desired mercy, and not sacrifice; and the knowledge of God more than burnt offerings.

In other words, mercy and knowledge of God are more important than the burnt offerings they were to bring. Not that they weren't to bring them, but it was a matter of the heart. It is always a matter of the heart. Many Christians quote Amos 5:22, "Though you offer me burnt offerings and your meat offerings, I will not accept [them]: neither will I regard the peace offerings of your fat beasts," as saying that the sacrifices were done away with. God is talking about the condition of their heart here. What he desired of them and desires of us is mercy, goodness, kindness, and faithfulness. No matter what you give or what you do for the Lord, nothing will earn you salvation, but if you want to please him, you will be good, kind, and faithful.

Good: I behave in a manner becoming to the word. I follow the commandments given to me.

Kind: I do mitzvah's for people, good deeds. I speak kindly, I act kindly, I am kind to those in my life.

Faithful: I have no other Gods before me.

38.   Matthew 9:36–38

36. But when he saw the multitudes, he was moved with compassion on them, because they fainted, and were scattered abroad, as sheep having no shepherd. 37. Then says he unto his disciples, The harvest truly [is] plenteous, but the laborers [are] few; 38. Pray you therefore the Lord of the harvest, that he will send forth laborers into his harvest.
Luke 10:2.

Remember who he is speaking to: The Jewish people. The religious leaders had let them down. They were telling them to do this and do that, yet they weren't keeping the commandments correctly, and, worse than that, they were adding to them! These people were desperately seeking a leader.

We all need to be workers in the field. We can't all be evangelists or pastors, but we can volunteer to teach and volunteer for many ministries in the church and in the community to get the people in before the harvest is over. There are so many people without a shepherd. The homeless organizations need help and many organizations that minister outside the churches. Volunteer. Get involved. Pray. Support. Be a shepherd.

Matthew Henry says this chapter is an "ordination sermon:"

39.   Matthew 10:5–15

5. These twelve Jesus sent forth, and commanded them, saying, Go not into the way of the Gentiles, and into [any] city of the Samaritans enter you not: 6. But go rather to the lost sheep of the house of Israel. 7. And as you go, preach, saying, The Kingdom of heaven is at hand. 8. Heal the sick, cleanse the lepers, raise the dead, cast out devils: freely you have received, freely give. 9. Provide neither gold, nor silver, nor brass in your purses, 10. Nor scrip for [your] journey, neither two coats, neither shoes, nor yet staves: for the workman is worthy of his meat. 11. And

into whatsoever city or town you shall enter, enquire who in it is worthy; and there abide till ye go thence. 12. And when you come into a house, salute it. 13. And if the house is worthy, let your peace come upon it: but if it is not worthy, let your peace return to you. 14. And whosoever shall not receive you, nor hear your words, when you depart out of that house or city, shake off the dust of your feet. 15. Verily I say unto you, it shall be more tolerable for the land of Sodom and Gomorrah in the Day of Judgment, than for that city.
1 Timothy 5:18, Luke 10:8, Luke 10:13, Psalms 35:13, Mark 6:11, Acts 13:51, Matthew 11:22–24.

These are specific instructions to the 12 disciples for training. Disciples can also be called emissaries, sheliachs — sent ones. Later on, he gives instructions to 72 more in Luke 10. Most translations say 70, but the NU–text says 72 in Luke 10.

These were mission trips such as we have today with young people in the churches. You notice the instruction in verses 12 and 13: "And when you go into a household, greet it." This greeting would be the typical Hebrew greeting as still done today. "Shalom aleichem" means *"peace be unto you."* The person you're speaking to is to say "aleichem shalom," which means *"unto you peace."* Yeshua/Jesus then says in verse 13: "If the household is worthy, let your peace come upon it. But if it is not worthy, let your peace return to you." In other words, if you're not welcome, it will be apparent by the way they greet you. "Whoever will receive you" goes along with the verse above where we were talking about not casting our pearls before swine. If they don't accept the gospel, "shake off the dust from your feet." Leave that city. The good news has been given. The choice has been made.

Chapter 10:6 is speaking about the exiles who have returned from the diaspora, "the lost sheep of the house of Israel," or the Northern Kingdom, house of Joseph/Ephraim, or just called Ephraim. Israel is known as the Northern tribes that split from Judah, which includes the tribes of Judah, Benjamin, and Levi. Israel consists of Zebulun,

Issachar, Asher, Naphtali, Dan, Manasseh, Ephraim, Reuben, and <u>Gad</u>. Their capital was first Shechem, then Samaria.

When "the lost sheep," or "the lost tribes" are spoken of, it is always the house of Israel. They are also spoken of as "those who are far" and Judah as "those who are near." The ones who are "far" is the house of Israel, the lost sheep of Israel. The ones who fell out of covenant with God. The ones who are "near" are from the house of Judah. They were still in covenant.

However, God had to restore his people back to him before he could graft in the gentiles. There are many promises in the Old Testament that he would do this. Therefore, going to the lost sheep of the house of Israel and first bringing restoration. That's what Yeshua/Jesus is all about, the restoration of all things. "To the Jew first, and also for the Greek." Romans 1:16b.

> Acts 3:21: Heaven must receive him until the time comes for the restoration of all things, which God has spoken through his holy prophets since the world began.
> See Matthew 4:25, Mark 5:20, and 7:31.

The Northern Tribes were those that did not accept Rehoboam as king after King Solomon died, which, as above, were all the tribes except Judah, Benjamin, and Levi. They rebelled against him. See 1 Kings 12:17–22. They are called "Israel" in the Word and Judah, Benjamin, and Levi are called "Judah." Later they were called "Jews," meaning "*from Judah*." Now we usually call any person of Israelite blood "Jews."

Nevertheless, the Ten Northern Tribes were scattered throughout the known world after their captivity. A lot of the descendants from the ten tribes had returned to Israel. These are the ones Yeshua/Jesus is talking about in this verse. They had lost touch with their Hebraic roots and were not following Torah. After all, it had been the year approximately 930 BC when they were taken into captivity. In this verse, it was several generations later. Their relatives had been set free in about 722 BCE. (Remember, we count up to the year one before the New Covenant.)

The disciples were sent to these villages to teach them about Torah and to preach the good news of the Kingdom. When the Bible says "the lost sheep of Israel," it isn't speaking of being lost in the sense of no one knowing who they are or where they are. It is in the sense that we would speak of a sinner being lost and away from God. We can see they weren't really "lost" because of several peoples being found today around the world knowing they are Jewish. Many of these have made alijah to Israel. The word "alijah" means "to go up."

When Yeshua/Jesus was born, there was a lady named Anna serving in the temple:

> Luke 2:36: And there was one Anna, a prophetess, the daughter of Phanuel, of the tribe of *Asher*: she was of a great age, and had lived with a husband seven years from her virginity.

She knew she was from the tribe of Asher. The apostle Paul knew he was a Benjamite.

So Yeshua/Jesus sent the disciples first to these with the good news. Also in Matthew 15 he says the same thing when the Gentile woman cries out to him.

> Verse 24: But he answered and said, "I was not sent except to the lost sheep of the house of Israel."

Remember our verse above that spoke of needing workers for the harvest? The heart's desire of our Lord was that these people hear the good news that the Kingdom of Heaven/God was at hand. What they had looked for over the years was coming to pass! In our verses in Matthew 10:5-6, he tells them not to go to the Gentiles or the Samaritans. It is said that it wasn't for about 15 years after the Holy Spirit was poured out in the Book of Acts that a Gentile was saved that we know of, Cornelius and his family. (Acts 10)

From Thayer's Greek Lexicon, *blueletterbible.org*: Samaritans: Strong's Concordance #G4541. "The origin of the Samaritans was as follows: After Shalmaneser (others say Esarhaddon, compare Ezra 4:2,10; but see Kautzsch in Herzog (Real–Encyclopädie für Protestantische Theologie und Kirche) edition 2, as referred to under the preceding word), king of Assyria, had sent colonists from Babylon, Cuthah, Ava, Hamath, and Sepharvaim into the land of Samaria which he had devastated and depopulated (see Samareia, 1), those Israelites who had remained in their desolated country (compare 2 Chronicles 30:6,10; 34:9) associated and intermarried with these heathen colonists and thus produced a mixed race."

When the Jews on their return from exile were preparing to rebuild the temple of Jerusalem, the Samaritans asked to be allowed to bear their part in the common work.

On being refused by the Jews, who were unwilling to recognize them as brethren, they not only sent letters to the king of Persia and caused the Jews to be compelled to desist from their undertaking down to the second year of Darius (Hystaspis) (B. C. 520), but also built a temple for themselves on Mount Gerizim, a place held sacred even from the days of Moses (compare Deuteronomy 27:12, etc.), and worshipped Jehovah there according to the law of Moses, recognizing only the Pentateuch as sacred.

This temple on Mount Gerizim was destroyed in 129 BC by John Hyrcanus.

Deprived of their temple, the Samaritans have nevertheless continued to worship on their sacred mountain quite down to the present time, although their numbers are reduced to some forty or fifty families.

Hence, it came to pass that the Samaritans and the Jews entertained inveterate (habitual) and unappeasable enmity (hostility) toward each other."

40.   Matthew 10:16–20

16. Behold, I send you forth as sheep in the midst of wolves: be you therefore wise as serpents, and harmless as doves. 17. But beware of men: for they will deliver you up to the councils, and they will scourge you in their synagogues; 18. And you shall be brought before governors and kings for my sake, for a testimony against them and the Gentiles. 19. But when they deliver you up, take no thought how or what you shall speak: for it shall be given you in that same hour what you shall speak. 20. For it is not you that speak, but the Spirit of your Father who speaks in you. Luke 10:3, Ephesians 5:15, Philippians 2:14–16, Mark 13:9, Acts 5:40, 22:19, 26:11, 2 Timothy 4:16, Luke 12:11–12, 21:14–15.

41.   Matthew 10:23

But when they persecute you in this city, flee you into another: for verily I say unto you, You shall not have gone over the cities of Israel, till the Son of Man comes.

These instructions were all written to the disciples. This passage has been debated back and forth for 2000 years. I'm in the company of several well-known scholars who believe that this saying, "Son of Man," is also used throughout scripture for depicting God being the one who brings punishment on Israel for not obeying his Word. In the Book of Revelation, Yeshua/Jesus warns Ephesus and Pergamum that he would come and bring punishment on them. So in our verse, Yeshua/Jesus is saying that he would be the one that allows the Romans to attack Israel because of their rebellion against him. In 66-70 AD that is what happened. Yeshua/Jesus knew what was ahead for them. He knew they would not have time to go throughout Israel with the gospel before the Roman-Jewish war started. The Siege of Jerusalem took place in 66-70 AD. So we see here in the history of Israel what happened to the first believers in Yeshua/Jesus as the Messiah. They were dispersed throughout the known world; thus the spread of the good news.

See the link below to an excellent article on this subject by Wayne Jackson of Christian Courier.

42.   Matthew 10:26–31

> 26. Fear them not therefore: for there is nothing covered, that shall not be revealed; and hid, that shall not be known. 27. What I tell you in darkness, [that] speak you in light: and what you hear in the ear, [that] preach you upon the housetops. 28. And fear not them which kill the body, but are not able to kill the soul: but rather fear him who is able to destroy both soul and body in hell. 29. Are not two sparrows sold for a farthing? One of them shall not fall on the ground without your Father. 30. But the very hairs of your head are all numbered. 31 Fear you not therefore; you are of more value than many sparrows.

These instructions are a continuation of his instruction to his disciples, but relevant today. Fear them not. God knows everything that has happened and will happen. He knows the hidden things and by his Holy Spirit will reveal them to you in due time.

He convicts through the Holy Spirit, with whom Yeshua/Jesus empowered them.

> John 14:26: The Spirit taught them all things, and brought to their remembrance all things that Jesus said to them.

Hold on there. He brought them to their remembrance. They had to KNOW all things formerly in order for God to bring them to their remembrance. They had studied the Torah their whole lives. Now that Yeshua/Jesus opened up the prophecies about him, they were expounding on what they knew already, just as Stephen in Acts 7 and Paul in Acts 13:17–41.

You have to have READ the Bible in order for God to bring it to your remembrance. You might think you don't know the Bible well. If you're faithful in studying it and read the whole thing through at least once, he will bring it to your remembrance when you need it. When you come up against false doctrine, it will slap you in the face, and you'll say, "Wait a minute! There's something wrong here! Let me check this out." He promises, but you have to LISTEN and know what's in the Bible first lest you be led astray.

What does he say in verse 27? "Whatever I tell you in the dark, speak in the light. What you hear in the ear, preach on the housetops." Sometimes you go to bed wondering about a certain thing or praying. The next morning you have the answer! He speaks to you while your mind and spirit are calmed down, and he can get through to you.

Wow. Aren't the rest of the verses awesome? Think of how much he loves us. More than we can ever possibly know.

43.   Matthew 10:34

Think not that I am come to send peace on earth: I came not to send peace, but a sword.
Luke 12:49.

If you don't think this is true, try witnessing. More and more we see Christians being laughed to scorn. Remember our verse about casting pearls? A one-on-one testimony is often fruitful. If a person gets saved and his family is not, it usually does bring a "sword," or separation. Light against darkness. Rejoice when they persecute you and ridicule you. There's a lot in the Scriptures about lightness and darkness, also in the Dead Sea Scrolls. The Bible says we're aliens here. We that are born again don't belong here. We are striving for the time when all things will be restored and like they were in the Garden of Eden, but for now we must be light and salt.

44.   Matthew 10:41–42

41. He that receives a prophet in the name of a prophet shall receive a prophet's reward. He that receives a righteous man

in the name of a righteous man shall receive a righteous man's reward. 42. Whosoever shall give a drink to one of these little ones a cup of cold [water] only in the name of a disciple, verily I say unto you, he shall in no wise lose his reward.
I Kings 17:10, Mark 9:41.

In other words, be hospitable. Always be ready to welcome believers into your home or help them out. Remember the widow that had a room for Elijah, I Kings 17? That was called "a prophet's room." Nowadays many people keep a "prophet's room" just for that purpose in case an evangelist, choirs traveling through, or people that need shelter for the night, etc., need it. Just be careful always to check people out with your church or even the police. And never leave your house open to them while you're gone. If it's a well-known person to your church or organization, you can be a little more lenient. Always be sure to use wisdom.

Sometimes we can't do what we'd like to do for the Lord, like give lots of money, but he says whatever you do in his name or in the name of a disciple receives a reward, not that we do it for a reward, but he's saying that whatever deed you do in his name is great to him. Be kind. Perform a mitzvah (kindness).

45.   Matthew 11:11–15

11. Verily I say unto you, Among them that are born of women there has not risen a greater than John the Baptist: notwithstanding he that is least in the Kingdom of heaven is greater than he. 12. And from the days of John the Baptist until now the Kingdom of heaven suffers violence, and the violent take it by force. 13. For before John came, all the prophets and the law prophesied to this present time. 14. And if you will receive [it], this is Elijah, who was to come. 15. He that has ears to hear, let him hear.
Luke 10:8, Luke 10:5, Psalms 35:13, Mark 6:11, Acts 13:51, Matthew 11:22, 24.

He's saying in 11:15: "Listen up! John the Baptist is the one with the spirit of Elijah!" And it is believed that one will come again during the Great Tribulation period with the spirit of Elijah and do miracles, as Elijah did. It is believed he is one of the two witnesses spoken about in the Book of Revelation.

However, Yeshua/Jesus is saying to listen! "He that has ears to hear" is a Hebrew idiom. Listen carefully. It's like some of us mothers say, "Open your ears." "Do you need your ears washed out?" Not only listen with your physical ears, but with your spiritual ears. He is saying to listen to what the spirit is saying to you. Study, pray, listen.

46.   Matthew 11:28–30

28. Come unto me, all [you] that labor and are heavy laden, and I will give you rest. 29. Take my yoke upon you, and learn of me; for I am meek and lowly in heart: and you shall find rest unto your souls. 30. For my yoke [is] easy, and my burden is light. John 6:35–37, Philippians 2:5, Zechariah 9:9, Jeremiah 6:16, I John 5:3.

Ah, one of our favorite verses, no? Who is he talking to? The yoke is the Torah/commandments as a moral compass. Learn of him. How do you learn of him if you don't read and study his Word personally? Delving into the Torah/Old Testament is a huge blessing, learning the Heart of God. Why should we read it? To know him better. He says it! Learn of ME. Immerse yourself in his Word. Meditate on it. If you just start at Matthew 1:1, you've missed half the story! Learn the History of the Jewish people. Learn what they went through crossing the wilderness. Learn about the battles they had, the doubts they had, the trials. Then internalize these. Meditate on them.

Do we have battles? Doubts? Trials? What did God say to them? How did he solve them? Meditate on the Psalms and Proverbs, Ruth, Ecclesiastes, Job. All the Torah is written FOR us, but it is not all written TO us. I'm not saying to spiritualize it. I'm saying to put yourself in their place. How does this story speak to your heart? Do you feel like you're standing there with them, fighting YOUR battle? Be strong and of a good courage, as he told Joshua:

> Deuteronomy 31:6-7: 6. Be strong and of a good courage, fear not, nor be afraid of them: for the Lord your God, it is he that goes with you; he will not fail you, nor forsake you. 7. And Moses called unto Joshua, and said unto him in the sight of all Israel, Be strong and of a good courage: for you must go with this people unto the land which the Lord has sworn unto their fathers to give them; and you shall cause them to inherit it.

Wow! Read the whole thirty-first chapter and put you and your trial/battle right there. Be so encouraged by these words. Research how many times "be strong" is in the Bible. Quote them out loud. Be strengthened by his Word.

David Stern in The Jewish New Testament Commentary on Matthew 11:28-30, page 44, says,

> "Judaism speaks of the "yoke of Heaven," the commitment any Jew must make to trust in God, and the "yoke of the Torah," the concomitant commitment an observant Jew makes to keep the generalities and details of halacha (the way one walks or the rules one follows). Yeshua speaks of his easy yoke and light burden. These two are sometimes contrasted in a way implying that in comparison with Judaism, Christianity offers "cheap grace." But this saying of Yeshua's must be put alongside remarks such as at Matthew 10:38 and Luke 9:23-24. The easy yoke consists in total commitment to Godliness through the power of the Holy Spirit. It at once requires both no effort and maximal effort—no effort in that the necessary moment-to-moment faith cannot be worked up from within, but is a gift of God, Ephesians 2:8-9; and maximal effort, in that there is no predetermined level of holiness and obedience sufficient to satisfy God and let us rest on our laurels."

But then in the Book of James, James tells us to show him our faith WITHOUT works, and he will show us faith WITH works.

> James 2:14–26: 14. What [does it] profit, my brethren, though a man say he has faith, and have not works? Can faith save him? 15. If a brother or sister be naked and destitute of daily food, 16. And one of you say unto them, Depart in peace, be [you] warmed and filled; notwithstanding you give them not those things which are needful to the body; what [does it] profit? 17. Even so faith, if it has not works, is dead, being alone. 18. Yes, a man may say, You have faith, and I have works: show me your faith without your works, and I will show you my faith by my works. 19. You believe that there is one God; you do well: the devils also believe, and tremble. 20. But will you know, O vain man, that faith without works is dead? 21. Was not Abraham our father justified by works, when he had offered Isaac his son upon the altar? 22. See you how faith wrought with his works, and by works was faith made perfect? 23. And the Scripture was fulfilled which says, Abraham believed God, and it was imputed unto him for righteousness: and he was called the Friend of God. 24. You see that a man is considered righteous by what he does and not by faith only. 25. Likewise also was not Rahab the harlot justified by works, when she had received the messengers, and had sent [them] out another way? 26. For as the body without the spirit is dead, so faith without works is dead also.

So the YOKE is the Torah/commandments. All of God's Word is Yeshua/Jesus, but he wasn't talking to all of us all the time. It may seem burdensome when you are a new Christian to see all the do's and don'ts in the New Covenant, then as you draw nearer to the Lord they aren't hard at all, but you delight in obedience. Obedience to what? Our commandments is what this study is about. Learning what Yeshua said for us as Gentiles to do and not do. We build our faith and security in him by knowing what he expects of us. We do not EARN our salvation by works, but it is the fruit that others can see in our lives that marks us as believers in Yeshua. If you continue deliberately sinning and have no desire to follow him and his commandments, then we have to question your salvation. Salvation makes you a new creature in him and changes your desire to sin, as in our next verse:

47.　　Matthew 12:33

Either make the tree good, and his fruit good; or else make the tree corrupt, and his fruit corrupt: for the tree is known by [his] fruit. Matthew 7:16–18.

What is the fruit we should produce?

John 15:16: You have not chosen me, but I have chosen you, and ordained you, that you should go and bring forth fruit, and [that] your fruit should remain: that whatsoever you shall ask of the Father in my name, he may give it you.

Romans 7:4–6: 4. Wherefore, my brethren, you also are become dead to the law by the body of Christ; that you should be married to another, [even] to him who is raised from the dead, that we should bring forth fruit unto God. 5. For when we were in the flesh, the motions of sins, which were by the law, did work in our members to bring forth fruit unto death. 6. But now we have been delivered from the law, being dead to what we were held by; so that we should serve in newness of Spirit, and not in the oldness of the letter.

Matthew 13:23: But he that received seed on the good ground is he that hears the Word, and understands [it]; who also bears fruit and brings forth, some a hundredfold, some sixty, some thirty.

John 15:1–8: 1. I am the true vine, and my Father is the husbandman. 2. Every branch in me that bears not fruit he took away: and every [branch] that bears fruit, he purges it, that it may bring forth more fruit. 3. Now you are clean through the Word which I have spoken unto you. 4. Abide in me, and I in you. As the branch cannot bear fruit of itself, except it abide in the vine; no more can you, except you abide in me. 5. I am the vine and you [are] the branches. He who abides in me and I in him brings forth much fruit; for without me you can do nothing. 6. If a man abides not in me, he is cast forth as a branch, and is withered; and men gather them, and cast [them] into the fire, and they are burned. 7. If you abide in me, and my words abide in you, you shall ask what you will, and it shall be done unto you. 8. By this is my Father glorified, that you bear much fruit; so will you be my disciples.

So what is the fruit?

Galatians 5:22–26: 22. But the fruit of the Spirit is love, joy, peace, longsuffering, gentleness, goodness, faith, 23. Meekness, temperance: against such there is no law. 24. And they that are Christ's have crucified the flesh with the affections and lusts. 25. If we live in the Spirit, let us also walk in the Spirit. 26. Let us not be desirous of vain glory, provoking one another, envying one another.

Philippians 1:9–11: 9. And this I pray, that your love may abound yet more and more in knowledge and [in] all judgment; 10. That you may approve things that are excellent; that you may be sincere and without offense till the day of Christ; 11. Being filled with the fruits of righteousness, which are by Jesus Christ, unto the glory and praise of God.

A changed life can be seen in the one who is genuinely saved. We have gone from death into life by the power of His death and resurrection. We become New Creatures in him. I believe this goes along with Yeshua's commandment to love your neighbor as yourself. (Matthew 22:36–40.) We have all the attributes of Galatians 5:22–26 if we sincerely and sacrificially love our neighbor as ourselves.

Also see Matthew 5:43, 19:19, 22:39, Mark 12:31, Romans 13:9, Galatians 5:14, James 2:8, Zechariah 8:17, and Luke 10:27.

48.   Matthew 13:9

Who has ears to hear, let him hear.
Matthew 11:15.

Hear what? Yeshua was teaching here about the Parable of the Sower.
He's saying, "Listen, pay attention!" And I think, "Beware!"

49.   Matthew 13:18

Hear you therefore the parable of the sower.
Mark 4:13–20.

Again he reminds us to hear. In verses 13:18–23 he explains the parable.

50.   Mathew 13:43

Then shall the righteous shine forth as the sun in the Kingdom
of their Father. Who has ears to hear, let him hear!
Daniel 12:3, Matthew 13:9.

Again, our commandment to listen!

51.   Matthew 15:3–9

3. But he answered and said unto them, Why do you also
transgress the commandment of God by your tradition? 4. For
God commanded, saying, Honor your father and mother: and,
he that curses father or mother, let him die the death. 5. But
you say, Whosoever shall say to [his] father or [his] mother, [It
is] a gift, by whatsoever you might be profited by me; 6. And
honor not his father or his mother, [he shall be free]. Thus have
you made the commandment of God of none effect by your
tradition. 7. [You] hypocrites, well did Isaiah prophesy of you,
saying, 8. This people draw nigh unto me with their mouth,
and honor me with [their] lips; but their heart is far from me.

9. But in vain they do worship me, teaching [for] doctrines the commandments of men.
Deuteronomy 5:16, Exodus 21:17.

Deuteronomy 5:16: Honor your father and your mother, as the Lord your God has commanded you; that your days may be prolonged, and that it may go well with you, in the land which the Lord your God gives you.

Exodus 21:17: "And he that curses his father or his mother shall surely be put to death."

Ephesians 6:2: Honor your father and mother; (which is the first commandment with promise).

What promise? "That your days may be long, and that it may be well with you in the Land which the Lord your God is giving you."

52.   Matthew 15:10

And he called the multitude, and said unto them, Hear, and understand.

Again, He's saying "listen" — shema in Hebrew! And adds here "understand" – da'at in Hebrew.

53.   Matthew 15:14

Let them alone: they are blind leaders of the blind. And if the blind lead the blind, both shall fall into the ditch.

We need to go back to the verse before, Matthew 15:13:

But he answered and said, Every plant, which my heavenly Father has not planted, shall be rooted up.

Then he says to leave them alone. Leave them alone. Isn't he saying what I said about receiving wrong doctrine? Leave them alone. These Pharisees know the Word. The people should know the Word. If they're adding to it or taking away, shouldn't they realize it? And they're still building these fences? Manmade laws. Wrong doctrine. Don't we see people that are in a wrong doctrine that won't listen to right doctrine? So, if they won't listen, leave them alone. Let them work out their salvation.

Peter asks him to explain this parable in the next verse, verse 15, and Yeshua gives the interpretation. He's giving a midrash (exposition or exegesis, storytelling that explores ethics and values in biblical texts) on the commandments of men (the Pharisees) about ritual hand washing, mentioned in verse 2.

> Matthew 15:16–20: 16. And Jesus said, Are you also yet without understanding? 17. Do not you yet understand, that whatsoever enters in at the mouth goes into the stomach, and is eliminated? 18. But those things which proceed out of the mouth come forth from the heart; and they defile the man. 19. For out of the heart proceed evil thoughts, murders, adulteries, fornications, thefts, false witness, blasphemies: 20. These are [the things] which defile a man: but to eat with unwashed hands defiles not a man.

There is no commandment here, but we need to look at this.

These are the "Traditions of men" or the "Traditions of the elders." The ritual of hand washing is called in Hebrew "*n'tilat yadayim.*" Yad is hand. Yadayim is plural for hands. They weren't "evil" practices as I said before, but fences they built around them in case they accidentally became ritually impure. This practice comes from the Temple Commandments where the priests had to be ceremonially pure before offering sacrifices or serving in the Temple. This is taught in the Oral Torah, the Mishnah and Talmud. The orthodox were so careful that they might break a commandment, so intent on obeying the commandments, that they built the fences and taught the people to do the same. It would be admirable if we were so careful to keep the commandments, but we need not make it a commandment where there is none. It won't make or break your salvation. This isn't for physical cleanliness, but spiritual.

When they came before the Lord bringing their Temple offering, korban, which means "drawing near," they had to get so close to the priest when handing over their sacrifice because symbolically they were handing it to God. They would have had to go through a mikveh (ritual bath) before coming into the Temple. Should we not consider this when we pay our tithe or bring an offering? Not going through a ritual bath, but making sure, as David said, "Cleanse me, O Lord." Making sure we have no unconfessed sin between us and God.

Should we not so yearn to "draw near" to him that we come close enough to touch him spiritually? Would it be different at church or wherever you give your tithes and offerings if we had this mindset? Not just throwing your tithe envelope into the offering basket, but with the thought as that basket comes closer and closer to you, "I'm drawing near to you Lord. I bring my tithe/offering to you because I want to draw closer to you." That obedience means so much to him. You should know how much it means to him for you to be obedient and bring that part of you with love and appreciation for what he provides for you.

Any commandment we do should be done with love and appreciation and a willing heart. In the Book of Isaiah (1:13–17), he talks about the futility of bringing offerings or sacrifices if your heart is not in it. He's not telling them to stop these, but not to even bother if they don't come with love and willingness in their heart. It doesn't mean a thing to him. He says not to bother to celebrate the New Moon or Festivals if your heart is not right before him. He says he won't hear your prayers!

He says in Isaiah 1:16-17: "Wash yourselves, make yourselves clean; Put away the evil of your doings from before my eyes. Cease to do evil. 17. Learn to do good; seek justice, rebuke the oppressor; defend the fatherless, plead for the widow."

The "wash yourselves" means to repent and come clean before the Lord. Wash –rachatz in Hebrew. Two Scriptures explain this:

Romans 12:2: And be not conformed to this world: but be you transformed by the renewing of your mind, that you may prove what [is] that good, and acceptable, and perfect, will of God.

Titus 3:5: Not by works of righteousness which we have done, but according to his mercy he saved us, by the washing of regeneration, and renewing of the Holy Ghost;

Paul speaking to husbands:

Ephesians 5:23–27: 23. For the husband is the head of the wife, even as Christ is the head of the church: and he is the Savior of the body. 24. Therefore as the church is subject unto Christ, so let the wives be to their own husbands in everything. 25. Husbands, love your wives, even as Christ also loved the church, and gave himself for it; 26. that he might sanctify and cleanse it with the washing of water by the Word, 27. that he might present it to himself a glorious church, not having spot or wrinkle, or any such thing; but that it should be holy and without blemish.

And how do we receive this "washing?" By reading the Word. Paul says by "the washing of water by the Word," hiding it in our hearts that we might not sin against him, and by prayer and repentance.

Reading the Word cleanses us. How? Reading the Word shows us the right and wrong way. It shows us what God expects of us so that we can repent of things in our lives that do not belong there and accept the things that he wants there and obey them.

Children like and need to know what their parents want them to do. It makes them feel secure when they know how to please their parents. We're the same way. God is our heavenly Father and in our hearts we want to please him.

54.   Matthew 16:6

Then Jesus said unto them, Take heed and beware of the leaven
of the Pharisees and of the Sadducees.
Luke 12:1.

What is "leaven?" Then the disciples try to figure it out and finally get
it in verse 12:

"They understood that he did not tell them to beware of the leaven
of bread, but of the doctrine of the Pharisees and Sadducees."

What was the doctrine of the Pharisees and Sadducees? Hypocrisy.
They were telling the people to build fences around the Word, but they
weren't doing it!

Research each group and see for yourselves what their doctrine is.
Yeshua is saying, I believe, to be careful of any supposed "Christian"
group you encounter and check their doctrine. It may not be apparent
at first. They may seem on the up and up doctrinally, but then you
may run into something that isn't scriptural, another "commandment
of men." We have lots of these in the Christian churches. Beware.
Check it out.

55.   Matthew 16:24

Then said Jesus unto his disciples, If any man will come after
me, let him deny himself, and take up his cross, and follow me.

What does "take up his cross" entail? You take up your cross the minute
you say, "I do," to him, the minute you're saved. It's being willing to
suffer if need be for your belief that Jesus came to earth as a little baby,
lived on earth and preached the gospel for about three and a half years,
died on the cross, and rose again to give us eternal life. We have to
enter into the covenant with him that says, "I accept you as my personal
Savior and will follow you."

56.   Matthew 17:5

While he yet spoke, behold, a bright cloud overshadowed them: and behold a voice out of the cloud, which said, This is my beloved Son, in whom I am well pleased; hear you him.
2 Peter 1:17, Mark 1:11, Matthew 3:17, 12:18, Deuteronomy 18:15, 19.

Here we have another "hear" commandment, except here we have The Father telling us to listen to His Son.

57.   Matthew 18:8-9

Wherefore if your hand or your foot offend you, cut them off, and cast them from you: it is better for you to enter into life halt or maimed, rather than having two hands or two feet to be cast into everlasting fire. 9. And if your eye offend you, pluck it out, and cast it from you: it is better for you to enter into life with one eye, rather than having two eyes to be cast into hell fire.
Matthew 5:29–30.

Of course, the Lord doesn't expect us to literally cut off our hand or foot or pluck our eye out, which is another form of hyperbole. He's trying to get our attention about always being aware not to sin.

The word in Greek here for "*offend*" is Strong's Concordance #G4624, *skandalizō*, and can mean "to put a stumbling-block or impediment in the way upon which another may trip and fall; metaphor "to cause." Also, "to entice to sin, to cause a person to begin to distrust and desert one whom he ought to trust and obey; to cause to fall away; to be offended in one, i.e. to see in another what I disapprove of and what hinders me from acknowledging his authority; to cause one to judge unfavorably or unjustly of another; since one who stumbles or whose foot gets entangled feels annoyed; to cause one displeasure at a thing; to make indignant; to be displeased, indignant."

You may have a habit that you think is not a sin. Most of us after we're saved gradually come into an awareness of something in our life that is sin. The Lord gives strict warning here and uses language that exaggerates to get our attention. He's saying that we need to deal with it. Only by the Holy Spirit can these things be made aware of and overcome. We need to pray daily for him to reveal any sin in our life that shouldn't be there and repent of it.

Remember when Yeshua/Jesus said in Luke 17:1-2:

1. Then said he unto the disciples, It is impossible but that offenses will come: but woe unto him, through whom they come! 2. It would be better for him if a millstone were hung about his neck, and he be cast into the sea than offend one of these little ones.

It is a serious thing to cause another to stumble because of something in your life or something you teach them that is false doctrine.

The Jews wear tzit–tzit on their garments. These are specially knotted ritual "fringes." There is supposed to be one blue thread woven amongst the white to remind them of heaven; heaven reminds them of God, so that if they think of sinning they look at the knotted threads and see the blue thread and remember the Commandments. The tzit-tzit are woven and tied in a manner that entails all 613 commandments they are supposed to keep and the center thread contains the Name of God. They wear a garment called a tallit, a prayer shawl, to which the tzit-tzit are attached. Many also wear an undergarment, kind of like a vest, in which the tzit-tzit are attached and hang outside their clothes. Some attach them to their belt loops, which is not proper as they are not to enter an unclean place with the tallit or the tzit-tzit and going to the bathroom entails an "unclean place." By the way, you shouldn't keep your Bible in the bathroom or anything with Scripture written on it.

So what can we do to remind us not to sin? Learn the Word. Hide it in our hearts that we may not sin against him.

1 John 3:7–10: 7. Little children, let no man deceive you: he that does righteousness is righteous, even as he is righteous. 8. He that commits sin is of the devil; for the devil has sinned from the beginning. For this purpose the Son of God was manifested, that he might destroy the works of the devil. 9. Whosoever is born of God does not commit sin; for his seed remains in him: and he cannot sin, because he is born of God. 10. In this, the children of God are manifest, and the children of the devil: whosoever does not righteousness is not of God, neither he that loves not his brother.

58.   Matthew 18:10

Take heed that you despise not one of these little ones; for I say unto you that in heaven their angels do always behold the face of my Father which is in heaven.

The "little ones" could be a child or a new believer. This verse proves that we all have "an angel." A guardian angel he is sometimes called.

Hebrews 1:14: Are they not all ministering spirits, sent forth to minister for them who shall be heirs of salvation?

God fights our battles for us, even those we cannot see. If we are offended or hurt, we shouldn't seek revenge, but let God handle it.

59.   Matthew 18:15–17

15. Moreover, if your brother shall trespass against you, go and tell him his fault between you and him alone: if he hears you, you have gained your brother. 16. But if he will not hear you, then take with you one or two more, that in the mouth of two or three witnesses every word may be established. 17. And if he shall neglect to hear them, tell it unto the church: but if he neglects to hear the church, let him be unto you as a heathen man and a publican.
Leviticus 19:17, James 5:20, Deuteronomy 17:6, 19:15, 2 Thessalonians 3:6, 14.

Here are our instructions to follow for people that we believe have something against us.

The word for *"trespass"* in Greek is hamartanō, Strong's Concordance #G264: "To be without a share in, to miss the mark, to err, be mistaken, to miss or wander from the path of uprightness and honor, to do or go wrong, to wander from the law of God, violate God's law, sin."

I've seen this done many times the opposite way, but we need to do what the Word tells us to do.

60.   Matthew 18:22

Jesus says unto him, I say not unto you, Until seven times: but, Until seventy times seven.

Forgive 490 times? Does that mean that when it reaches the 491st time you can NOT forgive him? No, it is that you're always to be ready to forgive. Don't keep count.

61.   Matthew 19:6

Wherefore they are no more twain, but one flesh. What therefore God has joined together, let not man put asunder.

The Scripture here is used in our marriage ceremonies. The words "joined together" means "to fasten to one yoke." To join together. To unite. The marriage covenant is the strongest bond in all relationships. The basic element in marriage is a contract or covenant.

Genesis 2:24: Therefore shall a man leave his father and his mother, and shall cleave unto his wife: and they shall be one flesh.

The word *cleave* in Hebrew is Strong's Concordance #H1692 – dabaq, or dabek. דָבַק. Dabek is the word for "glue" in Hebrew.

To cling, stay close, cleave, keep close, stick to, stick with, follow closely, join to, overtake, catch.

The Word is saying that this is how close a husband and wife should be. Our Father wants us to be that close to him too so that nothing can separate us from him.

> Malachi 2:14: NIV: You ask, "Why?" It is because the Lord is the witness between you and the wife of your youth. You have been unfaithful to her, though she is your partner, the wife of your marriage covenant.

When we marry, we agree to a covenant, a promise to our spouse. Breaking that covenant is a serious thing in God's eyes. Today it seems to be taken so lightly. I tell my great-grandchildren that God has the perfect soul mate for them and if they pray they will find that one. If we would all do that, pray for the "right one," then there wouldn't be so many divorces. Christians have just as many divorces as non-Christians. The saying, "The couple that prays together stays together" is true. If you will start out your marriage, or even before, having devotions together and discussing the Bible, it will put you on the right foundation. As you read and discuss the Word, things will come out that you didn't know the other believed or did not believe. God's Word is the perfect marriage counselor.

62.   Matthew 19:14

> But Jesus said, Suffer the little children and forbid them not to come unto me: for of such is the Kingdom of heaven.
> Matthew 18:3–4.

It's not up to us to decide if children are "old enough" to understand salvation. Only God knows the heart. The pure heart of a child is well able to understand God and His love. I got saved at age eight and understood immediately what happened. I was changed. God loved me. Jesus died for me! Give the little ones the chance to hear the salvation story often. We need to read Bible stories to them, buy Christian videos like Veggie Tales, take them to Sunday School, etc., so they can learn the Bible stories. When they're ready, they will commit. Present the salvation story to them lovingly.

In our next commandment, we have the story of the young man that came to Yeshua/Jesus and asked this question:

63.   Matthew 19:16–19

19. And, behold, one came and said unto him, Good Master, what good thing shall I do, that I may have eternal life? 17. And he said unto him, Why call you me good? There is none good but one, that is, God: but if you will enter into life, keep the commandments. 18. He says unto him, Which? Jesus said, You shall do no murder, You shall not commit adultery, You shall not steal, You shall not bear false witness, 19. Honor your father and your mother: and, you shall love your neighbor as yourself.

Here Yeshua/Jesus brings in a list of 6 of the Ten Commandments in Exodus 20 and Deuteronomy 5, and one other commandment from Leviticus.
Number one is the sixth commandment, "You shall not kill."
Number two is the seventh commandment, "You shall not commit adultery."
Number three is the eighth commandment, "You shall not steal."
Number four is the ninth commandment, "You shall not bear false witness against your neighbor."
Number five is the fifth commandment, "Honor your father and mother that your days may be long upon the land which the Lord your God has given you."
Number six is in Leviticus 19:18 and is known as the v'ahavta, part of the shema (Hear O Israel, the Lord our God is One) said every morning and every night. "You shall love your neighbor as yourself." V'ahavta l'reakha kamokha.

20. The young man said unto him, All these things have I kept from my youth up: what lack I yet? 21. Jesus said unto him, If you will be perfect, go and sell what you have and give to

the poor, and you shall have treasure in heaven: and come and follow me. 22. But when the young man heard that saying, he went away sorrowful: for he had great possessions. 23. Then said Jesus unto his disciples, Verily I say unto you, A rich man shall hardly enter into the Kingdom of heaven.

Jesus was proving a point with this young man. The young man had "great possessions." He was not willing to give any of that up to follow Jesus. In the end, he "went away sorrowful." Here we have the principle of giving. What are we willing to give up if asked? One of the main beliefs in Judaism is giving to charity. Many times in the Scriptures this commandment is taught, too many to go into here, but one is to take care of the widows and orphans.

Yeshua/Jesus was saying this to this young man because he knew his heart. He was testing him. He knows all of our hearts. He asks of all of us different things. He can see which direction our heart is leaning. He says these things to make us think and to turn us around if need be.

Again:

1 John 3:16–19: 16. Hereby perceive we the love of God, because he laid down his life for us: and we ought to lay down our lives for the brethren. 17. But whoso has this world's good, and sees his brother have need, and shuts up his bowels of compassion from him, how dwells the love of God in him? 18. My little children, let us not love in word, neither in tongue; but in deed and truth. 19. And hereby we know that we are of the truth, and shall assure our hearts before him.
John 3:16, John 10:11, 15:13, Deuteronomy 15:7, Ezekiel 33:31, John 18:37.

64.   Matthew 19:21

Matthew 19:21: Jesus said unto him, If you want to be perfect, go and sell what you have, and give to the poor, and you shall have treasure in heaven: and come and follow me.

Here is another "follow me" verse. He is talking to the young man here who asked what he lacked in his life. He told Yeshua/Jesus that he had kept the commandments his whole life. Yeshua/Jesus tells him how to be perfect.

65.   Matthew 20:25–28

25. But Jesus called them unto him, and said, You know that the princes of the Gentiles exercise dominion over them, and they that are great exercise authority upon them. 26. But it shall not be so among you: but whosoever will be great among you, let him be your minister; 27. And whosoever will be chief among you, let him be your servant: 28. Even as the Son of Man came not to be ministered unto, but to minister, and to give his life a ransom for many.
I Peter 5:3, Matthew 23:11, Matthew 18:4, John 13:4. Philippians 2:6–7, Luke 22:27, Isaiah 53:10–12, Romans 5:15, 19.

Yeshua/Jesus is teaching here the importance of being a servant to all. To serve is the highest honor to the King. "Whoever will be chief among you."

66.   Matthew 22:17–21

17. Tell us therefore, What do you think? Is it lawful to give tribute unto Caesar, or not? 18. But Jesus perceived their wickedness, and said, Why tempt you me, you hypocrites? 19. Show me the tribute money. And they brought unto him a denarius. 20. And he said unto them, Whose image is on this and what is the superscription? 21. They say unto him, Caesar's. Then he said unto them, Render therefore unto Caesar the things which are Caesar's; and unto God the things that are God's.

67.   Matthew 22:35–40

35. Then one of them, which was a lawyer, asked him a question, tempting him, and saying, 36. Master, which is the

great commandment in the law? 37. Jesus said unto him, You shall love the Lord your God with all your heart, and with all your soul, and with all your mind. 38. This is the first and great commandment. 39. And the second is like unto it, You shall love your neighbor as yourself. 40. On these two commandments hang all the law and the prophets.

Luke 10:25, 11:45–46, 52, and 14:3. (37) Deuteronomy 6:5, 10:12, 30:6. (39) Leviticus 19:18. (40) Matthew 7:12.

Here we have another instance of some of the Pharisees trying to trap him into teaching wrong doctrine. He never failed to come back with the perfect answer.

One famous account in the Talmud (Shabbat 31a) tells about a Gentile who wanted to convert to Judaism. This happened not infrequently, and this individual stated that he would accept Judaism only if a rabbi would teach him the entire Torah while he, the prospective convert, stood on one foot. First he went to Shammai, who, insulted by this ridiculous request, threw him out of the house. The man did not give up and went to Hillel. This gentle sage accepted the challenge, and said: "What is hateful to you, do not do to your neighbor. That is the whole Torah; the rest is the explanation of this — go and study it!"

So in our search of "Did Yeshua/Jesus tell us to obey the 10 Commandments," we have another one here. Leviticus 19:18 was already quoted in Matthew 19:17–19. These two commandments contain the moral compass of all the commandments. IF you love the Lord your God with all your heart, soul, and mind, and IF you love your neighbor as yourself, you will not break the other commandments.

68.   Matthew 23:1–7

1. Then spoke Jesus to the multitude, and to his disciples,
2. saying, The scribes and the Pharisees sit in Moses' seat:
3. All therefore whatsoever they bid you observe, that observe

and do; but do not you after their works: for they say, and do not. 4. For they bind heavy burdens and grievous to be borne, and lay them on men's shoulders; but they themselves will not move them with one of their fingers. 5. But all their works they do for to be seen of men: they make broad their phylacteries, and enlarge the borders of their garments, 6. and love the uppermost rooms at feasts, and the chief seats in the synagogues, 7. And greetings in the markets, and to be called of men, Rabbi, Rabbi. Nehemiah 8:4, 8, Romans 2:19, Luke 11:46, Matthew 6:1–6, 16–18, Luke 11:43, 20:46.

Moses' seat was a seat in the synagogue reserved for those that were honored. Yeshua/Jesus is talking about the teachings of the Pharisees, which were basically Biblical, but they tended to add "fences" to the commandments, which were a protection so that commandments could not possibly be broken, but Yeshua/Jesus says here that it is okay to observe and do, but not to do according to the Pharisee's works. These are not works that we do to honor God, but works that are manmade works added to the commandments. He reveals the source and purpose of this: Pride. If you find yourself being lifted up by men, honored because of your works, watch out. It is nice to be recognized for things we do, but watch your heart lest it lead you astray into loving honor among men above honor from God. Moses is said to be the humblest man that ever lived. His only goal in life was to obey God and do what he was commanded. Strive to be the servant of all.

69.   Matthew 23:8–10

8. But be not you called Rabbi: for one is your Master, even Christ; and all you are brethren. 9. And call no man your father upon the earth: for one is your Father, which is in heaven. 10. Neither be you called masters: for one is your Master, even Christ.

Here we see the stress again on servanthood. Don't esteem yourself above all men by letting people give you honor above God. Don't allow your congregation to give you honor above that given to the Lord. We're all just people. To be called a rabbi nowadays, you have to receive "*s'mikha*," or ordination. You have to be ordained by an organization that is qualified to give you that title.

Yeshua is also saying don't call any man here on earth your father. Of course, our earthly dads are our fathers. He's saying the same as above. Don't exalt another man to be higher than God to you. God is our Father, capital F. Of course, we should honor those over us, but don't honor them as higher than God.

He's also speaking to leaders here. A leader should have the heart of a servant. We should respect his office, but not exalt him as higher than God.

Signs of the Times

Here we come to Jesus' discourse on the Signs of the Times and the End of the Age.

70.   Matthew 24:4

And Jesus answered and said unto them, Take heed that no man deceive you.
Colossians 2:8, 18.

Study the Scriptures so you cannot be deceived.

71.   Matthew 24:6

And you shall hear of wars and rumors of wars: see that you be not troubled: for all these things must come to pass, but the end is not yet.
Revelation 6:2–4.

72.   Matthew 24:15–18

15. When you therefore shall see the abomination of desolation, spoken of by Daniel the prophet, stand in the holy place,

(whosoever reads, let him understand:) 16. Then let them which are in Judea flee into the mountains: 17. Let him which is on the housetop not come down to take anything out of his house: 18. Neither let him which is in the field return to take his clothes.

Mark 13:14, Daniel 9:27, 11:31, 12:11, Daniel 9:23.

73.   Matthew 24:20

But pray you that your flight be not in the winter, neither on the Sabbath day:

74.   Matthew 24:23

Then if any man shall say unto you, Lo, here is Christ, or there; believe it not.

75.   Matthew 24:26

Wherefore if they shall say unto you, Behold, he is in the desert; go not forth: behold, he is in the secret chambers; believe it not.

76.   Matthew 24:42

Watch therefore: for you know not what hour your Lord does come.

77.   Matthew 24:44

Therefore be you also ready: for in such an hour as you think not the Son of Man comes.

78.   Matthew 25:13

Watch therefore, for you know neither the day nor the hour wherein the Son of Man comes.

Chapter 25 tells the Parable of the Wise and Foolish Virgins. This is a warning to always be ready for the Coming of the Lord.

> Mark 13:1–3, Luke 21:5-6, 19:43-44, I Thessalonians chapter 5, Colossians 2:8, 18, John 5:43, Matthew 10:17, 2 Peter 2:1, 1 Timothy 4:1, 2 Thessalonians 2:3, Matthew chapter 10, Mark chapter 13, Daniel 9:26-27, 11:31, and 12:11. Daniel chapter 9. Luke 23:28–31, Isaiah 65:8-9, Luke chapter 17, 2 Thessalonians chapter 2. For Matthew 25:13: Mark 13:35–37, Matthew 24:36 and 42.

These are all warnings by Yeshua/Jesus for what was coming upon them in the future. Remember, all listening here were Jews. Again, In 70 AD, the Jewish Temple was destroyed by the Romans under Titus and many of the Jews were persecuted and fled to other countries. This was also an event that spread the gospel as many believing Jews took the gospel to other countries.

Yeshua/Jesus is also talking about a time to come, "that day," which is spoken of many, many times in the Torah/Old Testament. A time of terrible tribulation that is coming upon the earth.

Even so, come quickly, Lord Yeshua/Jesus.

79.   Matthew 26:26–29

26. And as they were eating, Jesus took bread, and blessed it, and broke it, and gave it to the disciples, and said, Take, eat; this is my body. 27. And he took the cup, and gave thanks, and gave it to them, saying, Drink you all of it; 28. For this is my blood of the New Testament, which is shed for many for the remission of sins. 29. But I say unto you, I will not drink henceforth of this fruit of the vine, until that day when I drink it new with you in my Father's Kingdom.
Mark 14:22–25, I Corinthians 11:23–34, I Peter 2:24, Exodus 24:8, Jeremiah 31:31, Matthew 20:28, Acts 10:41.

I Corinthians 11:23–26: 23. For I have received of the Lord that which also I delivered unto you, That the Lord Jesus the same night in which he was betrayed took bread: 24. And when he had given thanks, he broke it, and said, Take, eat: this is my body which is broken for you: this do in remembrance of me. 25. After the same manner also he took the cup, when he had supped, saying, This cup is the New Testament in my blood: this do you, as oft as you drink it, in remembrance of me. 26. For as often as you eat this bread, and drink this cup, you do show the Lord's death till he come.

Our instructions for the kiddush, which in Aramaic means "holy," or in Christianity we call it Communion, a beautiful time of fellowship and connection with our Lord and to each other as believers. A time of remembrance and a time of looking forward to the time we drink of the vine in the Kingdom with him. He wants us to remember every time we have Communion that the bread represents his body, the wine represents his blood, so that in partaking of this we are bound together in unity, one in him. WE are part of his body, all of us who believe. Since he died on the cross and was resurrected, believers have carried out this ceremony in his honor. He said he would not drink the wine until he drinks it in heaven with us. What a day that will be!

In the ceremony of Passover, this is the fourth cup, the cup of restoration. Some people drink it at this time and some people do not so they can wait to drink it with him at the Wedding Supper of the Lamb.

80.   Matthew 28:18–20

18. And Jesus came and spoke unto them, saying, All power is given unto me in heaven and in earth. 19. Go you therefore, and teach all nations, baptizing them in the name of the Father, and of the Son, and of the Holy Spirit: 20. Teaching them to observe all things whatsoever I have commanded you: and, lo, I am with you always, even unto the end of the world. Amen.

Known as "The Great Commission." Our instructions to be missionaries to the world. His promise that he is with us always, even unto the end. A great and wonderful promise that we can count on. But notice one thing that is usually not stressed: "Teaching them to observe all things whatsoever I have commanded you." I have commanded you. Thus, this book.

It is the burden of my heart that when a person becomes a believer, he is kind of left to drift along in his new life, most not being mentored on the New Covenant, Commandments, rules, or order. There are a couple of books I have that would be good for new believers to start them out.

One is by Max Anders titled *30 Days to Understanding the Bible*. The other is by Chuck Missler titled *Learn the Bible in 24 Hours*.

I believe the churches need to grasp hold of the fact that, yes, people may come to the altar and commit their lives to the Lord/Messiah/ Jesus, but then what? We need new believer classes in the churches, which many do have, but I believe we need to assign a mentor at that time to that person to be their Torah/Bible teacher, to lead them, guide them, and be there for them; also, to attend the class with them. This doesn't need to be a long, drawn out class, just an overview, like the two books above, and then get into a definitive study with them one on one, choosing any subject you agree on, but guiding them through the knowledge that the Bible is One Book, Old and New Covenants, One Story, His Story.

Many churches now have home groups where they study various things in the Bible. A new convert can be led to join one of these groups and learn there also and meet new believers that can help them grow and learn. These groups are also sustenance to our souls as we raise each other up in prayer and share each other's burdens. It is a connection that can't be made by only attending church. We all need fellowship and need to have intimate spiritual relationships with other believers. If you don't feel comfortable in one group, try another and another until you feel "this is the one."

In order to have mentors, the teacher in turn needs to be mentored, and so on. The Jews have a saying.

This is from Pirke Avot (Sayings of the Fathers), Chapter 1, Mishna 6(a): "Yehoshua ben (son of) Perachia and Nittai of Arbel received the transmission from them [the rabbis of Mishna 4]. Yehoshua ben Perachia said: Make for yourself a rabbi, acquire for yourself a friend, and judge every person favorably."

All of us need to be a rabbi (teacher), have a rabbi, be accountable to a friend, and judge every person favorably.

Commandments in the Book of Mark

Mark 1:1–4: 1. The beginning of the gospel of Jesus Christ, the Son of God; 2. As it is written in the prophets, Behold, I send my messenger before your face, which shall prepare your way before you. 3. The voice of one crying in the wilderness, Prepare you the way of the Lord, make his paths straight. 4. John did baptize in the wilderness, and preach the baptism of repentance for the remission of sins.

The Book of Mark begins in chapter one with the story I presented from the Book of Matthew on repentance.

Mark 1:2 begins with a quote from Malachi 3:1.

Malachi 3:1: 1 Behold, I will send my messenger, and he shall prepare the way before me: and the Lord, whom you seek, shall suddenly come to his temple, even the messenger of the covenant, whom you delight in: behold, he shall come, says the Lord of hosts.

This, of course, was John the Baptist. He was the forerunner of the Messiah. In Malachi, he is called "my messenger," which in Hebrew is "malachi." Therefore, there is a controversy concerning whether the Book of Malachi was written by a man named Malachi or is just signifying that it is a message from God. The Hebrew literally says, "The burden of the Word of the Lord to Israel by the hand of my messenger."

Nevertheless, the Book of Malachi prophesies concerning the coming of the messenger that will come before the Messiah.

It also begins with a quote from Isaiah 40:1–3.

> Isaiah 40:1–3: 1. Comfort you, comfort you my people, says your God. 2. Speak you comfortably to Jerusalem, and cry unto her, that her warfare is accomplished, that her iniquity is pardoned: for she has received of the Lord's hand double for all her sins. 3. The voice of him that cries in the wilderness, Prepare you the way of the Lord, make straight in the desert a highway for our God.

In verse one he says, "Comfort you! Comfort my people."

> As above, the word for "comfort" in Hebrew is *nacham*, Strong's Concordance #H5162. To be sorry, console oneself, repent, regret, comfort, be comforted.

So John the Baptist's message was to bring comfort to the people. He was "crying" in the wilderness. "Prepare the way of the Lord" would have spoken of the month of Elul, the month before Rosh HaShanah, the Jewish Civil New Year in which they were to prepare their hearts for the coming year and for Yom Kippur, the Day of Judgment.

Mark 1:4 begins with John the Baptist in the wilderness preaching a "baptism of repentance for the remission of sins." It says "all" the land of Judea and those from Jerusalem went out to him and were baptized by him in the Jordan River, confessing their sins. The verses go on to explain who John was. I've explained in Matthew chapter three what was going on at that time and the story behind it all.

81.   Mark 1:15

> And saying, The time is fulfilled, and the Kingdom of God is at hand: repent you, and believe the gospel.
> Galatians 4:4, Matthew 3:2, 4:17.

We have here a commandment to "repent" and "believe in the gospel." What exactly is *"the gospel*?" In Greek, it is *euaggelion*, Strong's Concordance #G2098. "A reward for good tidings."

> The Thayer's Greek Lexicon from Blueletterbible.org says, "The glad tidings of the Kingdom of God soon to be set up, and subsequently also of Jesus the Messiah, the founder of this Kingdom. After the death of Christ, the term comprises also the preaching of (concerning) Jesus Christ as having suffered death on the cross to procure eternal salvation for the men in the Kingdom of God, but as restored to life and exalted to the right hand of God in heaven, thence to return in majesty to consummate the Kingdom of God."

In a Jewish perspective, it means that the long awaited Messiah has come. Although Yeshua/Jesus fulfilled perfectly the prophecies about him, and most remarkably the one in Daniel concerning the 70 weeks, their eyes were blinded to this fact by God so the Gentiles could be brought into the Kingdom. Many Jewish people have accepted Yeshua/Jesus, however, when they reason out his qualifications and their eyes are opened, as with his aunt and uncle on the road to Emmaus, Luke 24:18, Mary and Cleopas, spelled Cleophas elsewhere, John 19:25. This Mary was the sister of Jesus' mother Mary, or Miriam in Hebrew. God tells his plan for the world in Isaiah 49.

> Isaiah 49:5-6: 5. And now, says the Lord that formed me from the womb to be his servant, to bring Jacob again to him, though Israel be not gathered, yet shall I be glorious in the eyes of the Lord, and my God shall be my strength. 6. And he said, It is a light thing that you should be my servant to raise up the tribes of Jacob, and to restore the preserved of Israel: I will also give you for a light to the Gentiles, that you may be my salvation unto the end of the earth.

> "Light thing," is Strong's Concordance #7043, *'qalal,'* to be slight, to be swift, be trifling, be of little account, be light."

It would have been a very simple thing for them to recognize Yeshua/ Jesus as their Messiah as he landed right smack on target according to the Book of Daniel, but, for our sakes, their eyes were blinded.

The word there for "salvation" is "Yeshua." Remember when the angel told Joseph he should name Mary's son Jesus?

> Matthew 1:20-21: 20. But while he thought on these things, behold, the angel of the Lord appeared unto him in a dream, saying, Joseph, you son of David, fear not to take unto you Mary your wife: for that which is conceived in her is of the Holy Spirit. 21. And she shall bring forth a son, and you shall call his name JESUS: for he shall save his people from their sins.

> The word *Jesus* in Hebrew is Yeshua. Strong's concordance #H3444. Salvation, deliverance.

So in our verse in Isaiah, God is saying, You should be my Yeshua/ Salvation to the ends of the earth." The Jewish Nation was chosen by God to carry that light and through Mary it was fulfilled.

The Jewish people were fervently watching and waiting for their Messiah to bring deliverance from the Roman Empire. Only by the Holy Spirit working in their lives could they have missed seeing it was him! In other words, it was an easy thing for God to send the Messiah and they would recognize him, but God had another plan. He was sending the nation of Israel to be a "light to the nations," to bring salvation to the goyim. Ultimately, God came as a man, born as a baby to a virgin named Mary, grew up, preached the gospel, was crucified, and rose again for salvation to all those who believe.

> Romans 1:16: For I am not ashamed of the gospel of Christ: for it is the power of God unto salvation to everyone who believes; to the Jew first, and also for the Greek.

> Romans 2:10: But glory, honor, and peace, to every man that works good, to the Jew first, and also to the Gentile.

Doesn't John 3:16 say,

> "For God so loved the WORLD, that He sent his only begotten Son, that whosoever believes in him should not perish, but have everlasting life."

The plan. It would have been an easy thing for God to reveal the Jewish Messiah to His people, but the plan was for "salvation" for the entire world if they would only believe.

Some have condemned the Jewish people for rejecting him, for not seeing him for who he was and is, but if people are doing that, they are condemning God because it was his idea!

Many Jews did believe however. The first believers were all Jewish, than the Gentiles began to come in. Eventually, with persecution beginning shortly after Yeshua/Jesus died on the cross, the Jewish people were scattered. This has continued to this day, but every day they are finding Jewish people in every corner of the world worshipping the One God and acting out Jewish rituals and practices. A lot of them are coming back to Israel.

In the meantime, we're still in the Age of the Gentiles. I believe this will continue until the start of The Great Tribulation, whose purpose is finally to bring God's Chosen People back to him. We're told at the end of this critical period in time, they will all believe. Their eyes will be opened when they see him.

> Romans 11:26: And so all Israel shall be saved: as it is written, There shall come out of Zion the Deliverer, and shall turn away ungodliness from Jacob:

> John 19:37: And again another Scripture says, They shall look on him whom they pierced.

Revelation 1:7: Behold, he comes with clouds; and every eye shall see him, and they also which pierced him: and all kindreds of the earth shall wail because of him. Even so, Amen.

Zechariah 12:10: And I will pour upon the house of David, and upon the inhabitants of Jerusalem, the spirit of grace and of supplications: and they shall look upon me whom they have pierced, and they shall mourn for him, as one mourns for his only son, and shall be in bitterness for him, as one that is in bitterness for his firstborn.

Zechariah 13:6: And one shall say unto him, What are these wounds in your hands? Then he shall answer, Those with which I was wounded in the house of my friends.

That will be a great and mighty day. The plan of salvation is woven all through the entire Bible.

Hebrews 10:7: NKJV: Then I said, 'Behold, I have come—In the scroll of the book it is written of me—To do your will, O God.'

Psalms 40:7: NKJV: Then I said, Behold, I come; in the scroll of the book [it is] written of me.

From the first Hebrew letter bet that begins Genesis to the last Greek letter in the Book of Revelation, the Bible is about him. It lays out the plan of God's salvation for mankind. The Festivals of the Lord tell of the early and latter rains. They plan out the salvation of the world in the spring festivals and the result of not accepting him in the fall festivals.

82.   Mark 1:17

And Jesus said unto them, Come you after me, and I will make you to become fishers of men.
Matthew 13:47-48.

God not only calls you from where he finds you, he uses your talents, your occupation, and your gifts in order for you to serve him. He chose four fishermen who had the training to seek out those that could not be found and used that talent to teach them to seek men.

Remember our story about the fishers and the hunters in Matthew chapter four and Jeremiah 16:16?

God seeks you out, and when you turn to him with everything you've got, he uses the best talent in you. He teaches us all to become "fishers of men."

In the parable in Mark 4 concerning the sower, we have another "listen" commandment.

83.   Mark 4:9

And he said unto them, He that has ears to hear, let him hear. Matthew 13:9, 13:18, 13:43, Mark 4:23, Mark 7:16, Luke 8:8, Luke 14:35.

As we've learned before, "ears to hear" is a Jewish idiom meaning, "Listen!" Shema!

84.   Mark 4:23

If any man have ears to hear, let him hear. Matthew 11:15, 13:9, 43.

There is a reward for those that truly "hear." If you read God's Word and listen to sermons, study, and pray, he will reveal more of his Word to you over time. If you never open the Word, never pray, never study, you'll stay a baby Christian and never grow. Paul gives Timothy the commandment to "study," one of our key verses.

2 Timothy 2:15: Study to show yourself approved unto God, a workman that needs not to be ashamed, rightly dividing the word of truth.

For "*study*," Strong's Concordance #G4704: *spoudazō, study*:
1. to hasten, make haste
2. to exert one's self, endeavor, give diligence

Make an effort! That's all he asks! Then he will pour out blessings on you and reveal more and more of his Word to you.

85.   Mark 6:7–11

7. And he called unto him the twelve, and began to send them forth by two and two; and gave them power over unclean spirits; 8. And commanded them that they should take nothing for their journey, save a staff only; no scrip, no bread, no money in their purse: 9. But be shod with sandals; and not put on two coats. 10. And he said unto them, In whatever place you enter into a house, there abide till you depart from that place. 11. And whosoever shall not receive you, nor hear you, when you depart thence, shake off the dust under your feet for a testimony against them. Verily I say unto you, It shall be more tolerable for Sodom and Gomorrah in the day of judgment, than for that city.
Mark 3:13–14, Ecclesiastes 4:9–10, Ephesians 6:15, Matthew 10:11, Matthew 10:14, Acts 13:51, 18:6.

These are commandments given to his twelve disciples for training purposes. We also need training in our endeavors. Certainly, God gives the gifts, but we need discipline and training from elders to carry out those gifts. We can't start out our Christian life pastoring a church, heading up a Christian organization, teaching, or any ministry we might feel called to. It takes discipline and training. We need to be discipled in order to disciple someone else.

86.   Mark 7:14

And when he had called all the people unto him, he said unto them, Hearken unto me every one of you, and understand.
Matthew 15:10, Matthew 16:9, 11, 12.

87.　　**Mark 7:16**

If any man have ears to hear, let him hear.
Mark 4:23, Matthew 11:15.

Two commandments here to "hear." If you don't listen, how are you going to learn? He also adds here, "understand." How can we understand? If you've never been to church before in your life, never read the Bible, and have never been taught, how can you "understand." If you don't have a good study Bible, someone to mentor you, a group to study with, study tools, and a good church to go to and hear the Word, how can you understand?

There are lots of scriptures on "understanding." It is used 160 times to be exact in the King James Version.

How does the Word make "entrance" into our minds? By hearing, reading, and listening!

Psalms 119:130: NKJV: The entrance of your words gives light; It gives understanding to the simple.

Proverbs 1:5: NKJV: A wise [man] will hear and increase learning, and a man of understanding will attain wise counsel.

Proverbs 9:10: NKJV: The fear of the Lord [is] the beginning of wisdom, and the knowledge of the Holy One [is] understanding.

As above, there are many more times "*understanding*" is used. In fact, it is used 32 times in the Old Testament. It is "*binah*" in Hebrew, Strong's Concordance #H998. How can we understand God's Word if we don't study it?

Mark 8:12: And he sighed deeply in his spirit, and says, Why does this generation seek after a sign? verily I say unto you, There shall no sign be given unto this generation.
Mark 7:34, Matthew 12:39.

Not a commandment, but an admonition.

Yeshua/Jesus says this is a wicked and adulterous generation that seeks after a sign. He's given us his Word. Seek that and find answers for your life. Don't be deceived.

I absolutely believe that the Holy Spirit can use a person to give you a word from God. Again, verify this with other circumstances and happenings in your life. Or just wait and see if it comes to pass. If it doesn't, no harm to you. Just go on with your life. In church a few Sundays ago, a lady who was sitting on the same row of chairs as I came over to me and told me that my family was going to be saved. That was nice, but I already know that. It was nice of her to fulfill what she felt the Lord wanted her to tell me and I appreciated that, but always be sure it confirms something else in your life or some circumstance that you know couldn't come to pass without the power of God.

88.   Mark 8:15

And he charged them, saying, Take heed, beware of the leaven of the Pharisees, and of the leaven of Herod.
Luke 12:1.

Leaven: What is it used for? To make bread rise for one thing. These Pharisees were "puffed up" with their own pride.

Strong's Concordance on *leaven*: #G2219: *Zyme*: Metaphor for inveterate mental and moral corruption, viewed in its tendency to infect others.

Notice please, these were only "some Pharisees." In my commentary on Matthew, Chapter 16 verse 6, I explain what Yeshua is talking about. Yeshua is saying to check carefully the "doctrine" of various church organizations to be sure they are in line with Scripture. That is your duty. It is up to you whether you know the Word or not. If you get led off into some false doctrine, it is because you didn't "rightly divide the Word of God."

89. Mark 8:34

And when he had called the people unto him with his disciples also, he said unto them, Whosoever will come after me, let him deny himself, and take up his cross, and follow me.

What is Yeshua saying here? Deny yourself. Take up your cross. Follow me.

He goes on to say,

> Mark 8:35–38: 35. For whosoever will save his life shall lose it; but whosoever shall lose his life for my sake and the gospel's, the same shall save it. 36. For what shall it profit a man, if he shall gain the whole world, and lose his own soul? 37. Or what shall a man give in exchange for his soul? 38. Whosoever therefore shall be ashamed of me and of my words in this adulterous and sinful generation; of him also shall the Son of Man be ashamed, when he comes in the glory of his Father with the holy angels.

Not a commandment, but, again, an admonition.

If you have come to the Messiah, you didn't earn that salvation by any works that you could ever do; you came by faith, believing, and asked him to come and live in your heart. From that point, you are a new creature in Yeshua/Jesus. That means restoration. He came to restore all things as they were in the Garden of Eden, bringing mankind back into relationship with the Creator. If you have truly repented and truly meant it when you said "I do" to him, then you are changed. Your desires change. Your habits change. Your heart is changed. We can't see on the outward person the change that is inward, but inwardly you are being reconciled to God as that "New Creature." Nothing can make you turn back. You're dedicated to becoming everything you can be in him.

But just as we cannot earn or pay for that salvation, Yeshua's brother says,

James 2:18: NKJV: "But someone will say, 'You have faith, and I have works.' Show me your faith without your works, and I will show you my faith by my works."

One way to tell if someone is truly "saved" is his behavior and desires. Showing your faith by works is the same as a husband and wife. If we get married and then we go and spend all our time with our old friends and relatives and never speak to one another or see one another, that is not really a marriage. In a marriage, you respect the other person. You do things that make each other happy and show your love by your "works." That isn't earning the other party's love, it IS love. I love my husband and want to be the kind of wife he deserves and is proud of. If we give our lives to Yeshua, we need to show our gratitude and live for him, live like he says to live, BE that light to others. Only God can judge the heart and many will be saved on that day, but when you and I stand before him, can we look him in the eye and say we've tried to do our best? And how do you know how to do your best if you don't read the Word he's given to us?

But what are "works?" Actions. It is said, "Actions speak louder than words." But what actions?

Yeshua/Jesus said, "If you love me, you will keep my commandments."

Notice that every commandment is an action. Hear, do, keep, obey, believe. Faith is an action word. All of these are verbs and a verb is an action word. So where do we begin? We go back over all the commandments in the New Covenant and check our hearts to see if we are obedient to them. The Ten Commandments are our guide, and yes, they are given by Yeshua/Jesus in the New Covenant except one, the one to keep the Sabbath, but he kept it, didn't he? When asked by his disciples, he told them what the two most important ones were:

Matthew 22:36–40: 36. Master, which is the great commandment in the law? 37. Jesus said unto him, You shall love the Lord your God with all your heart, and with all your soul, and with all your mind. 38. This is the first and great commandment. 39. And the second is like unto it, You shall love your neighbor as yourself.

If you love God first and your neighbor second, it will be easy for you to follow the rest of the commandments. In both of these, all the others are wrapped up.

90.   Mark 9:35–37

35. And he sat down, and called the twelve, and said unto them, If any man desires to be first, the same shall be last of all, and servant of all. 36. And he took a child, and set him in the midst of them: and when he had taken him in his arms, he said unto them, 37. Whosoever shall receive one of such children in my name, receives me: and whosoever shall receive me, receives not me, but him that sent me.
Luke 22:26, 27. Mark 10:13–16, Matthew 10:40.

Right before this, Yeshua is talking to the disciples about who will be the greatest. They think he doesn't hear them discussing this subject. (verse 34). In Mark 9:35 he gives the criteria for who will be the greatest. The one who is the servant of all. That is what he did for us. He became the servant for all mankind. He is the suffering servant as in Isaiah 53, but he's coming back as the conquering King! If you humble yourself and become like a servant, he will reward you in the end.

Isaiah 53:1–12: NKJV:
1. Who has believed our report? And to whom has the arm of the Lord been revealed?
2. For he shall grow up before him as a tender plant, and as a root out of dry ground. He has no form or comeliness; and when we see him, [there is] no beauty that we should desire him.
3. He is despised and rejected by men, a man of sorrows and acquainted with grief. And we hid, as it were, [our] faces from him; he was despised, and we did not esteem him.

4. Surely he has borne our griefs and carried our sorrows; yet we esteemed him stricken, smitten by God, and afflicted.

5. But he [was] wounded for our transgressions, [he was] bruised for our iniquities; the chastisement for our peace [was] upon him, and by his stripes we are healed.

6. All we like sheep have gone astray; we have turned, every one, to his own way; And the Lord has laid on him the iniquity of us all.

7. He was oppressed and he was afflicted, yet he opened not his mouth; he was led as a lamb to the slaughter, and as a sheep before its shearers is silent, so he opened not his mouth.

8. He was taken from prison and from judgment, and who will declare his generation? For he was cut off from the land of the living; for the transgressions of my people he was stricken.

9. And they made his grave with the wicked — but with the rich at his death, because he had done no violence, nor [was any] deceit in his mouth.

10. Yet it pleased the Lord to bruise him; he has put [him] to grief. When you make his soul an offering for sin, he shall see [his] seed, he shall prolong [his] days, and the pleasure of the Lord shall prosper in his hand.

11. He shall see the labor of his soul, [and] be satisfied. By his knowledge my righteous servant shall justify many, for he shall bear their iniquities.

12. Therefore I will divide him a portion with the great, and he shall divide the spoil with the strong, because he poured out his soul unto death, and he was numbered with the transgressors, and he bore the sin of many, and made intercession for the transgressors.

91.   Mark 9:38–41

38. And John answered him, saying, Master, we saw one casting out devils in your name, and he follows not us: and we forbad him, because he follows not us. 39. But Jesus said, Forbid him not: for there is no man who shall do a miracle in my name, that

can lightly speak evil of me. 40. For he that is not against us is on our part. 41. For whosoever shall give you a cup of water to drink in my name, because you belong to Christ, verily I say unto you, he shall not lose his reward.

The Bible doesn't tell us who this person or who these persons were, but Yeshua gives a teaching on how to treat others who don't belong to your organization or believe exactly as you do. We need to try to have an open dialogue with other people about their beliefs and try to come together on the things we do agree on. Or not. If we find it turning into arguments and shouting matches, walk away and pray the Holy Spirit will speak to their hearts. Or yours.

92.   Mark 9:43–48

43. And if your hand offend you, cut it off: it is better for you to enter into life maimed, than having two hands to go into hell, into the fire that never shall be quenched: 44. Where their worm dies not, and the fire is not quenched. 45. And if your foot offend you, cut it off: it is better for you to enter halt into life, than having two feet to be cast into hell, into the fire that never shall be quenched: 46. Where their worm dies not, and the fire is not quenched. 47. And if your eye offend you, pluck it out: it is better for you to enter into the Kingdom of God with one eye, than having two eyes to be cast into hell fire: 48 Where their worm dies not, and the fire is not quenched.

Isaiah 66:24 is quoted three times here.

Isaiah 66:24: And they shall go forth, and look upon the carcasses of the men that have transgressed against me: for their worm shall not die, neither shall their fire be quenched; and they shall be an abhorring unto all flesh.

I am told that never was it reported that any Jewish person cut his hand or foot off or plucked out his eye. This verse, again, is hyperbole,

Hebrew figurative speaking. This verse is right after the incident of believers that didn't belong in their group who were casting out demons in Yeshua's Name. This also speaks of repentance. Be sincere about repenting for your sins. If you don't feel sorry, pray to the Father until you do. Sin is sin and no matter what the sin, the Holy Spirit is the one that has to reveal it and bring sorrowful repentance because you have hurt the Father and gone against His Word.

93. Mark 9:50

Salt is good: but if the salt has lost its saltiness, wherewith will you season it? Have salt in yourselves, and have peace one with another. Matthew 5:13. Luke 14:34.

See our study in Matthew 5:13. Salt in the past and today is used as a preservative and to keep flesh from corrupting, such as bacon, ham, fish, or jerky. If the salt has lost its saltiness, you'll have a rotten mess! In other words, "watered down." We need to be careful to recognize a "watered down" gospel. Many today are teaching that there is more than one way to be saved. Some are joining up with unbelievers in our God, Yahweh, such as Muslims or Islamists, just to become a "seeker friendly" church, accepting every doctrine, which comes to denying the true gospel of Yeshua/Jesus, our Messiah. Be careful! They've lost their saltiness and are preaching a watered down gospel. We need to love people of all faiths without accepting doctrine that goes against God's Word. Allah, the sun and moon God, is NOT OUR TRUE GOD, YAHWEH!

So we as believers, if we have let our convictions slide, if we have not stayed in the Word daily, if we have not had a prayer life daily, if we have forsaken the assembling of ourselves together with other believers, if we have gone our own way, we have lost our "saltiness." We are no good to God or anyone else as far as living our faith and being a witness for him concerning salvation.

We are to be a light to others, revealing the working of the Holy Spirit to others as apparent in our spiritual growth, our love for the brothers and sisters, our love for Yeshua/Jesus, our faithfulness in serving, our love for the lost, and our readiness to show that light. It's a dangerous thing to drift away from the faith. Sometimes we don't even realize we're doing it until we're so far that it takes true, heartfelt repentance, prayer, and study to get back on the right path. The way to avoid this is to stay daily in the Word, in prayer, and fellowship with believers.

What does it mean to have "peace with one another?" Shalom, peace, is a sign of fellowship. If you've gotten off track, your brothers and sisters can sense it. Go to them and have them pray with you that you will get back on track. Maybe set a time to study and pray with one or two of them. Building one another up in the faith.

1 Thessalonians 5:11: Wherefore comfort yourselves together, and edify one another, even as also you do.

Hebrews 3:12-13: 12. Take heed, brethren, lest there be in any of you an evil heart of unbelief, in departing from the living God. 13. But exhort one another daily, while it is called Today; lest any of you be hardened through the deceitfulness of sin.

Act 14:22: Confirming the souls of the disciples, and exhorting them to continue in the faith, and that we must through much tribulation enter into the Kingdom of God.

Act 16:5: And so were the churches established in the faith, and increased in number daily.

Romans 14:1: Him that is weak in the faith receive you, but not to doubtful disputations, or disputes over doubtful things, which profits nothing.

1 Corinthians 16:13: Watch, stand fast in the faith, be brave, be strong.

2 Corinthians 13:5: Examine yourselves as to whether you are in the faith. Test yourselves. Do you not know yourselves, that Jesus Christ is in you? — unless indeed you are disqualified.

Reprobates. *Adokimos,* Strong's Concordance #G96. Not standing the test, not approved. Properly used of metals and coins. That which does not prove itself such as it ought. Unfit for, unproved, spurious, reprobate.

Check to see if you are walking according to the gospel that you professed. A "certain one" who is not standing the test is reprobate. One who is not living according to the Word. Paul says, "Examine yourselves." We aren't to be fruit inspectors for one another, but check our own fruit! This doesn't mean you're not saved, but that you need to get in line with the Word. Talk the talk and walk the walk!

Colossians 2:6–7: 6. As you therefore have received Christ Jesus the Lord, so walk in him, 7. rooted and built up in him and established in the faith, as you have been taught, abounding in it with thanksgiving.

If you are in a situation where you've gotten into some doctrine that you find is not Biblical and you've strayed from right doctrine, don't fear to call out to others for help. Most of us have been there at one time or another. Fear will drive us even further from the road back. Just jump in, turn around (teshuva, repentance), and begin the journey back. Your experiences from what you've learned from this will help others greatly in the end when you've come back and have been strengthened.

94. Mark 10:2–12

2. And the Pharisees came to him, and asked him, Is it lawful for a man to put away his wife? Tempting him. 3. And he answered and said unto them, What did Moses command you? 4. And they said, Moses suffered to write a bill of divorcement, and to put her away. 5. And Jesus answered and said unto them, For the hardness

of your heart he wrote you this precept. 6. But from the beginning of the creation God made them male and female. 7. For this cause shall a man leave his father and mother, and cleave to his wife; 8. And they twain shall be one flesh: so then they are no more twain, but one flesh. 9. What therefore God has joined together, let not man put asunder. 10. And in the house his disciples asked him again of the same matter. 11. And he says unto them, Whosoever shall put away his wife, and marry another, commits adultery against her. 12. And if a woman shall put away her husband, and be married to another, she commits adultery.

Mark Chapter 10 is all about marriage, divorce, and children. This Scripture goes back to Genesis and the first man and woman. They were to leave their father and mother and "cleave" to one another. Be glued to one another.

Let's begin with verse 2. The Pharisees were again trying to trap him into something that was not in the Torah; therefore, showing he was not the Messiah if he went against the Torah/Word of God.

We went over this in Matthew chapter 5 verses 31 and 32. Remember in my commentary the vav of purpose? "In order to."

Also, as above, in the Delitzsch Hebrew Gospels for Luke 16:18 it says, Or, "sends away his wife in order to marry."

What therefore God has joined together, let not man put asunder.

95.   Mark 10:14

But when Jesus saw it, he was much displeased, and said unto them, Suffer the little children to come unto me, and forbid them not: for of such is the Kingdom of God.

I Peter 2:2: As newborn babes, desire the sincere milk of the Word, that you may grow thereby:

In my life, I've spent many years in children's ministry and have seen many children come to the Messiah. I, myself, got saved at age eight. I understood then that I was a sinner in need of a Savior. I remember the change I felt in my heart and life that Jesus loved me and I belonged to him now! I have a granddaughter that, out of the blue at age two said she wanted to ask Jesus into her heart. I was blown away! Could hardly breathe! I didn't ask her, I was just telling her the story of Jesus' birth with a little open and close nativity set. I told her the story and said, "If we believe in Jesus and ask him into our hearts, we will be saved." She said, "I want to do that!" What a privilege. Never overlook the little ones in your life. Never think they're too young to understand their need for a Savior.

In our growth as believers in him, we all have to come as little children. We can't start out as Bible scholars, knowing all the answers, but daily we read, listen, pray, and grow.

I'm teaching a beginning Hebrew class as I write this. I tell my students, "We have to come as little children, like in kindergarten." We enter in admitting, "I don't know this, but I want to humble myself and learn."

96.   Mark 10:19

You know the commandments, Do not commit adultery, Do not kill, Do not steal, Do not bear false witness, Defraud not, Honor your father and mother.
Exodus 20:12–16, Deuteronomy 5:16–20.

Here we have the sixth, eighth, and fifth commandments. Yeshua tells us not to defraud people.

The word for "defraud" here is Strong's Concordance #650, apostereo. It means to defraud, rob, despoil, deprive of a thing. To fail a person or thing. Used of persons not present at the right time.

Yikes! People who are late? Oh, me. Also, to cause to fail, to withdraw, take away from. It is used six times in the New Covenant: For "defraud" four times, "destitute" one time, and "keep back by fraud" one time.

How much fraud do we have in the world today? Let us be careful in all things not to defraud anyone.

1 Thessalonians 4:6: That no [man] go beyond and defraud his brother in [any] matter: because that the Lord [is] the avenger of all such, as we also have forewarned you and testified.

The word for defraud here is a different number. It is Strong's Concordance #G4122. It is used five times in the New Covenant: It is used for "to make again" two times, "defraud" two times, and "get an advantage" one time:

1. To have more, or a greater part or share;
2. to be superior, excel, surpass, have an advantage over;
3. to gain or take advantage of another, to overreach.

In First Corinthians 7:5, Paul is speaking of marital relations.

1 Corinthians 7:5: Defraud you not one the other, except [it be] with consent for a time, that you may give yourselves to fasting and prayer; and come together again, that Satan tempt you not for your incontinency.

97.   Mark 10:21

Then Jesus beholding him loved him, and said unto him, One thing you lack: go your way, sell whatsoever you have, and give to the poor, and you shall have treasure in heaven: and come, take up the cross, and follow me.

This is a continuation of the story begun in this chapter about the man that wanted to follow Yeshua/Jesus, but then decided not to after Jesus said these words.

If he asks us to sacrifice something in our lives, to give up something we love for him, are we willing? I think of the dedication of the many missionaries I have known that have left home, family, and nation to go preach the gospel in other lands. Their children, when school age, must go away to a mission school, usually for the year, coming home only on holidays. They must give up the niceties of their lives, grocery stores, nice hospitals, washers and dryers, etc., to go forth and win the lost.

Is there something in your life the Lord is asking you to give up, leave behind, or lay down? From all the testimonies I have heard from these missionaries, it was worth it all. If today you are holding back because you don't think you are ready to pay the price, be assured that the reward way outweighs the sacrifice and God will give you the strength and power to accomplish what he asks.

98.   Mark 11:22

And Jesus answering says unto them, Have faith in God.

In Hebrew, the word for faith is "*emun*," masculine singular. "Emuna," pronounced "emunah", emphasis on the "nah," is the feminine singular. "Faithful trusting, firmness, fidelity, steadfastness, steadiness." Strong's Concordance #H529.

Remember, faith is a verb. An action word.

We could write a book on the words "faith, faithful, and faithfulness." You may have done a study before on this.

I was praying one day and told the Lord I had complete faith in him. I felt him say to my heart, "I have complete faith in you too."

God has faith in me? I was overwhelmed. I constantly pray that I will not fail him. I try to live for him, draw close to him, learn about him, pray to him. But God has faith in ME? Not that I'm anything more spectacular than any of you, but this is how God sees us. When we come to believing faith in him, become his child, believe that Yeshua/Jesus died for our sins according to the Scriptures, that he was buried, and that he rose again the third day according to the Scriptures (I Corinthians 15:3–4), then we open the door to his Kingdom.

If we read the Word and learn, pray, fellowship with others, not forsake the assembling of ourselves together, we grow and grow in him. Our faith grows. So when he says, "I have faith in YOU," he's saying, "I see that you are obedient to my Word and that you are drawing near to me and I love you with an everlasting love that will never die." If you open the door just a crack to him, he will pour out on you blessing after blessing. This is not financially I am speaking of, but spiritually. When we develop a great desire to learn of him, reading his Word, reading books that grow your faith and teach you, etc., he will supply your spiritual need immensely.

Sometimes I've come to the end of a book or the end of a study and I'll say, "Okay, Lord. I'm bored now. I need to be fed." And wow! Again he pours it out on me. Ask him. He has faith in you.

In Greek, the word for "faith" is "*pistis*," Strong's Concordance #G4102.

1. Conviction of the truth of anything, belief; in the NT of a conviction or belief respecting man's relationship to God and divine things, generally with the included idea of trust and holy fervor born of faith and joined with it relating to God.
2. The conviction that God exists and is the creator and ruler of all things, the provider and bestower of eternal salvation through Christ. Relating to Christ.
3. A strong and welcome conviction or belief that Jesus is the Messiah, through whom we obtain eternal salvation in the Kingdom of God. The religious beliefs of Christians.

4. Belief with the predominate idea of trust (or confidence) whether in God or in Christ, springing from faith in the same. Fidelity, faithfulness. The character of one who can be relied on.

As a little child, we place our hand in his hand and say, "I will follow you."

99.   Mark 11:24–26

24. Therefore I say unto you, What things soever you desire, when you pray, believe that you receive them, and you shall have them. 25. And when you stand praying, forgive, if you have ought against any: that your Father also who is in heaven may forgive you your trespasses. 26. But if you do not forgive, neither will your Father who is in heaven forgive your trespasses. Matthew 7:7, Colossians 3:13, Matthew 6:15, 18:35.

Here we are back to repentance! Another place says not to bring your offering to the altar until you repent and go ask a person to forgive you, or if they think you have wronged them, you be the one to go to them. The world thinks differently. We're children of the King and Kingdom. We're different. New creatures. Be obedient to the Holy Spirit. Go to him in repentance before you ask. Sincerely spend time with him and focus in on anything that might be between you and him or you and another person until you get an answer. Then ask.

The key here is forgiveness. Again, if there is something blocking your prayers, it is most likely that you have something against some person or that they have something against you. If we ask the Lord by his Holy Spirit to help us forgive people, he will. Sometimes in our humanity it seems impossible to forgive the things some people have done to us, but if you pray sincerely and ask the Holy Spirit to help you, he will.

If you have sinned against a person or persons and you go to them and apologize and ask their forgiveness, but they reject your apology, you've done your part. You have been obedient to the Word.

If someone has done something against you and you pray and ask the Lord to go with you and help you forgive that person or persons, then you go to that person and tell them you forgive them and they don't accept it, you've done your part.

It's all a matter of the heart. God wants YOUR heart to be right before him.

100.   Mark 12:12–17

NIV: 12 Then the chief priests, the teachers of the law and the elders looked for a way to arrest him because they knew he had spoken the parable against them. But they were afraid of the crowd; so they left him and went away. 13 Later they sent some of the Pharisees and Herodians to Jesus to catch him in his words. 14 They came to him and said, "Teacher, we know that you are a man of integrity. You aren't swayed by others, because you pay no attention to who they are; but you teach the way of God in accordance with the truth. Is it right to pay the imperial tax to Caesar or not? 15 Should we pay or shouldn't we?" But Jesus knew their hypocrisy. "Why are you trying to trap me?" he asked. "Bring me a denarius and let me look at it." 16 They brought the coin, and he asked them, "Whose image is this? And whose inscription?" "Caesar's," they replied. 17 Then Jesus said to them, "Give back to Caesar what is Caesar's and to God what is God's." And they were amazed at him.
Matthew 22:17–21.

This story starts in verse 12. Some of the Pharisees had been outwitted by him, again, in the Parable of the Vinedressers in verses 12:1–11. They were out to get him, again.

Simple. Pay to your government what is due them and to God what is due him.

Remember when Yeshua/Jesus sent Peter to catch a fish when the taxes were due? Amazing story.

Matthew 17:24–26: 24. And when they were come to Capernaum, they that received tribute [money] came to Peter, and said, Does not your master pay tribute? 25. He said, Yes. And when he was come into the house, Jesus anticipated him, saying, What think you, Simon? Of whom do the kings of the earth take custom or tribute? Of their own children, or of strangers? 26. Peter says unto him, Of strangers. Jesus says unto him, Then are the children free.

This was done to build up Peter's faith. God provides in mysterious and awesome ways. Trust in him. Obey the laws of the land unless they are against his Word.

101.   Mark 12:28–34

28. Then one of the scribes came, and having heard them reasoning together, perceiving that he had answered them well, asked him, "Which is the first commandment of all?" 29. And Jesus answered him, "The first of all the commandments is, Hear, O Israel; The Lord our God is one Lord: 30. And you shall love the Lord your God with all your heart, and with all your soul, and with all your mind, and with all your strength: this is the first commandment." 31. And the second is like, namely this, "You shall love your neighbor as yourself. There is none other commandment greater than these." 32. So the scribe said to him, "Well [said], Teacher. You have spoken the truth, for there is one God, and there is no other but he. 33. And to love him with all the heart, with all the understanding, with all the soul, and with all the strength, and to love one's neighbor as oneself, is more than all the whole burnt offerings and sacrifices." 34. Now when Jesus saw that he answered wisely, he said to him, "You are not far from the Kingdom of God." But after that no one dared question him.
Matthew 22:34–40. 29. Deuteronomy 6:4–5. 30. Deuteronomy 10:12, 30:6. 31. Leviticus 19:18, Romans 13:9. 32. Deuteronomy 4:39. 33. Hosea 6:6. 34. Matthew 22:46. Ten Commandments: Exodus 10:1–17 and Deuteronomy 5:4–21.

This scribe had great understanding of the Scriptures. Yeshua/Jesus first says "Hear O Israel." As I said before for Matthew 16:16–19, this is part of what is called the "shema." Shema means "hear." To hear that the Lord our God, the Lord is one. Not one God, but one. In Hebrew, echad, one. If we say "one God," then there must be others, right? And the second in verse 30 is part of the shema also. In Verse 31, he says this is the second most important, to love your neighbor as yourself. This is also part of the shema.

Deuteronomy 6:4–9 is said, then Deuteronomy 6:5–9, then Deuteronomy 11:13–21, then Numbers 15:37–41.

This is said in the morning and in the evening, during synagogue services, and upon the death of a loved one. If they are unable to say it before they die, it is recited by someone else for them.

Here we have the first of the Ten Commandments: "I am the Lord your God. You shall have no other Gods before me." Yeshua/Jesus is expounding on that commandment. Not only shall you not have any other Gods before the One True God, but you shall love the Lord your God with all your heart, with all your mind, and with all your strength. This second part is a compilation of commandments five through ten, which relate to our treatment of other people. The Jewish people standing there with him knew completely what he was talking about.

If twice a day we sing the Shema, we remind ourselves that God is God and he is the only God. There should be no other in our lives that we worship or bow down to. If there is, we need to repent. Search your soul morning and evening.

102.   Mark 12:38–40

38. And he said unto them in his doctrine (teaching), Beware of the scribes, which love to go in long clothing, and love salutations in the marketplaces, 39. And the chief seats in the synagogues, and the uppermost rooms at feasts: 40. Which

devour widows' houses, and for a pretense make long prayers:
these shall receive greater damnation.
Mark 4:2, Matthew 23:14.

Again, he wasn't speaking of all scribes, only those who had become
drunk with power, taking advantage of people by flaunting their position
over them. Scribes were important, truly, but some of them lacked any
humility at all and took advantage of the office.

If you're a person in power and have a great influence over people, be
careful that you don't become like these scribes and lord it over the people.
Be a servant. Be humble. Don't desire to be worshipped by the people.

The most famous scribe in the Bible is Ezra, who was also a priest.
A scribe transcribed documents and interpreted documents from
other languages. They were teachers, philosophers, counselors, and
performed many duties that the people needed. They held public offices
and performed judicial procedures. They were able to sit on the ruling
authority board, the Sanhedrin. They were loyal to the chief priests
and leaders because their standing depended on them, even though in
Jesus' day these offices were corrupt. Some scribes and some Pharisees
constantly tried to trip Jesus up, but it never worked.

103.   Mark 13:5-6

5. And Jesus answering them began to say, Take heed lest any
man deceive you: 6. For many shall come in my name, saying,
I am Christ; and shall deceive many.
Ephesians 5:6.

Over the centuries, there have been multitudes that have said they are
the Messiah. In Jesus' day, there were many rabbis teaching that they
were the Messiah. After he lived here on earth, there have been many
who have said they were the Messiah or people have thought they might
be the Messiah. There were two famous men especially who were
thought to be the Messiah.

Simon bar Kokhba, otherwise known as Simon ben Kosiba, led a revolt against the Romans in 132 AD. He established an independent Jewish state which he ruled for three years as prince. He was defeated in 135 by the Romans following a two-and-a-half year war. Many thought he was the Messiah until he was defeated.

In our day, some of the orthodox Jews thought Rabbi Menachem Mendel Schneerson was the Messiah. He was a great rabbi, but he died in 1994. The last time I was in Israel, we went to Tzfat and they still had posters of him in the streets. He was a wonderful person and helped his people very much. I read the story of his life and it was amazing. He did not believe he was the Messiah. He was a very humble person.

If we watch television today, many try to draw you in by offering you riches, power, or a better life if you will just give money to them. Run! Yeshua/Jesus never promised this. If you are being taken in by any of these people, it is your own fault. You're being deceived! You don't know the Word or you would know this is false teaching. There are many on television and on the internet that pretend to be prophets. Their lives are built around this lifestyle. There are conferences held constantly with these people. Run! Yeshua/Jesus gave the criteria for being a true prophet. If the prophecy comes to pass, it is of God.

It would take another book to expound on what is going on today in the "prophecy" ministry. Whole churches are given to this. Whole television networks are given to this. I know people that are so caught up in this that they don't have time for anything else. It's like an addiction. They run from conference to conference, church to church, hoping they will be "prophesied over." They lose touch with being a well-rounded believer. They are certainly in deception. They don't really study the Scriptures, but let others tell them what the Word says, and it is usually misused.

A pastor once said that if a church is focused on only one gift of the Spirit, it is a church off balance. We need to have well-rounded churches, operating in all the gifts of the Spirit.

I believe in a Word of knowledge from a believer. However, that word needs to be confirmed in the mouth of two or three witnesses. Don't go running to Mexico to become a missionary on the word of one person saying "God told me to tell you this." You'll find yourself in Mexico sitting under a cactus wondering where God is. Well, he'll be right back there where you left him. Wait on the workings of the Holy Spirit. If he wants you to go to Mexico, several things will happen to confirm it. Always be in deep prayer and in touch with the Holy Spirit's leading.

It's a shame that we don't teach new believers this. So many cling to a church, a ministry, a TV network, etc., to get their answers. It's the easy way. No sacrificial seeking him. No daily Bible study, searching the Word. Only the words of people that have given themselves to deception.

Yeshua/Jesus gives us warnings:

> Matthew 12:39: But he answered and said unto them, An evil and adulterous generation seeks after a sign; and there shall no sign be given to it, but the sign of the prophet Jonas:

> Luke 11:29: And when the people were gathered thickly together, he began to say, This is an evil generation: they seek a sign; and there shall no sign be given it, but the sign of Jonas the prophet.

> Matthew 16:4: A wicked and adulterous generation seeks after a sign; and there shall no sign be given unto it, but the sign of the prophet Jonas. And he left them, and departed.

104.   Mark 13:7–23

7. And when you shall hear of wars and rumors of wars, be you not troubled: for such things must needs be; but the end shall not be yet. 8. For nation shall rise against nation, and kingdom against kingdom: and there shall be earthquakes in diverse places, and there shall be famines and troubles: these are the

beginnings of sorrows. 9. But take heed to yourselves: for they shall deliver you up to councils; and in the synagogues you shall be beaten: and you shall be brought before rulers and kings for my sake, for a testimony against them. 10. And the gospel must first be published among all nations. 11. But when they shall lead you, and deliver you up, take no thought beforehand what you shall speak, neither do you premeditate: but whatsoever shall be given you in that hour, that speak you: for it is not you that speak, but the Holy Spirit. 12. Now the brother shall betray the brother to death, and the father the son; and children shall rise up against their parents, and shall cause them to be put to death.

13. And you shall be hated of all men for my name's sake: but he that shall endure unto the end, the same shall be saved. 14. But when you shall see the abomination of desolation, spoken of by Daniel the prophet, standing where it ought not, let (him that reads understand,) then let them that are in Judea flee to the mountains: 15. And let him that is on the housetop not go down into the house, neither enter in to take anything out of his house: 16. And let him that is in the field not turn back again for to take up his garment. 17. But woe to them that are with child, and to them that give suck in those days!

18. And pray you that your flight is not in the winter. 19. For in those days shall be affliction, such as was not from the beginning of the creation which God created unto this time, neither shall be. 20. And except that the Lord had shortened those days, no flesh should be saved: but for the elect's sake, whom he has chosen, he has shortened the days. 21. And then if any man shall say to you, Lo, here is Christ; or, lo, he is there; believe him not: 22. For false christs and false prophets shall rise, and shall show signs and wonders, to seduce, if it were possible, even the elect. 23. But take you heed: behold, I have foretold you all things.

Yeshua/Jesus in these passages was warning the people of the sorrows coming upon the earth. All these things happened to the Jewish people about 40 years after this. During the years between 66-70 AD, Titus came in and destroyed the Temple. The persecution that the Jewish people faced in that day drove them into "all the world." Through these tribulations, the gospel was preached throughout the world.

Through the years, there have been many wars, persecutions, and trials for Jewish people and Christians alike. There is still to come upon the world the Great Tribulation as spoken of by John in the Book of Revelation and by Daniel in the Book of Daniel. There is a great rise in antisemitism and hatred for Christians right now in our day. I believe the Age of the Gentiles is drawing to a close soon.

Whatever trials and persecution we have to go through, Yeshua/Jesus said he would never leave us or forsake us. Stand strong!

105.   Mark 13:28-29

28. Now learn a parable of the fig tree; When her branch is yet tender, and puts forth leaves, you know that summer is near:
29. So you in like manner, when you shall see these things come to pass, know that it is nigh, [even] at the doors.
Luke 21:29, Matthew 24.

What is "it" is near? The passages before this tell us of "those days." Days of Great Tribulation. The fig tree is thought by many to be a symbol of the Nation of Israel. How do we know the fig tree is Israel?

Hosea 9:10: I found Israel like grapes in the wilderness; I saw your fathers as the firstfruits in the fig tree at her first time: but they went to Baalpeor, and separated themselves unto that shame; and their abominations were according as they loved.

Jeremiah 24:5: Thus says the Lord, the God of Israel; Like these good figs, so will I acknowledge them that are carried away captive of Judah, whom I have sent out of this place into the land of the Chaldeans for their good.

On May 14, 1948, Israel was declared a state. The fig tree had begun putting on leaves symbolically. Yeshua/Jesus says, "When you see these things happening, know that "it" is near... at the doors." What? Those days. We are living right on the edge of "those days."

One well-known scholar denies that the fig tree represents Israel. In fact, in quoting Mark 13:28: "Look at the fig tree," he adds "and all the trees" as if it is part of the verse. It absolutely does not say that. I have checked several translations. A lot of other well-known scholars agree that Israel is represented by the fig tree.

One of my favorite stories in the New Covenant is the calling of Nathanael.

> John 1:47–51: 47. Jesus saw Nathanael coming to him, and says of him, Behold an Israelite indeed, in whom is no deceit! 48. Nathanael said unto him, How do you know me? Jesus answered and said unto him, Before Philip called you, when you were under the fig tree, I saw you. 49. Nathanael answered and said unto him, Rabbi, you are the Son of God; you are the King of Israel. 50. Jesus answered and said unto him, Because I said unto you, I saw you under the fig tree, believe you? You shall see greater things than these. 51. And he said unto him, Verily, verily, I say unto you, Hereafter you shall see heaven open, and the angels of God ascending and descending upon the Son of Man.

This might not mean anything to you. It meant a great deal to Nathanael. That is because Nathanael knew Yeshua/Jesus was speaking of the Millennial Kingdom. Yeshua/Jesus was seeing Nathanael in the future. Nathanael absolutely understood. It made him declare Yeshua/Jesus to be the Son of God and King of Israel! No one on earth could see the future except God!

Here in these verses we see that each man dwelt in safety under his own vine and fig tree when King Solomon reigned:

1 Kings 4:25: And Judah and Israel dwelt safely, every man under his vine and under his fig tree, from Dan even to Beersheba, all the days of Solomon.

From Dan to Beersheva is a Hebrew idiom that means "from one end of Israel to the other." Dan is in the north and Beersheva in the south.

2 Kings 18:31: Hearken not to Hezekiah: for thus says the king of Assyria, Make an agreement with me by a present, and come out to me, and then eat you every man of his own vine, and every one of his fig tree, and drink you every one the waters of his cistern:

Same verse in Isaiah:

Isaiah 36:16: Hearken not to Hezekiah: for thus says the king of Assyria, Make an agreement with me by a present, and come out to me: and eat you every one of his vine, and every one of his fig tree, and drink you every one the waters of his own cistern;

Micah 4:4: But they shall sit every man under his vine and under his fig tree; and none shall make them afraid: for the mouth of the Lord of hosts has spoken it.

Zechariah 3:10: In that day, says the Lord of hosts, shall you call every man his neighbor under the vine and under the fig tree.

What a wonderful day that will be for all of us that believe!

The fig tree speaks of the Nation of Israel. "Gathering figs" is also is a Jewish idiom for studying. Yeshua/Jesus sees right into the heart of Nathaniel. "An Israelite in whom is no guile." Or deceit, an illusion to Jacob. The ladder imagery also recalls Jacob's dream in Genesis 28:12. But Yeshua tells Nathaniel now that HE will see heaven open and the angels ascending and descending upon the Son of Man. Yeshua/Jesus is the connector between heaven and earth and Nathaniel becomes his

disciple and will soon see this. Nathaniel sees right away that Yeshua/
Jesus is The King of Israel.

The title "Son of Man" takes us back to the Book of Daniel.

> Daniel 7:13: I saw in the night visions, and, behold, one like the
> Son of Man came with the clouds of heaven, and came to the
> Ancient of days, and they brought him near before him.

So there is a lot going on here in these verses.

106.   Mark 13:32-33

> 32. But of that day and that hour knows no man, no, not the
> angels which are in heaven, neither the Son, but the Father.
> 33. Take you heed, watch and pray: for you know not when the
> time is.

What day? Here Yeshua/Jesus is speaking of the Day that ends the Great
Tribulation period and the Millennial reign begins. It is spoken of often
in the Torah/Old Testament as "That Day."

107.   Mark 13:35–37

> 35. Watch you therefore: for you know not when the master
> of the house comes, at even, or at midnight, or at the cock-
> crowing, or in the morning: 36. Lest coming suddenly he find
> you sleeping. 37. And what I say unto you I say unto all, Watch.

Whatever your belief in the events of eschatology, Yeshua/Jesus says to
"watch." Watch and pray. Be ready.

By the way, there are no chickens or roosters allowed within the city
walls of Jerusalem or any city in Israel. That is a Hebrew idiom for the
watchers on the wall that sounded the trumpet at watches during the
night. The "cock's crow" was not a chicken, but a place on top of the wall

that surrounded the temple. They found a rock with the inscription, "to the place of trumpeting," in the ruins of the temple that was destroyed in 70 AD. You can see it if you go to Israel or check it out online. The watchers would sound the trumpet at designated times.

There were three watches the Israelites kept of about four hours each: The beginning watch, the middle watch, and the morning watch. These were:

First watch	Sunset, or 6:00 p.m. to 10:00 p.m.
Second watch	10:00 p.m. to 2:00 a.m.
Third watch	2:00 a.m. to sunrise, or 6:00 a.m.

During the time the Romans ruled there were four watches: The fourth watch as in Matthew 14:25, or "even." In the evening, at midnight, at cock crowing, or morning, as in Mark 13:35. These were:

First watch	6:00 p.m. to 9:00 p.m.
Second watch	9:00 p.m. to 12:00 a.m., or midnight
Third watch	12:00 a.m. to 3:00 a.m.
Fourth watch	3:00 a.m. to 6:00 a.m.

108.   Mark 14:22

And as they did eat, Jesus took bread, and blessed, and broke [it], and gave to them, and said, Take, eat: this is my body.
I Corinthians 11:23–25, I Peter 2:24.

This was part of the Passover Seder and part of our Communion service. There are four cups that are drunk during the Passover Seder. Yeshua/ Jesus said he would not drink the fourth cup here, but he would drink it with us in the Kingdom. The bread and wine represent his body and blood. When we partake of this, let us remember the sacrifice he made for us and not let it just become a ritual. We also need to dwell on the fact that we are part of him. He has made us a part of his family. We have communication with him and with other Christian brothers and sisters because we are one in him.

Mark 14:30,68,72: 30. And Jesus said unto him, Verily I say unto you, That this day, even in this night, before the cock crow twice, you shall deny me thrice. 68. But he denied, saying, I know not, neither understand I what you say. And he went out into the porch; and the cock crew. 72. And the second time the cock crew. And Peter called to mind the word that Jesus said unto him, Before the cock crow twice, you shall deny me thrice. And when he thought thereon, he wept.

As above, this wasn't a rooster, as translated in some translations, but the watches of the night.

109.   Mark 14:38

Watch you and pray, lest you enter into temptation. The spirit truly is ready, but the flesh is weak.

Here we have the commandment to "watch" and "pray." Our spirit always thinks we can withstand temptation, but our flesh is weak. We need to be watchful all the time for things that might come into our life that tempt us. Prayer is the way we stay close to the Lord.

In John 16, he explains the workings of the Holy Spirit and what he will do for us. He says it is expedient that he go away so the Holy Spirit can come. We need to draw near to the Lord and he will speak to us and warn us of all things through His Holy Spirit.

110.   Mark 16:15–16

15. And he said unto them, Go into all the world and preach the gospel to every creature. 16. He that believes and is baptized shall be saved; but he that believes not shall be damned.

Here we have a command to "go." Go where? Go into all the world. Wherever you are, that is your world.

Another command is to be baptized. Does baptism save you? No, but it is an outward declaration to the world that you believe in the Messiah, Yeshua/Jesus. Are you going to hell if you aren't baptized? No. The thief on the cross next to Yeshua/Jesus wasn't baptized. But this is a commandment. If you have not been baptized, make an appointment today to do this. Most churches have "baptism classes" to teach you what it is all about. Baptism is a sign of faith and belief.

Commandments in the Book of Luke

In the third chapter of Luke, we have the same scene as told about in the books of Matthew and Luke of John the Baptist preaching on the banks of the Jordan River and baptizing in the Jordan with one exception: Luke 3:1–6 gives the background of why he is there instead of in the Temple serving. As I have explained in Matthew and Mark, there was an illegal priesthood serving in the temple. The office was sold in those days when the Romans ruled; therefore, John would not serve under that priesthood. He chose to go out to the banks of the Jordan and preach and baptize. The people came to him there.

> Luke 3:1–6: 1. Now in the fifteenth year of the reign of Tiberius Caesar, Pontius Pilate being governor of Judaea, and Herod being tetrarch of Galilee, and his brother Philip tetrarch of Ituraea and of the region of Trachonitis, and Lysanias the tetrarch of Abilene, 2. Annas and Caiaphas being the high priests, the Word of God came unto John the son of Zacharias in the wilderness. 3. And he came into all the country about Jordan, preaching the baptism of repentance for the remission of sins; 4. As it is written in the book of the words of Isaiah the prophet, saying, The voice of one crying in the wilderness, Prepare you the way of the Lord, make his paths straight. 5. Every valley shall be filled, and every mountain and hill shall be brought low; and the crooked shall be made straight, and the rough ways shall be made smooth; 6. And all flesh shall see the salvation of God. Matthew 27:2, Acts 4:6, Luke 1:13, Mark 1:4, Luke 1:77, Isaiah 40:3–5, Isaiah 52:10.

Thus Luke goes a little further than Matthew and Mark did. He quotes Isaiah, saying "all flesh shall see the salvation of God," showing that salvation is for all people.

> Verse 7: Then he said to the multitudes that came out to be baptized by him, "Brood of vipers! Who warned you to flee from the wrath to come?"

111.   Luke 3:8

> Bring forth therefore fruits worthy of repentance, and begin not to say within yourselves, We have Abraham to our father: for I say unto you, That God is able of these stones to raise up children unto Abraham.

My husband and I have run into this very thing. We went to a synagogue once in a while where we lived in California. The people were very nice and friendly. However, just as we read above, one lady we talked to didn't feel she needed to read the Bible or study. She felt that just because she was a Jew she didn't need to come to repentance or do anything at all except go to the synagogue. We tried to talk to her about the Festivals of the Lord and she didn't even know that much about them, only that they celebrated them at the synagogue, yet she was raised in an Orthodox home.

It is the same with some Christians. They get saved and warm a pew for 60 years or so and think that that is "good enough." Of course, we do not and cannot "earn" our salvation, but as in the chapter on Mark, James says:

> James 2:18: If you fulfill the royal law according to the Scripture, You shall love your neighbor as yourself, you do well:

John was a "hell fire and brimstone" preacher. He was trying to wake the people up to come to repentance. He told them that just because they were the descendants of Abraham, they still had to do "works" to show their faith.

112.   Luke 3:10–14

10. And the people asked him, saying, What shall we do then?
11. He answered and said unto them, he that has two coats, let him impart to him that has none; and he that has meat, let him do likewise. 12. Then also came publicans to be baptized, and said unto him, Master, what shall we do? 13. And he said unto them, Exact no more than that which is appointed you. 14. And the soldiers likewise demanded of him, saying, And what shall we do? And he said unto them, Do violence to no man, neither accuse any falsely; and be content with your wages.

References for the above verses:

10: Acts 2:37-38, 16:30-31.
11. 2 Corinthians 8:14, Isaiah 58:7.
12. Luke 7:29.
13. Luke 19:8.
14. Exodus 20:16, 23:1.

So here we have John on the banks of the Jordan in the month of Elul preaching a baptism of repentance before Rosh HaShanah and Yom Kippur for the remission of sins (John 3:3). This was in preparation for the Holy Days. He went into all the region around the River Jordan.

We need to prepare our hearts and lives to face our redeemer. We need to live daily in an attitude of preparation. Not that we need to flog ourselves or mourn over our sins, but repent daily, search our hearts, and make sure our lives are free from sin.

David said,

Psalms 139:23-24: 23. Search me, O God, and know my heart: try me, and know my thoughts: 24. And see if there is any wicked way in me, and lead me in the way everlasting.

The word here for "*search*" is *chaqar* in Hebrew, Strong's Concordance #H2713. "To search, search for, search out, examine thoroughly, investigate."

In other words, if you say you truly want to live for the Lord and let your light shine, you must repent daily and search your heart.

When we got saved, we asked the Lord to forgive us for our sins, to come into our lives and help us live for him. It doesn't end there. Repentance is a daily activity we should be doing in order to draw near to the Lord.

The word for "*thoughts*" there is *saraph, saraphim* for plural thoughts, Strong's Concordance #H8312. It means "disquieting thoughts or thoughts."

We all have trouble with our thought life sometimes, but we need to get in the habit of recognizing when we're sliding back into thoughts that aren't acceptable to the Lord. Stop and repent right there the minute a bad thought starts to creep in. We need to begin to pray or quote Scripture or sing a praise song. Soon you'll get into the habit of recognizing a thought that is not pleasing to the Lord and be able to develop a mind that is pleasing to the Lord.

Remember, if the thought is a thought of condemnation, it is not from you or from God. It is an accusation from Satan. The accuser of the brethren.

Romans 8:1: There is therefore now no condemnation to them which are in Christ Jesus, who walk not after the flesh, but after the Spirit.

If the thought is specific to one thing in your life, then it could be from the Holy Spirit, warning you to repent.

Psalms 139:24: And see if there is any wicked way in me, and lead me in the way everlasting.

The word here for wicked is *otzev*, Strong's Concordance #G6090. Another word for wicked or evil is *ra* in Hebrew. This word, otzev, means pain, sorrow, or idol.

In the Gesenius' Hebrew-Chaldee Lexicon in Blue Letter Bible it says for *wicked*, which is *otseb*, Strong's Concordance #H6090, "The image of an idol, as in Isaiah 48:5, Psalms 139:24, worship of idols." Also, "sorrow, as in 1 Chronicles 4:9 and Isaiah 14:3."

Short Hebrew lesson here. The reason the two words look different for "wicked" is because in Hebrew the letter bet can be a B or a V. The bet has a marker in it that looks like a dot called a dagesh. If the dagesh is in the bet, it is pronounced B. If the dagesh is not, it is pronounced V. Also, some choose to use a TZ to sound out the tsade, a Hebrew letter that does sound like our Z, but some choose TS,, as above. So otzev and otseb are the same word.

Do you think you have any idols in your life? I'm amazed that a lot of Christians know the movie actors and actresses, popular singers of the day, and TV stars much better than they do the Word of God. There's even a TV show called "American Idol." Worship of people just because they can sing great or are great actors benefits nothing in our life. What can these people do for you? Nothing. The Creator of the Universe wants to get to know you personally. Shouldn't we try to draw closer to him and make him the only idol in our life?

Your idol could be anything that you put above Yahweh. Our homes, cars, or any material thing. Our job could be an idol. Our spouse or children could be our idols. Search your heart and ask God to help you make him the one you worship above anything on this earth. Put him first.

I want to say a word here about worry. Worry is sin. It indicates distrust in God. You can overcome worry the same way you do the sinful thoughts you may have, as above. Satan is the one that torments you with worry. Overcome this by the same spiritual exercises as above and read all the Scriptures pertaining to worry as you pray.

113. Luke 4:4

And Jesus answered him, saying, It is written that man shall not live by bread alone, but by every Word of God.

114. Luke 4:8

And Jesus answered and said unto him, Get you behind me, Satan: for it is written, You shall worship the Lord your God, and him only shall you serve.

115. Luke 4:12

And Jesus answering said unto him, It is said, You shall not tempt the Lord your God.

Yeshua/Jesus is quoting Deuteronomy 8:3 in Luke 4:4. In verse 4:8 he is quoting Deuteronomy 6:13. In verse 4:12 he is quoting Deuteronomy 6:16.

Chapter four tells about the temptation of the Messiah when he was led into the wilderness by the Holy Spirit. He fasted and prayed for 40 days and then Satan came along and taunted him and tempted him. If Yeshua/Jesus battled Satan with Scripture, we should take his example and do the same. Satan knows the Word of God better than we do, but he also knows how powerful it is.

Notice the three temptations are the ones we deal with every day. The lust of the flesh, the lust of the eyes, and the pride of life. Every sin fits into one of these categories.

Luke 22:40: And when he was at the place, he said unto them, Pray that you enter not into temptation.

Chapter 22 of Luke tells about the night the soldiers came to arrest Yeshua/Jesus. He and the disciples had gone to the Mount of Olives to pray. He knew what was coming upon him, but his thoughts were for his beloved disciples. He wanted to strengthen them and make them understand what was coming upon them too.

As mothers when one of our loved ones is leaving home, don't we do the same thing? "Don't forget your coat! Make sure to eat! Don't drive too fast!" But here our Savior is telling his disciples the most important thing: "Pray that you may not enter into temptation." As Barney Fife would say, "Nip it in the bud!" Think about it! Recognize when these are coming upon you. Shouldn't we pray this every day: "Lord, please don't let me enter into temptation today."

We are going to be tempted every day, it is part of our journey, but remember to pray every day that we don't give in to anything that would keep us from our fellowship with the Lord.

116.   Luke 5:10

> And so was also James and John, the sons of Zebedee, which were partners with Simon. And Jesus said unto Simon, Fear not; from henceforth you shall catch men.

Oh, I love this verse. This was at the beginning of his ministry when he began to call his disciples to follow him. Luke chapter five tells the story of Yeshua/Jesus telling Simon Peter to "launch out into the deep and let down your nets for a catch." They had fished all night and had caught nothing. They obeyed him and caught a multitude of fish. His commandment to us here is "Fear not."

The Word says Yeshua/Jesus got into Simon Peter's ship, Luke 5:3, and the other future disciples were in another ship, Luke 5:7. They were all fishing partners. "James and John, the sons of Zebedee, which were partners with Simon."

Yeshua/Jesus tells us not to be afraid. These disciples were worried about making their living. We all do that when we aren't bringing in any money or our business is down. He says, "From now on, you will catch men." The thing that is the most important in our lives is winning souls and being witnesses for him. Then he will supply, just as with Peter and the fish he caught with the coin in its mouth, and just as here, when they listened to him, they caught so many their nets were breaking.

The sea represents to us the world and the fish the people. Yeshua/Jesus was giving an object lesson here also. We have to use the right "bait" for people. The gospel needs to be told in a manner that fits the person, their customs, and their way of thinking. For centuries, missionaries have gone into foreign lands to preach the gospel, but first they have to learn that country's language, what certain phrases would mean to them, and their customs. The people's "idioms" might not have any meaning to the ones in the Bible. They have to learn what to do and what not to do, what might be offensive and different ways they greet people, etc. We have to meet people at their level before they will listen to us. The greatest thing to remember is that the Holy Spirit does the work. We need to be trained, but it is him who gives the anointing and understanding to the individual.

So why do people say they were "poor, unlearned fishermen?" What an insult! Have you ever known anyone that had a fishing fleet? These guys are not poor! Or unlearned. They certainly knew the Scriptures!

I watched a documentary on a fishing company in Israel once on Day of Discovery. The fishing business is a huge enterprise in Israel! These friends of Yeshua/Jesus were commercial fishermen! Do you think they would leave their father high and dry with no business coming in? That would be against the commandment to honor your father and mother! Their father probably had many more men that worked for him. He may even have had more sons. He was probably also very Torah observant and put God first in his life. When his sons were called to be disciples, I think he probably had an inkling of who this Teacher was.

To add to my theory, look at the story in John chapter 21. In verse three, it says, they entered into *"a ship."* This wasn't a tiny *little boat.*

Strong's Concordance G4143. *Ploion.* Then in verse eight it says the other disciples came in a *"little ship"* So, Peter jumps out of the main ship and swims to shore and the others come along in another ship which is called *"a little ship,"* or *ploiarion*, Strong's Concordance #G4142. This word is used six times in five verses. *Ploion* is used 67 times in 64 verses.

> Mark 4:36: And when they had sent away the multitude, they took him even as he was in the ship, *Ploion.* And there were also with him other little ships, *ploiarion.*

I am reading between the lines, sure, but think about it. Zebedee probably had sent his sons to yeshiva, school. Unlearned? Don't you think they knew the Torah backwards and forwards? I believe that all twelve Yeshua/Jesus called were very learned. I believe they were Torah scholars. He called them because they would put two and two together because they knew the Torah so well. He didn't have to start with teaching them the basics. They were well beyond basics. He only had three and a half years after all!

That's how you and I should be. We should know the Torah so well that when we read the New Covenant our minds go back to the example given in the Torah about the same subject.

By the way, the Sea of Galilee is not a little lake. Like its name, SEA of Galilee, it is an enormous sea. It is 13 miles long and 8.1 miles wide, 141 feet deep in places, of a size to accommodate a commercial fishing company. When we were in Israel we saw what looked like big freighters on it. It is harp-shaped; thus, its name, which in Hebrew is Kinneret, from the harp called the kinnor. It was sometimes in ancient times called the Sea of Tiberius and Sea of Ginosar, or Genneseret, "garden of riches," for the fertile plain of Genosar on its western side. It was Jesus' favorite place in all of Israel and you can see why when you go there.

As above, as I saw on Day of Discovery, the Sea of Galilee today has commercial fishing boats. The fish most notably caught and sold from there is Tilapia, or Saint Peter's Fish. Tons of Tilapia are taken out of the Sea of Galilee annually and from fish farms in the Negev, The Israeli Desert.

The St. Peter's fish is popular on the menu in restaurants around the Sea of Galilee. I ordered it when we were in Israel in the year 2000. It came with a coin in its mouth. I'm told that only the ladies are served with it that way. This tradition is to commemorate Jesus telling Peter to go to the sea, cast his hook, and take up the fish that first comes up. He told him he would find a piece of money and for Peter to take the coin and pay the tax for him and Peter. Matthew 17:24–27.

117.   Luke 5:27

And after these things he went forth, and saw a publican, named Levi, sitting at the receipt of custom: and he said unto him, Follow me.
John 12:26, 21:19, 22.

Here is another "follow me" verse. We went over this in Matthew 4:19.

From the David Stern Jewish New Testament Commentary, page 118: Luke chapter six verses 20–49 are known as *"The Sermon on the Plain,* or *"the level place"* of verse 17. This can be compared with the Sermon on the Mount in Matthew 5:3–7:29. It is believed that Yeshua/Jesus may have preached the same sermon many times with variations in length, emphases, and illustrations, depending on the needs of his audience.

118.   Luke 6:23

Rejoice you in that day, and leap for joy: for, behold, your reward is great in heaven: for in like manner did their fathers unto the prophets.
James 1:2, Acts 7:51.

This verse is pretty much exactly the same verse as Matthew 5:12. In Matthew it says,

"Rejoice, and be exceeding glad: for great is your reward in heaven: for so persecuted they the prophets who were before you.

The commandment here is to "rejoice and be exceeding glad."

119.   Luke 6:27–29

27. But I say unto you which hear, Love your enemies, do good to them which hate you, 28. Bless them that curse you, and pray for them which despitefully use you. 29. And unto him that smites you on the one cheek offer also the other; and him that took away your cloak forbid not to take your coat also
Romans 12:20 quotes Proverbs 25:21. Matthew 5:38–48 also speaks of love for our enemies.

Yeshua/Jesus is speaking of being kind here. Verse 29 speaks of being a peacemaker, looking out for the welfare of those who need help. If someone is so needy that they need to take your coat, give them some more clothing. Don't just give the minimum, but go the maximum. Give them more than they need. Direct them to where they can get more help.

This was at a time when religious persecution was elevating. Yeshua/Jesus knew that only their love would keep them strong.

We certainly have religious persecution in our day. Antisemitism is rampant on college campuses and around the world. Christians are being called the enemy in our own country. Our religious freedoms are being taken away from us daily and rapidly. Freedom of speech and freedom of religion is what our country was founded on.

Islam is rampant around the world, trying to erase every trace of Christianity and Judaism. Their theme is "Kill the Jews!" Their children are taught this from birth and songs are sung in the kindergartens that teach this.

So what does Yeshua/Jesus tell us to do? Pray for those that are persecuting us. That is very hard, but we need to ask the Holy Spirit to help us pray and what to pray.

120.   Luke 6:30-31

30. Give to every man that asks of you; and of him that took away your goods ask them not again. 31. And just as you want men to do to you, you also do to them likewise.

In The Delitzsch Hebrew Gospels, it says for verse 30, "The Hebrew implies, 'do not demand it from him in court.'"

Yeshua/Jesus isn't saying to be foolish and give to people that are trying to defraud you. Be wise as a serpent and harmless as a dove. Give as you are able. A wise thing to do nowadays is to give to a charity for the homeless that screens people to make sure they're not trying to defraud. We have organizations such as the Salvation Army, our local missions, etc. Pray about where the Lord would have you give and support that organization. The main support in the Torah is for the widows and orphans.

Paul gives stipulations for supporting widows:

1 Timothy 5:3–5: 3. Honor widows who are widows indeed. 4. But if any widow has children or nephews, let them learn first to show piety at home, and to requite their parents: for that is good and acceptable before God. 5. Now she that is a widow indeed, and desolate, trusts in God, and continues in supplications and prayers night and day.

Deuteronomy 15:7-8: 7. If there be among you a poor man of one of your brethren within any of your gates in your land which the

Lord your God gives you, you shall not harden your heart, nor shut your hand from your poor brother: 8. But you shall open your hand wide unto him, and shall surely lend him sufficient for his need, in that which he wants.

Again:

1 John 3:17-18: 17. But whoso has this world's good, and sees his brother have need, and shuts up his bowels of compassion from him, how does the love of God dwell in him? 18. My little children, let us not love in word, neither in tongue; but in deed and truth.

121.   Luke 6:32–36

32. For if you love them which love you, what thank have you? For sinners also love those that love them. 33. And if you do good to them which do good to you, what thank have you? For sinners also do even the same. 34. And if you lend [to them] of whom you hope to receive, what thank have you? For sinners also lend to sinners, to receive as much again. 35. But love you your enemies, and do good, and lend, hoping for nothing again; and your reward shall be great, and you shall be the children of the Highest: For he is kind unto the unthankful and to the evil. 36. Be you therefore merciful, as your Father also is merciful. Romans 13:10, Hebrews 13:16, Psalms 37:26, Matthew 5:46.

Here is a valuable lesson to learn. Let go. My husband and I learned years ago that when people ask for a "loan," to consider it as giving to the Lord and not to expect anyone to pay it back. We make sure that this is in cases where the person needs the money for something concerning his livelihood or wellbeing. He may need help to save his house or money for food for his family. If you know his circumstances and you know his situation, when you let go of that money, give it as unto the Lord, not expecting anything in return. Give the guy a boost in life. Take some of the burden off his back. I can testify that it will bring you great joy and peace. If you're not willing to have this attitude, don't give it. Don't get into a situation where the guy owes you money, he's back on his feet, he hasn't spoken to you in months, he hasn't called to tell you when he's repaying you. You've gotten where this situation is robbing you of everything joyful in your life. Resentment creeps in. And so forth. It's not worth it. Just let it go or don't give it at all if you can't give as unto the Lord.

Give, expecting nothing in return.

I might comment here also on tithing. When you tithe, as soon as you drop that envelope into the offering plate, let go. It's up to the pastor and elders on what to do with that money. If you don't like the way the money is being handled, you haven't let go. You think it's still yours. You have a string tied to it that is conditional. God doesn't want your money if you have that attitude. None of it is your money anyway. He only asks for 10 percent. He allows you to keep 90 percent. If you have this problem, pray about it and ask the Lord to help you be a cheerful giver and to let go when you give. Thank him and be grateful for the 90 percent. There are also offerings. Give out of the abundance of your heart. Of course, if you find out that the ones you're giving your tithe to are doing something wrong with the money, go to a different church or confront them about it.

Never give your tithe money to any organization or ministry except your church. That is where it belongs. You can give as many offerings as you like to other places. The word *tithe, ma'aser* in Hebrew, means *tenth*. Aser is the number ten.

122.   Luke 6:37

Judge not, and you shall not be judged: condemn not, and you shall not be condemned: forgive, and you shall be forgiven. Isaiah 65:5, Matthew. 7:1–5, Matthew 18:21–35, Mark 4:24-25, Romans 2:1-2, Romans 14:3, 4, 10–16, I Corinthians 4:3–5, James 4:11, Luke 11:39–52; Galatians 6:1-2.

The word for *judge* in this sentence is *"krino"* in Greek, Strong's Concordance #G2919. It means to separate, put asunder, to pick out, select, choose, to approve, esteem, to prefer, to be of opinion, deem, think.

We talked about this when going over Matthew 7:1–5. This word is the same word used in that Scripture.

In the Talmud in HaShanah 16b, "Rabbi Isaac further said, 'Three things call a man's iniquities to mind, namely, a shaky wall, the scrutinizing of prayer, and calling for [Divine] judgment on one's fellow man.'" For Rabbi Abin said, "He who calls down [Divine] judgment on his neighbor is himself punished first [for his own sins], as it says, And Sarah said unto Abram, 'My wrong be upon you,' and it is written later, And Abraham came to mourn for Sarah and to weep for her."

What should we say when someone says, "Don't judge me?" As our study in Matthew, it could mean they think we're being critical. We aren't called of God to be fruit inspectors; but, are we our brothers' keeper?

We usually answer them with, "I'm not judging." The confusion here is that we come at it with an attitude of condemnation. If you're telling someone such things as, "You shouldn't have gone to see that movie. It is not right for a Christian to go to R-rated movies," that person isn't going to take it nicely. You've hit him in the face with a judgment call.

You can't change people by being the chastiser. They don't need a chastiser, they need someone to love them and pray for them. The Holy Spirit can do more work in a person's life in seconds than we can do in their lifetime. No one accepts criticism well.

We see things all the time in other Christian's lives that we don't approve of, but prayer is the only way to convict them, or us, of sin. Maybe you or I are doing something other Christians think is wrong, and I'm sure we are, but pray about it.

Here's the danger of just letting it go however:

> Ezekiel 3:18–21: 18. When I say unto the wicked, You shall surely die; and you give him not warning, nor speak to warn the wicked from his wicked way, to save his life; the same wicked man shall die in his iniquity; but his blood will I require at your hand. 19. Yet if you warn the wicked, and he turn not from his wickedness, nor from his wicked way, he shall die in his iniquity; but you have delivered your soul. 20. Again, When a righteous man does turn from his righteousness, and commit iniquity, and I lay a stumbling-block before him, he shall die: because you have not given him warning, he shall die in his sin, and his righteousness which he has done shall not be remembered; but his blood will I require at your hand. 21. Nevertheless if you warn the righteous man, that the righteous sin not, and he does not sin, he shall surely live, because he is warned; also you have delivered your soul.

In the case of a friend, the answer is to go about this with an attitude of prayer and loving kindness. If you have not prayed for this person before you approach them, it's going to go badly and you will probably lose a friend. Let the Holy Spirit prepare their heart beforehand. Take some counseling lessons on how to approach people in a Godly manner. Check your heart to make sure there is no hidden sin in your life. Pray about approaching them. Take the Word with you and Scriptures you have looked up and compiled for this sin. If you feel a warning from the Holy Spirit, don't do it. If you feel an attitude of resentment coming from the other person, don't do it. Stop and end the conversation and go home and continue to pray for this one. And yourself. Maybe it's your attitude and the other person can sense it.

The better thing to do is report it to your pastor and the elders. This must all be done in love. If it's done in condemnation, this one is going to be lost. The Scripture that condemns this action must be brought forth in love and discussed. The person has to be prayed with and loved and it must be stressed to them that they aren't alone in this, that all of us have gone through situations like this, that we all at times need counseled through things in our lives.

Many people have been driven away from churches by other Christians' attitudes about them or telling them they shouldn't do this and shouldn't do that. We have to have faith that the Holy Spirit will work on us and others and sometimes just pray. Just? The most important part.

If you see a person who is teaching Sunday School or leading a group in the church going into a bar and later coming out staggering, you must report it to your pastor and elders. If you see any other behavior unbecoming to a Christian and they're not a friend or even an acquaintance in the church, but you know they go to your church, you must report it to the pastor and elders. It's not your place to counsel this person, it's your pastors and the elders. We have to be wise in what to talk to people about and what not to. The Lord has given us pastors and leaders to handle these things. We need to pray for the person or persons concerned and let the authorities deal with them.

Most churches now have excellent counselors, trained in every situation. I had a son-in-law who was in a desperate situation in his life. He was nearly out of his mind with grief. I asked him to go talk to a counselor at our church. This counselor was our pastor's dad. He was one of the most awesome people I've ever known, he and his wife. He and his wife had founded churches all over the world. He was now "retired," but, like most pastors, they never really retire. Our son-in-law in one session with Pastor Paul received a grip on life that never left him from the counseling he received. Pastor Paul's middle name could have been Love. He loved people into the Kingdom and helped them with situations in their lives and how to deal with them. Our son-in-law went back many times to see him and loved Pastor Paul more than a father. Pastor Paul was his life-line to open up Jesus to him.

Are you that life-line to someone today? Are you willing to give up self and become Jesus to someone? We have no answers. We are just a lump of dirt. But when we turn everything over to him and let him minister through us, we become that life-line to others.

Your church's reputation is dependent upon all of us being watchmen. We are not being "holier than you," but making sure our church represents Jesus and how he wants us to live. You may save a soul by reporting them. They may have drifted off into a habit or an action and need to just be brought back with love and prayer. And don't gossip. God hasn't shown you this to ruin this person's reputation. Remember, that is akin to murder.

123. Luke 6:38

Give, and it shall be given unto you, good measure, pressed down, and shaken together, and running over, shall men give into your bosom. For with the same measure that you mete withal it shall be measured to you again.
See Luke 6:30–31 above. Proverbs. 19:17, 28:27, Psalms 26:4, 79:12, James 2:13, Siriach 1:29, 32:15.

In The Delitzsch Hebrew Gospels for verse 38, it says, "Give and it will be given to you; they will return to your lap a beautiful measure pressed, crammed full, and overflowing. For with the measure that you use to measure, it will be measured to you. For the word "they:" i.e., God." (In Hebrew, the third-person plural without a precedent is an indirect way to speak to God or the heavenly court.)"

It is God that gives out the rewards. We should not give to get, but in obedience and as a Godly action. Doesn't God give everything to us that we have? If we want to be like him, we give to others our best. We don't give them a ragged coat, we give them our best coat. We buy them a coat. We make sure they have other things they need. However; if we aren't doing this through the Holy Spirit with God's love, we might as well not give at all. Giving done grudgingly is nothing. Pleasing the Father is foremost.

124.   Luke 6:41-42

41. And why behold you the mote that is in your brother's eye, but perceive not the beam that is in your own eye? 42. Either how can you say to your brother, Brother, let me pull out the mote that is in your eye, when you behold not the beam that is in your own eye? You hypocrite, cast out first the beam out of your own eye, and then shall you see clearly to pull out the mote that is in your brother's eye.
Matthew 7:3–5.

In other words, simply, look in the mirror! Criticism of other people is often a trait we don't see in ourselves. We need to be sure we're not being a hypocrite. Love others and try to see the good in them. Pray for them. Pray for yourself that you don't become a critic and hypocrite.

The Parable of the Sower: Luke 8:5–15:

The commandment:

125.   Luke 8:8

And other fell on good ground, and sprang up, and bear fruit a hundredfold. And when he had said these things, he cried, He that has ears to hear, let him hear. Luke 14:35 – hear. Matthew 13:10–23. Isaiah 6:9. 1 Peter 1:23. Luke 5:1, 11:28. 1 Timothy 6:9–10.

Listen. Hear. Study.

126.   Luke 8:18

Take heed therefore how you hear: for whosoever has, to him shall be given; and whosoever has not, from him shall be taken even that which he seems to have.
Matthew 25:29, Matthew 13:12. Luke 19:26.

Luke 19:26: For I say unto you, That unto every one which has shall be given; and from him that has not, even that he has shall be taken away from him.

Here we have HEAR again! Listen! Shema!

But "has" what? Money? Earthly riches? No. Yeshua/Jesus here is speaking of the parable of the sower still. The riches are the Word of God! It's up to you how much of it you learn, how much you study, whatever is the desire of your heart to draw closer to the Lord. That is what will matter at the end of the day.

In The Delitzsch Gospel in this verse it says, "Therefore, watch out how you hear." In Hebrew "see."

In other words, check out the doctrine. Check out the meaning of words and verses yourself. It is up to you to "see" correctly. Check everything against the Word.

127.   Luke 9:3–5

3. And he said unto them, Take nothing for your journey, neither staves, nor scrip, neither bread, neither money; neither have two coats apiece. 4. And whatsoever house you enter into, there abide, and thence depart. 5. And whosoever will not receive you, when you go out of that city, shake off the very dust from your feet for a testimony against them.

Here we have the instructions for the disciples again, as in Luke 10:4–12, Matthew 10:1-2, 7-8, 14. John 14:12, Mark 6:10, and Acts 13:51.

The instruction given in these verses are the disciples' training maneuvers. This was their internship. We also need training and a mentor when we come to the Lord for direction and guidance. Find a wise Christian person or believer that will be willing to study with you and teach you. Take this example from the Lord and don't go running off into what you think the Lord is calling you to; on the other hand, don't let others squelch what you feel is from the Lord. Pray and ask for Divine Guidance yourself. Ask him to open doors for you or close doors. Calm down and be patient and wise, but don't lose your zeal. Keep that fire burning.

When he moves in our lives, it is so exciting and amazing. It is hard to wait to make sure this is our leading, but do try to be sure you are hearing and seeing his leading and call on your life.

128.　　Luke 9:23–27

23. And he said to them all, If any man will come after me, let him deny himself, and take up his cross daily, and follow me. 24. For whosoever will save his life shall lose it: but whosoever will lose his life for my sake, the same shall save it. 25. For what is a man advantaged, if he gain the whole world, and lose himself, or be cast away? 26. For whosoever shall be ashamed of me and of my words, of him shall the Son of Man be ashamed, when he shall come in his own glory, and in his Father's, and of the holy angels. 27. But I tell you of a truth, there are some standing here, which shall not taste of death, till they see the Kingdom of God. Matthew 4:19, Mark 8:34, Matthew 10:38, 16:13–20, 16:24, Mark 8:27–30, John 6:67–71.

Here Yeshua/Jesus is speaking of discipleship. This is personal to each and every one of us. He asks that we give up our plans for our life and follow him. He reminds us that if we agree to this, it is a daily commitment. We go into this agreement without knowing the future or what this commitment might entail, but agree wholeheartedly. We talked about "follow me" in Matthew and what that entails.

Luke 9:49-50: 49. And John answered and said, Master, we saw one casting out devils in your name; and we forbade him, because he follows not with us. 50. And Jesus said unto him, Forbid him not: for he that is not against us is for us.

Matthew 12:30, Luke 11:23, Numbers 11:26–29 concerning Elded and Medad.

Luke 11:23: He that is not with me is against me: and he that gathers not with me scatters.

There are only two choices given here: Either you believe in him and follow him completely or you don't.

For verse 27, I believe he is talking about his resurrection. The witnesses "saw" the Kingdom of God in the resurrected Messiah and understood at that time what it was all about.

Here is a story about two men named Elded and Medad in the Book of Numbers:

Numbers 11:25–30: 25. And the Lord came down in a cloud, and spoke unto him, and took of the spirit that was upon him, and gave it unto the seventy elders: and it came to pass, that, when the spirit rested upon them, they prophesied, and did not cease. 26. But there remained two of the men in the camp, the name of the one was Eldad, and the name of the other Medad: and the spirit rested upon them; and they were of them that were written, but went not out unto the tabernacle: and they prophesied in the camp. 27. And there ran a young man, and told Moses, and said, Eldad and Medad do prophesy in the camp. 28. And Joshua the son of Nun, the servant of Moses, one of his young men, answered and said, My Lord Moses, forbid them. 29. And Moses said unto him, Envy you for my sake? Would God that all the Lord's people were prophets, and that the Lord would put his spirit upon them! 30. And Moses went into the camp, he and the elders of Israel.

Again, verse 29: "Would God that all the Lord's people were prophets, and that the Lord would put his spirit upon them!"

Don't we?

Oh, that we don't find ourselves envious of others that have a gift from the Lord that we don't have but seek to minister in the gifts he has given us personally.

These two men are a mystery, only mentioned in verses 26 and 27, but obviously they loved God and he loved them. These verses remind me of the verses in John 21:

> John 21:20–23: 20. Then Peter, turning about, saw the disciple whom Jesus loved following; which also leaned on his breast at supper, and said, Lord, which is he that betrays you? 21. Peter seeing him said to Jesus, Lord, and what shall this man do? 22. Jesus said unto him, If I will that he tarry till I come, what is that to you? Follow you me. 23. Then went this saying abroad among the brethren, that that disciple should not die: yet Jesus said not unto him, he shall not die; but, If I will that he tarry till I come, what is that to you?

In other words, "Mind your own business." We all have our own ministry and our own calling on our heart. We need to respect that in others and support one another. We need to keep our opinions to ourselves if they're not uplifting to people and their ministry. If they're not doing it like we would do it, pray for them, but let them run their ministry, them and God.

129. Luke 9:59–60

> 59. And he said unto another, Follow me. But he said, Lord, suffer me first to go and bury my father. 60. Jesus said unto him, Let the dead bury their dead: but go you and preach the Kingdom of God.

See the commentary on Matthew 8:21-22 in the Matthew chapter.

Was Yeshua saying our family is not important?

David Stern's Commentary says on page 35, Matthew. 8:21-22: Don't suppose this would-be talmid (disciple) is traveling around with Yeshua while his father's corpse is waiting at home, stinking in the sun. The father is not dead yet! If he had been, the son would have been at home, sitting shev'ah (the seven-day mourning period). The son wishes to go home, live in comfort with his father till his death perhaps years hence, collect his inheritance and then, at his leisure, become a disciple. See Luke 9:57–62.

130.   Luke 10:2

Therefore said he unto them, The harvest truly is great, but the laborers are few: pray you therefore the Lord of the harvest, that he would send forth laborers into his harvest.
Mark 6:7, John 4:35, 2 Thessalonians 3:1.

What is the commandment here? Pray. What is "the harvest?"

In this chapter, in verse 1, Yeshua/Jesus is sending out 70 disciples. In Chapter 9:3 He sends out the 12. Only in Luke's gospel does it mention 70 disciples. He sends them out two by two to (2) "every city and place where he himself was about to go."

These verses remind me of the Billy Graham Crusades. My husband and I went to a class to train us to be altar workers for one of Billy's crusades, to train us in the way he wanted things done. Yeshua/Jesus is sending them out to "prepare the way" for him. He's training them, just as we need to be trained.

The "harvest" is the reaping of those who will believe on Yeshua/Jesus, that he IS the Messiah for whom they were looking.

Are we preparing "the harvest" in our time? He says in verse 2 that the laborers are few. That is certainly true in our day. There are many, many churches throughout the world of every denomination and a lot that are "non–denominational," but is the True Gospel being preached? If your church isn't preaching the True Gospel, then leave, or pray for the pastor and try to talk to him. If the blood of Yeshua/Jesus isn't preached, leave that church. If your church doesn't give altar calls or an invitation to accept Yeshua/Jesus as Savior, leave that church.

What is the True Gospel? What does being "saved" entail?

> 1 Corinthians 15:3–4: 3. For I delivered unto you first of all that which I also received, how that Christ died for our sins according to the Scriptures; 4. And that he was buried, and that he rose again the third day according to the Scriptures:

But is it enough to believe?

> James 2:18-19: 18. Yes, a man may say, You have faith, and I have works: show me your faith without your works, and I will show you my faith by my works. 19. You believe that there is one God; you do well: the devils also believe, and tremble.

Do our works save us? Of course not. If they did, Yeshua/Jesus wouldn't have had to come to earth, spend time on earth, die on a cross, rise again, and return to heaven to save us. But our "works" are proof that we believe and are his.

> Throughout the Torah/Old Testament, the word for "*works*" is Strong's Concordance #H4639, *ma'*aseh, and is used in Exodus 5:4 where Pharaoh is asking Moses and Aaron if they really think he's going to let the Jewish people go worship the True God. Their "works" were, of course, building with bricks for the king. The word means *a deed, a work, a thing done, labor.* Therefore, it is a verb. Verbs are action words. In 1 Chronicles 9:12, this word is also used as a proper name: Maasiah, which means "work of the Lord." This word, *ma'aseh*, occurs 235 times in 221 verses in Genesis through Deuteronomy and is used as "work, deed, needlework (with #H7551), acts, labor, doing, and art.

All of these are actions. So what is James saying? "Show me your faith without your works, and I will show you my faith by my works."

There are 36 different words for "work" in the Torah/Old Testament, but they are all action words. There are 18 different words in the New Covenant for work or works. They are all action words.

Let's look at the verses in Chapter two of James:

James 2:14–26: 14. What does it profit, my brethren, though a man say he has faith, and have not works? Can faith save him? 15. If a brother or sister be naked, and destitute of daily food, 16. And one of you say unto them, Depart in peace, be you warmed and filled; notwithstanding you give them not those things which are needful to the body; what does it profit? 17. Even so faith, if it has not works, is dead, being alone. 18. Yes, a man may say, You have faith, and I have works: show me your faith without your works, and I will show you my faith by my works. 19. You believe that there is one God; you do well: the devils also believe, and tremble. 20. But will you know, O vain man, that faith without works is dead? 21. Was not Abraham our father justified by works, when he had offered Isaac his son upon the altar? 22. Seeing how faith wrought with his works, and by works was faith made perfect? 23. And the Scripture was fulfilled which says, Abraham believed God, and it was imputed unto him for righteousness: and he was called the Friend of God. 24. You see then how that by works a man is justified, and not by faith only. 25. Likewise also was not Rahab the harlot justified by works, when she had received the messengers, and had sent them out another way? 26. For as the body without the spirit is dead, so faith without works is dead also.

We went over this extensively in Matthew 11:28–30 and went over what the "yoke" is. It is good to reiterate this. We must understand that being saved is the important thing, the key to the door let's say, but living for him is where we learn and grow.

Yeshua/Jesus expects US to be the laborers, to go one by one to friends and neighbors and prepare them for the harvest. The last harvest will be when he returns and sets his feet on the Mt. of Olives and many believe in him at that point. At that time, the Millennial Reign of 1000 years begins.

Be sure you're ready for That Day.

Then Yeshua/Jesus gives the 70 disciples instructions on how to go out and minister.

> Luke 10:3–12: 3. Go your ways: behold, I send you forth as lambs among wolves. 4. Carry neither purse, nor scrip, nor shoes: and salute no man by the way. 5. And into whatsoever house you enter, first say, Peace be to this house. 6. And if the son of peace be there, your peace shall rest upon it: if not, it shall turn to you again. 7. And in the same house remain, eating and drinking such things as they give: for the laborer is worthy of his hire. Go not from house to house. 8. And into whatsoever city you enter, and they receive you, eat such things as are set before you: 9. And heal the sick that are therein, and say unto them, The Kingdom of God is come nigh unto you. 10. But into whatsoever city you enter, and they receive you not, go your ways out into the streets of the same, and say, 11. Even the very dust of your city, which cleaves on us, we do wipe off against you: notwithstanding be you sure of this, that the Kingdom of God is come nigh unto you. 12. But I say unto you, that it shall be more tolerable in that day for Sodom, than for that city.
>
> Verse 3: Isaiah 40:11.
> Verse 4: II Kings 4:29.
> Verse 6: I John 4:1. Test the spirits.
> Verse 7: This doesn't mean not to eat kosher as they were going to Jewish people only at this time. He's saying, as we do to our children when invited to someone's home, "Eat what they serve us. Be polite."

Also see Matthew 9:37, Matthew 10:7–16, Luke 9:3–5, 2 Kings 4:29 (see above) 1 Corinthians 10:27, 1 Timothy. 5:18.

There is a lot of wisdom in these verses for all of us, especially those in a ministry like evangelism.

Why not go from house to house? They needed to have a headquarters where there would be peace and quiet. It is hard work to minister to people. We're going from our ordinary realm to the heavenly when ministering. Our mortal bodies are being used of the Holy Spirit to minister to others and "coming down" from that height takes a lot out of a person. I know after I speak somewhere, I am just zapped. I need to be somewhere alone where it is quiet. If I'm with one family afterwards, it is easier to relax and not be expected to keep ministering. If they had gone from house to house, each family would want to talk and talk about their ministry, their lives, etc. They need to use their energies wisely.

We don't have so much of that nowadays. If we do, the church usually puts them up in a hotel and feeds them, which is nice. In the Torah/ Old Testament, people had rooms for the prophets. That is what was happening in the story in 1 Kings 16-17 where Elijah was sent to the woman of Zarephas. It tells us in Chapter 17 verse 19 that he stayed in a loft.

There are entire ministries that have prophet rooms for ministers that come through or are ministering in their church.

131.   Luke 10:20

Notwithstanding in this rejoice not, that the spirits are subject unto you; but rather rejoice, because your names are written in heaven.

This verse is in answer to the seventies' joy in returning saying, "Lord, even the demons are subject to us in your name, verse 10:17.

Then he goes on to tell them, "I saw Satan fall like lightning from heaven." Then in verse 18, our verse, "Do NOT rejoice because of the fact even demons are subject to you, but do rejoice because your names are written in heaven."

What an eye opener for us. Can you even start to imagine that YOUR name is written in heaven?

David Stern's commentary, page 122, concerning names written: Judaism features prominently the idea that the names of the forgiven are recorded in heaven. The liturgy for Rosh HaShanah (the New Year) includes a prayer for being written in the Book of Life and the Yom Kippur (Day of Atonement) liturgy nine days later has a prayer for being "sealed" in the Book of Life, the idea being that the decision is made final on that day.

He also notes John 7:37 and Revelation 20:12b.

Yeshua/Jesus speaking about "Satan falling from heaven" goes back to Isaiah 14:12, proving Yeshua/Jesus is God and was there when Satan and his angels got thrown out of heaven. He has defeated Satan, sin, and death, and conquered the grave.

Revelation 1:4: NKJV: John, to the seven churches which are in Asia: Grace to you and peace from him who is and who was and who is to come, and from the seven Spirits who are before His throne.

Rev. 1:8: NKJV: "I am the Alpha and the Omega, the Beginning and the End," says the Lord, "who is and who was and who is to come, the Almighty."

Rev. 4:8: NKJV: The four living creatures, each having six wings, were full of eyes around and within. And they do not rest day or night, saying: "Holy, holy, holy, Lord God Almighty, Who was and is and is to come!"

Rev. 11:17: NKJV: "We give You thanks, O Lord God Almighty, The One who is and who was and who is to come, Because You have taken Your great power and reigned."

Almighty, *Shaddai*, Strong's Concordance #7706: Almighty, most powerful, Shaddai, the Almighty (of God).

Also, see Ezekiel chapter 28 about the King of Tyre, but a metaphor for Satan. The Bible doesn't tell us his name. Satan, Lucifer, Abbadon, and so on, are descriptions of him or titles. If you do a word search on all of his titles, you will learn a lot about who he is and what his goal is.

132.   Luke 10:25–28

25. And, behold, a certain lawyer stood up, and tempted him, saying, Master, what shall I do to inherit eternal life? 26. He said unto him, "What is written in the law? How read you?" 27. And he answering said, "You shall love the Lord your God with all your heart, and with all your soul, and with all your strength, and with all your mind; and your neighbor as yourself." 28. And he said unto him, "You have answered right: this do, and you shall live."
Deuteronomy 6:5, Deuteronomy 10:12, Deuteronomy 30:6, Leviticus 19:18, Matthew 19:17–19, Matthew 22:37–40, Mark 12:31.

Then the lawyer wants to know who IS his neighbor. Yeshua/Jesus goes into the story of the Good Samaritan, Luke 10:30–37.

133.   Luke 10:37

And he said, he that showed mercy on him. Then said Jesus unto him, "Go, and do you likewise."

Our commandment here is, "Go and do likewise." We as believers in Yeshua/Jesus should be the "first responders" when we see those in need.

Proverbs 14:21: He that despises his neighbor sins: but he that has mercy on the poor, happy is he.

Again:

1 John 3:17: But whoso has this world's good, and sees his brother have need, and shuts up his bowels of compassion from him, how does love of God dwell in him?

How to Pray

134.   Luke 11:2–4

2. And he said unto them, When you pray, say, Our Father who art in heaven, Hallowed be your name. Your Kingdom come. Your will be done, as in heaven, so in earth. 3. Give us day by day our daily bread. 4. And forgive us our sins; for we also forgive every one that is indebted to us. And lead us not into temptation; but deliver us from evil.

This prayer given by the Lord is our pattern on how to pray to the Father. Also, see Matthew 6:9–13.

Verse 11:4: Ephesians 4:32: And be you kind one to another, tenderhearted, forgiving one another, even as God for Christ's sake has forgiven you.

Not a commandment, but look at Luke 11:8: "Because of his persistence." The word in Hebrew is "chutzpah."

David Stern's Commentary, page 123, says: A colorful Hebrew and Yiddish word that means "boldness, audacity, effrontery, insolence, gall, brazen nerve, presumption, arrogance, persistence and just plain 'guts.'" In varying combinations, proportions, and intensities. To me it seems the ideal rendering of Greek *anaideia*, which Arndt and Gingrich's A Greek–English

Lexicon of the New Testament translates as "impudence, shamefulness."

From the Thayer's Greek Lexicon, *Blueletterbible.org*, the word here is *"importunity."* Strong's Concordance #G335. Feminine noun: Shamelessness, impudence, as above.
1. Self-confidence: boldness coupled with supreme self-confidence;
2. rudeness: impudent rudeness or lack of respect
Late 19th century. Via Yiddish < Aramaic *ḥuṣpā*
Thesaurus: NOUN

Synonyms: gall, cheek, boldness, nerve, impudence, fearlessness, effrontery, audacity, brass neck.

135.   Luke 11:9–13

9. And I say unto you, Ask, and it shall be given you; seek, and you shall find; knock, and it shall be opened unto you. 10. For everyone who asks receives, and he who seeks finds, and to him who knocks it will be opened. 11. If a son asks for bread from any father among you, will he give him a stone? Or if [he asks] for a fish, will he give him a serpent instead of a fish? 12. Or if he asks for an egg, will he offer him a scorpion? 13. If you then, being evil, know how to give good gifts to your children, how much more will [your] heavenly Father give the Holy Spirit to those who ask him!" John 15:7, Isaiah 55:6b, Matthew 7:9, James 1:17.

Is Yeshua/Jesus talking about earthly riches here? A "get rich scheme?" No, he certainly was not a "prosperity preacher."

See my commentary to Matthew 7:7–12.

136.   Luke 11:33–36

Luke 11:33–36: 33. No man, when he has lit a candle, puts it in a secret place, neither under a bushel, but on a candlestick, that they which come in may see the light. 34. The light of the body is the eye: therefore when your eye is single, your whole body also is full of light; but when your eye is evil, your body also is full of darkness. 35. Take heed therefore that the light which is in you be not darkness. 36. If your whole body therefore be full of light, having no part dark, the whole shall be full of light, as when the bright shining of a candle does give you light. Mark 4:21, Matt 5:15, Matt 6:22–23.

What are we commanded to do here? To be sure we have right doctrine and are following the Scriptures correctly, as in verses 35 and 36.

From David Stern's Commentary on the NT, Page 32 on Matt 6:22–23: "The eye is the lamp of the body." Apparently, Yeshua quotes a common proverb and comments on it. If you have a "good eye." This is in the Greek text, but the explanation, that is, if you are generous, is added by me the translator because in Judaism "having a good eye" an 'ayin tovah, means "being generous," and "having a bad eye," an 'ayin ra'ah, means "being stingy." That this is the correct interpretation is confirmed by the context; greed and anxiety about money being the topic in both the preceding and following verses. This passage is another link in the chain of evidence that NT events took place in Hebrew; I made this point when analyzing v. 23 in Section I of the JNT Introduction. (Jewish New Testament.)

In verse 11, what is "the lamp?" This is God's Word!

Psalms 119:105: Your word is a lamp unto my feet, and a light unto my path.

Let God's Word lead us and be the Light on our path.

137.   Luke 11:41

But rather give alms of such things as you have; and, behold, all things are clean unto you.
Luke 12:33, 16:9.

From David Stern's Commentary on the NT, Page 123-124. A difficult text in the original Greek. One possibility: Give to the poor what is inside your cups and dishes, here understood no longer as robbery and wickedness (v. 39), but food, good things in general. Another: Give truly, from your heart, i.e., from what is inside. A third: Luke, working from an Aramaic source misread "zakki" (give alms) for "dakki" (clean, as in the parallel passage, Matthew 23:23).

138.   Luke 12:1

In the meantime, when there were gathered together an innumerable multitude of people, insomuch that they trod one upon another, he began to say unto his disciples first of all, Beware of the leaven of the Pharisees, which is hypocrisy.
Mark 8:15, Matt 16:12.

Leaven, usually a symbol of sin or evil, as is clear at Matthew 16:12. See 1 Corinthians 5:6–8. Matzah represents purity and truth. Chametz means "sour."

The Talmud says, "Leaven represents the evil impulse of the heart."

In Matthew 16:12 it says to beware of the "doctrine" of the Pharisees. Leaven, of course, represents sin in our lives, as spoken of in Matthew 16:6–12. The "sin" of the Pharisees was in telling the people to do things that they did not do themselves.

139.   Luke 12:4-5

4. And I say unto you my friends, Be not afraid of them that kill
the body, and after that have no more that they can do. 5. But I will
forewarn you whom you shall fear: Fear him, which after he has
killed has power to cast into hell; yes, I say unto you, Fear him.
Isaiah 51:7-8, 12-13, John 15:13–15. (5) Psalms 119:120.

Who has the power to cast into hell? God, of course. Fear him!

Yeshua/Jesus knew that in the future terrible times would come upon
the Jewish people. In 70 AD, the Temple was destroyed, the Romans
came in and invaded Israel and many of the Jewish people fled. He said,
"Don't fear them!" Fear Me! We should have no fear of death as he has
conquered the grave!

140.   Luke 12:7

But even the very hairs of your head are all numbered. Fear not
therefore: you are of more value than many sparrows.
Matthew 10:30–31

Never think that he doesn't care about you. He knows everything about
you and I and still loves us. Would he have come and died on the cross
for us if he didn't care? Here again we hear him say, "Do not fear."
Fear is a zapper of our faith. When fear comes in, get into the Word,
quote Scripture as he did to Satan, and listen to an uplifting sermon or
uplifting praise music.

141.   Luke 12:11–12

11. And when they bring you unto the synagogues, and unto
magistrates, and powers, take you no thought how or what thing
you shall answer, or what you shall say: 12. For the Holy Spirit
shall teach you in the same hour what you ought to say.
Mark 13:11, John 14:26.

Yeshua/Jesus knew what was coming upon the world to those listening to him at that time. Not only that, he speaks to all of us who have lived since that time. He will teach us what to say when persecuted or brought before judges for being believers. We only have to believe and have no fear. This life is but a moment in eternity. What counts here is our stand for him.

142.   Luke 12:15

And he said unto them, Take heed, and beware of covetousness: for a man's life consists not in the abundance of the things which he possesses.
I Tim 6:6–10.

David Stern says of verses 13 through 34: "No passage could be more to the point for modern man than these verses about the nature, origin, and cure of greed."

Amen. And:

143.   Luke 12:22-23

22. And he said unto his disciples, Therefore I say unto you, Take no thought for your life, what you shall eat; neither for the body, what you shall put on. 23. Life is more than food, and the body [is more] than clothing.

"Take no thought for your life." That is really hard, isn't it? He's saying, "Concentrate on what's important in life."

144.   Luke 12:24

Consider the ravens: for they neither sow nor reap; which neither have storehouse nor barn; and God feeds them: how much more are you better than the fowls?
Matthew 6:25–33, Job 38:41.

He says in verse 24, "Consider the ravens." They're just out there flying around finding food, water, and shelter with no problems.

145.   Luke 12:27-28

27. Consider the lilies how they grow: they toil not, they spin not; and yet I say unto you, that Solomon in all his glory was not arrayed like one of these. 28. If then God so clothe the grass, which is today in the field, and tomorrow is cast into the oven; how much more will he clothe you, O you of little faith?
I Kings 10:4–7, 2 Chronicles 9:6, Matthew 6:30, 8:26, 14:31, 16:8.

The lilies are out there growing, getting sunlight, rain, and nourishment. They don't ask for it, they just expect it. No problem.

In 2 Chronicles 9:6–8, when the Queen of Sheba came to visit King Solomon and she saw his glorious Kingdom and the magnificence of it all, she said,

"6. Howbeit I believed not their words, until I came, and mine eyes had seen it: and, behold, the one half of the greatness of your wisdom was not told me: for you exceed the fame that I heard. 7. Happy are your men, and happy are these your servants, which stand continually before you, and hear your wisdom. 8. Blessed be the Lord your God, which delighted in you to set you on his throne, to be king for the Lord your God: because your God loved Israel, to establish them forever, therefore made he you king over them, to do judgment and justice.

Friends, as I sit here writing this, I am fat and healthy, warm, have lots of food, a beautiful home, clothes to wear, my limousine to drive (which is my 1994 Plymouth Voyager), a wonderful husband, beautiful, healthy children, grandchildren, great-grandchildren, friends, about 20 different Bibles, the internet to use to study and stay in contact with friends and family, a wonderful church, and I'm thinking, "The half has not been told of what God has done for my husband and I through these many years." As I think back on all the times the Lord has rescued us, saved us, guided us, healed us, provided for us, and blessed us, it would surely fill another book. He has always been there for us and has never failed us.

Stop and look around you right now. Mentally list all your blessings. Look through other people's eyes at how they must look at you. We are so blessed.

Solomon, in spite of breaking every rule in the Book, was blessed beyond any human being ever in this world materially. Yet, he failed God. Don't let the cares of this world keep you from the most important thing in our lives, serving God. Put him first. He will take care of the rest.

> Luke 8:14-15: 14. And that which fell among thorns are they, which, when they have heard, go forth, and are choked with cares and riches and pleasures of this life, and bring no fruit to perfection. 15. But that on the good ground are they, which in an honest and good heart, having heard the Word, keep it, and bring forth fruit with patience.

God help us not to hear the Word and let it fall on stony ground or among thorns. Let us put your Word first in our lives and not worry about the cares of this world. Don't let us be like Solomon and ignore your commandments. Help us to be like you and live as you did.

146.   Luke 12:29

And seek not you what you shall eat, or what you shall drink, neither be you of doubtful mind.

147.   Luke 12:31

But rather seek you the Kingdom of God; and all these things shall be added unto you.

148.   Luke 12:32

Fear not, little flock; for it is your Father's good pleasure to give you the Kingdom.

149.   Luke 12:33–34

33. Sell that you have, and give alms; provide yourselves bags which wax not old, a treasure in the heavens that fails not, where no thief approaches, neither moth corrupts. 34. For where your treasure is, there will your heart be also.
Matthew 6:20, 6:31–33, 11: 25–36, 19:21, Luke 11:41, Isaiah 40:11, Zechariah 13:7.

Here in verse 33 we have a commandment concerning generosity. "Sell what you have and give alms." In other words, as the Christians in the Book of Acts, they sold all and pooled it, none having more than the other. Ideal, but in this day and age, impossible, except in Israel where they have kibbutzim (kibbutzes) and a lot of people live this way. They are amazing.

In this day and age, we can sell what we are not using and do not need and give to the poor and widows. "Money bags which do not grow old." Investments in the future. You can't take it with you, so invest in people, in giving to organizations or ministries that will carry on after you're gone. Many Christian colleges and schools have annuities, etc. Leave a heritage for learning about the Word. See Philippians 4:19.

Where is your heart today?

150.   Luke 12:35-36

35. Let your loins be girded about, and your lights burning; 36. And you are like men that wait for their Lord, when he will return from the wedding; that when he comes and knocks, they may open unto him immediately.

Verse 12:36: We are to be ready immediately for service. See Romans 1:1. Paul uses the image of a bondservant in describing his relationship to God.

"Girding up your loins" is an idiom for pulling up the back hem of your robe, under your legs, and tucked into your belt in the front so you can run. A lamp was usually only used at night in those days. Both of these are pictures of being ready. We need to be ready at any time for the Lord to come for us or to be ready if he calls us to do something. "Be instant in season and out of season," 2 Timothy 4:2.

> Verses 12:37–39. 37. Blessed [are] those servants whom the master, when he comes, will find watching. Assuredly, I say to you that he will gird himself and have them sit down [to eat], and will come and serve them. 38. And if he should come in the second watch, or come in the third watch, and find [them] so, blessed are those servants. 39. But know this that if the master of the house had known what hour the thief would come, he would have watched and not allowed his house to be broken into.

Girding here is as a servant would do to serve others.

Verse 12:37: Blessed are those who watch attentively for their master's return.

12:38: Blessed are those servants who, no matter how late they think his coming is, they are watching and waiting. The faithful servant is in constant readiness.

151.   Luke 12:40

Be you therefore ready also: for the Son of Man comes at an hour when you think not.
I Peter 1:13, Matthew 25:1–3, Matthew 24:46, Revelation 3:3, 16:15, Mark 13:33.

What are the watches? See Mark 13:35 above.

We have the watches in Lamentations 2:19 and Judges 7:19. These are the middle watch. The morning watch is in Exodus 14:24 and 1 Samuel 11:11.

152.   Luke 12:58-59

58. When you go with your adversary to the magistrate, as you are in the way, give diligence that you may be delivered from him; lest he drag you to the judge, and the judge deliver you to the officer, and the officer cast you into prison. 59. I tell you, you shall not depart from there till you have paid the very last mite. Isaiah 55:6.

Proverbs 25:9-10: 9. Debate your cause with your neighbor himself; and discover not a secret to another: 10. Lest he that hears it put you to shame, and your infamy turn not away.

In other words, keep your personal business to yourself; don't give outsiders a chance to blow it out of proportion. Your business is between you and the other party in the matter.

On the other hand, this can mean to become reconciled to God before the judgment comes.

153.   Luke 13:24

Strive to enter in at the strait gate: for many, I say unto you, will seek to enter in, and shall not be able.
Matthew 7:14, John 7:34, 8:21, 13:33.

The "narrow gate" is salvation through Yeshua HaMashiach only. It is sometimes stated by different ministers or pastors that there are other roads to God. There are not. Either you believe the entire Bible or you don't.

1 Timothy 2:5–6: 5. For there is one God, and one mediator between God and men, the man Christ Jesus; 6. Who gave himself a ransom for all, to be testified in due time.

"And know that a person needs to traverse a very, very narrow bridge, but the fundamental and most important principle is to have no hesitation or fear at all." (Rabbi Nachman of Breslev in Likutey Moharan II, 48).

154.   Luke 14:8–10

8. When you are bidden of any man to a wedding, sit not down in the highest room; lest a more honorable man than you be bidden of him; 9. And he that bade you and him come and say to you, Give this man place; and you begin with shame to take the lowest room. 10. But when you are bidden, go and sit down in the lowest room; that when he bade you come, he may say unto you, Friend, go up higher: then shall you have worship in the presence of them that sit at meat with you.

Yeshua/Jesus teaches manners! This verse can also speak to us of when we get to heaven. We are saved by the blood of Yeshua, but there will be rewards. Some boastful people will think they're first in line, but here comes the little widow, the least of all, to the head of the line, escorted by the angels, because she gave ALL.

Brothers and sisters, try not to be boastful of your accomplishments in life or ministries, but be humble, as Yeshua was, the Servant of all. Realize you're the lowest on the totem pole, but when Yeshua, who invited you, beckons you to come higher, you'll be so happy and surprised! Nothing we do in this life is possible without him. We should give him the glory daily.

1 Corinthians 6:19-20: 19. What? Know you not that your body is the temple of the Holy Spirit which is in you, which you have of God, and you are not your own? 20. For you are bought with

a price: therefore glorify God in your body, and in your spirit, which are God's.

155.   Luke 14:12–14

12. Then said he also to him that bade him, when you make a dinner or a supper, call not your friends, nor your brethren, neither your kinsmen, nor your rich neighbors; lest they also bid you again, and a recompense be made you. 13. But when you make a feast, call the poor, the maimed, the lame, and the blind: 14. And you shall be blessed; for they cannot recompense you: for you shall be recompensed at the resurrection of the just. See Luke 6:30, 38 above, Luke 12:33–34.

Who appreciates being provided for more than anyone? Those that have nothing. Give, not asking anything in return. Bless them with "all you have," see the above, "sell all you have," Luke 12:33-34.

In this day and age, we can't just go drive around and pick up people to invite to our homes because of the danger, but we can give to the missions and homeless shelters. We can provide food and clothing for them.

156.   Luke 14:34-35

34. Salt is good: but if the salt has lost its saltiness, how shall it be seasoned? 35. It is neither fit for the land, nor yet for the dunghill; but men cast it out. He that has ears to hear, let him hear.
Matthew 5:13, Mark 9:49-50, Colossians 4:6, James 3:12.

Salt was used in the temple to salt the sacrifices. The ramp to the altar was salted. Leviticus 2:3.

Don't lose your zeal for the gospel! Don't lose the fire of the Word! Keep that "spice" in your life. How powerful can we be in our testimony if we've become salt-less?

In Chapter 16 of Luke, Jesus tells about a rich man who had a manager. A report was brought to the rich man that the manager was squandering his property. The rich man called the manager before him and asked him to give an accounting of his management. The manager, filled with fear of losing his position, summoned all the rich man's debtors to him and cut a deal with them over their debt, thinking the rich man would be happy about such a deal. Well, surprise, surprise! The rich man was happy!

Then comes our verse:

157.   Luke 16:9

And I say unto you, Make to yourselves friends of the money of unrighteousness; that, when you fail, they may receive you into everlasting habitations.

"Unrighteous money."

For the love of money is the root of all evil: which while some coveted after, they have erred from the faith, and pierced themselves through with many sorrows. 1 Timothy 6:10.

Note: The LOVE of money.

But use "unrighteous money" (the things of this world) for good for the Kingdom.

Read Luke 16:9–13. See also 1 Timothy 6:6–10, 17–19, James 1:9–11, 5:1–6. Some say "friends" are Yeshua and the Father, that though WE fail, even though our money fails, they will receive us into our everlasting home.

Other commentators say there is no real explanation for this verse. Amy-Jill Levine says in The Jewish Annotated New Testament, "The parable defies any fully satisfactory explanation."

158.   Luke 17:3-4

3. Take heed to yourselves: If your brother trespasses against you, rebuke him; and if he repent, forgive him. 4. And if he sins against you seven times in a day, and seven times in a day returns to you, saying, 'I repent,' you shall forgive him."
Matthew 18:15–17. Proverbs 17:10. (The NU–Text omits "against you.")

Luke 17:5 And the apostles said unto the Lord, Increase our faith.

I think it's humorous and human here that the disciples say to the Lord, "Increase our faith." All of us need our faith increased if someone sins against us once in a day, let alone seven times in one day! We usually say, "Lord, give me strength!" Yet the Lord still says to forgive them! This action is not natural to us, but is supernatural if we are led by the Holy Spirit. In our flesh, we cannot do this; only through his Holy Spirit can we do this. Most of us do not want to "rebuke our brother," but, as above, Jesus commands us to, as in Ezekiel 3:20–21: 20.

Again, when a righteous man does turn from his righteousness, and commit iniquity, and I lay a stumbling-block before him, he shall die: because you have not given him warning, he shall die in his sin, and his righteousness which he has done shall not be remembered; but his blood will I require at your hand. 21. Nevertheless if you warn the righteous man, that the righteous sin not, and he does not sin, he shall surely live, because he is warned; also you have delivered your soul.

Could the Bible make it any plainer? There are ways of going about this and the Bible gives us further instruction when it talks about going to a brother that has "ought" against us. We talk to these people privately, not pointing out their sin to the entire congregation, and then if they do not listen, then we take the next steps.

See the commentary on Matthew 18:15.

Luke 17:6–9: 6. And the Lord said, If you had faith as a grain of mustard seed, you might say unto this sycamore tree, Be you plucked up by the root, and be you planted in the sea; and it should obey you. 7. But which of you, having a servant plowing or feeding cattle, will say unto him by and by, when he is come from the field, Go and sit down to meat? 8. And will not rather say unto him, Make ready wherewith I may sup, and gird yourself, and serve me, till I have eaten and drunken; and afterward you shall eat and drink? 9. Does he thank that servant because he did the things that were commanded him? I think not.

Then our commandment verse:

159.   Luke 17:10

So likewise you, when you shall have done all those things which are commanded you, say, We are unprofitable servants: we have done that which was our duty to do.

Here Yeshua compares us to the "unprofitable servants." We have only done our duty! Shouldn't we wake up and realize any "works" that we do for the Lord are only what he has asked us to do and we shouldn't expect a great reward for doing what we're supposed to do? We're only obeying his Commandments.

160.   Luke 17:32

Remember Lot's wife.

What a lesson in obedience! She paid with her life. We should take heed when we think we can change God's Word around to suit us, when we think we will follow his Word, but then add in or take away whatever doesn't suit us. Marcion of Sinope who lived between 85–160 AD was said to have cut out (literally) from the Bible those parts he didn't agree with! It was because of him and this wicked deed that prompted the church to develop the canon we have today. He was excommunicated.

161.   Luke 18:6

Then the Lord said, "Hear what the unjust judge says."

Here we have another "hear" verse. What did the unjust judge say? This verse is from the parable of the "persistent widow." The judge only gave her what was due her because he was tired of her coming back and asking him to help her over and over. He says, verse 5: "Yet because this widow troubles me, I will avenge her, lest by her continual coming she weary me."

So is the Lord pointing out here to us to continually ask, ask, ask. One of my favorite verses to teach my students in Sunday School for 29 years was Luke 11:9:

> "And I say unto you, Ask, and it shall be given you; seek, and you shall find; knock, and it shall be opened unto you."

I would write it in big invisible letters in the air to get across my point.

Ask, ask, ask. Pray, pray, pray.

> Luke 18:7: And shall God not avenge his own elect who cry out day and night to him, though he bears long with them?

> David Stern in the Jewish New Testament Commentary, page 136, gives Psalm 35:17 and Psalm 74:10 as references.

> Psalm 35:17: Lord, how long wilt you look on? Rescue my soul from their destructions, my darling from the lions.

> Psalms 74:10: O God, how long shall the adversary reproach? Shall the enemy blaspheme your name forever?

He also says, "If a corrupt judge gives in to a widow's pestering, how much more will God, who is altogether just, respond to his chosen people's continual prayers (as opposed to the widows occasional visits)," and gives the above Scriptures, as we also see in Daniel where he was praying and praying for help to come."

Daniel 10:12–13: 12. Then said he unto me, Fear not, Daniel: for from the first day that you did set your heart to understand, and to chasten yourself before your God, your words were heard, and I am come for your words. 13. But the prince of the Kingdom of Persia withstood me one and twenty days: but, lo, Michael, one of the chief princes, came to help me; and I remained there with the kings of Persia.

As we see here, this encourages us never to give up. We need to be faithful in praying and we need to have faith that God hears our prayers and will answer.

162.   Luke 18:16

But Jesus called them unto him, and said, Suffer little children to come unto me, and forbid them not: for of such is the Kingdom of God.

What is our commandment here? To never think that any child is "too young" to understand the gospel.

163.   Luke 18:18–20

18 And a certain ruler asked him, saying, Good Master, what shall I do to inherit eternal life? 19. And Jesus said unto him, Why call you me good? None is good, save one, that is, God. 20. You know the commandments, Do not commit adultery, Do not kill, Do not steal, Do not bear false witness, Honor your father and your mother.

Here we have five of the 10 Commandments.

Yeshua is saying to the ruler, "You shouldn't have to ask me how to inherit eternal life, you know the commandments." Then he tells him to sell all that he has and distribute it to the poor and he will have treasure in heaven and then come and follow him.

Verse 23 says, "But when he heard this, he became very sorrowful for he was very rich."

Was this man looking for an easy way to heaven? Did he think this rabbi had a new plan? How many people do we know that want to take a shortcut to eternal life, to make Yeshua's sacrifice for us on the cross as a way to skate into heaven? There's only one way to salvation and that is through the blood, but there are commandments/works to follow after salvation. Following the commandments does not save you, but the New Covenant sets down the way to walk as Christians, what God expects of us. The Jewish word is *"halacha."* Our walk. That's what we're here to learn. What ARE these commandments? That's what this book is about.

By the way, this man was a "ruler." See Acts 13:42. He would be the ruler, or leader of a synagogue. He should know the Scriptures, shouldn't he?

164.   Luke 20:21–25

21. And they asked him, saying, Master, we know that you say and teach rightly, neither accept you the person of any, but teach the way of God truly: 22. Is it lawful for us to give tribute unto Caesar, or no? 23. But he perceived their craftiness, and said unto them, Why tempt you me? 24. Show me a denarius. Whose image and superscription has it? They answered and said, Caesar's. 25. And he said unto them, Render therefore unto Caesar the things which be Caesar's, and unto God the things which be God's.
I Peter 2:13–17, Matthew 22:15, Mark 12:14.

This is in answer to the question the Pharisees asked Yeshua:

> Luke 20:20: And they watched him, and sent forth spies, who pretended to be just men, that they might take hold of his words, that so they might deliver him unto the power and authority of the governor.

"They" in this verse are the Pharisees. (Remember, not all the Pharisees were against him.) They followed him around during his ministry trying to trap him into something that was against Torah. Their goal was to do this in order to turn him over to the ruling authority.

This question concerned the poll tax to Rome, which was different from the taxes collected by the tax collectors. The poll tax was a citizenship tax paid directly to Rome, as an indication that Israel was subject to that Gentile nation. The Pharisees' query was a trick question. If Jesus answered yes, the people would be angry because he respected a foreign power. If he answered no, he could be charged with sedition.

Jesus' reply was clever. He had the Pharisees pull out a coin, indicating that they already recognized Roman sovereignty by using Roman coins themselves. A denarius was a silver coin that usually had a picture of a Roman ruler on it. The coins of Tiberius were inscribed *Tiberius Caesar, Augustus, son of divine Augustus*. On some of them the reverse bore an image of Tiberius's mother, Livia, portrayed as a goddess of peace with the inscription "high priest."

> Luke 20:25: And he said unto them, Render therefore unto Caesar the things which be Caesar's, and unto God the things which be God's.

The Pharisees could not twist Jesus' wise reply into a charge of sedition

> Luke 23:2: And they began to accuse him, saying, We found this fellow perverting the nation, and forbidding to give tribute to Caesar, saying that he himself is Christ a King.

Bad translation. They didn't say, "He himself is Christ a King." They might have said, "He himself is a leader of the people." Or, another translation, "He claims to be the Messiah and King of the Jews." Nevertheless, watch the translations.

According to Jesus, Caesar, as the ruler of the empire, had the right to collect taxes. Yet at the same time, God should be honored above any ruler. Honoring God does not make a person exempt from supporting the basic functions of the state (see Romans 13:1–7), "for all figures of authority have been ordained by God." This answers a lot of questions concerning what, as believers, we are to obey concerning our government. We have heard of people that refuse to pay taxes in our country because they think they should be exempt.

This also goes along with the story of Yeshua and Peter in Matthew 17:24–27:

24. And when they were come to Capernaum, they that received tribute money came to Peter, and said, Does not your master pay tribute? 25. He says, Yes. And when he was come into the house, Jesus anticipated him, saying, What think you, Simon? Of whom do the kings of the earth take custom or tribute? Of their own children, or of strangers? 26. Peter says unto him, Of strangers. Jesus says unto him, Then are the children free. 27. Notwithstanding, lest we should offend them, go you to the sea, and cast a hook, and take up the fish that first comes up; and when you have opened his mouth, you shall find a piece of money: that take, and give unto them for me and you.

165.   Luke 20:45–47

45. Then in the audience of all the people he said unto his disciples, 46. Beware of the scribes, which desire to walk in long robes, and love greetings in the markets, and the highest seats in the synagogues, and the chief rooms at feasts; 47. Which

devour widows' houses, and for a show make long prayers: the same shall receive greater damnation.

See Matthew 23:1–7, 14, Luke 11:43, 14:7. Matthew 6:5–6.

We've all seen these people. Pray to the Lord that none of us are them. Pray to be humble before the Lord.

166.   Luke 21:8

And he said, Take heed that you be not deceived: for many shall come in my name, saying, I am Christ; and the time draws near: go you not therefore after them.

In the first and second centuries there was a great expectation, awaiting the Messiah. There were many at that time saying they were the Messiah. The people so wanted the Messiah to come and set them free from Roman rule. Again, he is warning them about doctrine here. Beware of false doctrine, check the Scriptures.

How much more in these days and times should we be aware of those that say they have come in his name? How do we avoid that? By being so familiar with the Word that we recognize false doctrine when we hear it. As above, it is said of the FBI that when they are trained to spot a counterfeit bill that they are not shown counterfeit bills, but study the real bills to become so familiar with them that they can spot any flaw or discrepancy. That's how we should be with the Word of God, so familiar with it that anything askew instantly sends up a signal, "Warning, warning! This does not compute."

167.   Luke 21:9

But when you shall hear of wars and commotions, be not terrified: for these things must first come to pass; but the end will not come right away.

So many things we're hearing in our day. He says, "Be not terrified!" Heed not. When people say, "The end of the world is coming," that in itself is a false statement. First the Great Tribulation period will come, then the Millennial Reign. So if the Great Tribulation started today, we still have 1007 years or so to finish out on this earth. This is Yeshua's teaching on "When will all these things be" in chapter 21.

See Matthew 24:3–14, Mark 13:3–13.

168.   Luke 21:14

Settle it therefore in your hearts, not to meditate before what you shall answer.

Don't we all study and study when we're coming to meet with someone to discuss a passage of Scripture or to speak on a passage, as we well should, but here is his promise, verse 15:

"For I will give you a mouth and wisdom, which all your adversaries shall not be able to gainsay nor resist."

In other words, "contradict." What a promise! How many of you have had this happen to you? I always think I don't know Scripture well and I study and study and then when it comes time to speak, the Lord DOES fill my mouth. He's with us all the time. The key here is YOU have to study in order to expect him to fill your mouth. It has to be downloaded in order to upload it.

See Luke 12:11, Acts 6:10.

169.   Luke 21:19

In your patience possess you your souls.

Patience. Oy vey. How many of us need to practice patience more? Yeshua is speaking to us here to be patient about his coming. To be patient in all things in our lives, but pray fervently. Stay faithful and don't grow weary in well doing.

Luke 21:21: Then let them which are in Judaea flee to the mountains; and let them which are in the midst of it depart out; and let not them that are in the countries enter therein.

Yeshua was speaking to the generation standing in front of him that would go through the invasion of the Roman army and the destruction of the Temple once again in 70 AD. Many, many places in the Scriptures the people are warned of the coming judgment on them. This was the beginning of the age of the Gentiles. The Temple was destroyed, the people were scattered, and never has the Temple been rebuilt since that time.

There is a group in Israel called the Temple Institute that has been working to rebuild the temple since 1987. They have many of the items made that will be needed for this Temple. They have the priestly garments, the breastplate, the utensils, and have trained the Levitical Priesthood living today to serve in that Temple. They are faithful in fulfilling God's commandment to them that says to build him a Temple. "Build me a house." As believers in Yeshua, a lot of us believe Yeshua will build the Millennial Temple. Our house, our bodies here on earth, are spiritual houses and we need to be building them also. The people at the Temple Institute have been so faithful in carrying out what God commanded them. If we could only be as faithful and diligent to keep his commandments.

170.   Luke 21:28

And when these things begin to come to pass, then look up, and lift up your heads; for your redemption draws nigh.

From the same sermon as above concerning the destruction of Jerusalem in 70 AD. The Lord is encouraging the people to stay faithful and do not despair, "For your redemption draws near." As should we when it seems things are so bad, our country is in such disrepair, and we long for his soon coming. But, brother and sister, do not despair. He IS coming. We must be faithful and watch for him.

See also Romans 8:19, 23. Signs of His coming also: Matthew 24:29–31, Mark 13:24–27.

171.   Luke 21:29–31

29. And he spoke to them a parable; Behold the fig tree, and all the trees; 30. When they now shoot forth, you see and know of your own selves that summer is now nigh at hand. 31. So likewise you, when you see these things come to pass, know you that the Kingdom of God is nigh at hand.

"Know you." The fig tree is the Nation of Israel. See Mark 13:28–29.

172.   Luke 21:34

And take heed to yourselves, lest at any time your hearts be overcharged with surfeiting, and drunkenness, and cares of this life, and so that day come upon you unawares.

Take heed. Again, don't lose sight of his soon coming. Guard your soul from becoming callous. Stay close to him by reading the Word, praying, and having fellowship with other believers. Be ready! "The Day of the Lord" in Scripture is the day he returns to this earth "with all his saints," I Thessalonians 3:13, following the seven year period called The Great Tribulation.

See also 1 Thessalonians 5:6, Luke 8:14.

See Wikipedia article on The Day of the Lord.

173.   Luke 21:36

Watch you therefore, and pray always, that you may be accounted worthy to escape all these things that shall come to pass, and to stand before the Son of Man.

"Watch." Again, he is speaking to those of the generation that were alive when the destruction of the temple came in 70 AD, but also to us here in our day. Here he reminds us to "watch, pray always."

See 1 John 2:28. Matthew 24:42, 25:13. Luke 18:1, 20:35, Ephesians 6:13.

174.   Luke 22:17-18

17. And he took the cup, and gave thanks, and said, Take this, and divide it among yourselves: 18. For I say unto you, I will not drink of the fruit of the vine, until the Kingdom of God shall come.

We studied this in Matthew 26. Here we have the institution of the Communion, represented here at Passover by the wine and the bread. Each time we partake of these emblems, we praise him for shedding his blood for us, for his body that was broken for us.

175.   Luke 22:19

And he took bread, and gave thanks, and brake it, and gave unto them, saying, This is my body which is given for you: this do in remembrance of me.

The commandments here are "take this, and this do." We shouldn't take the Communion service lightly. We are commemorating what the Christian life is all about. He died on the cross for us, shedding his blood for us, and sacrificing his body that we might be saved. I suggest you do this also with your family once a week. Some people do this every day.

See 1 Corinthians 11:23–26. Mark 14:25. Matthew 26:26. 1 Peter 2:24. 1 Corinthians 10:16.

176.   Luke 22:25–30

25. And he said unto them, The kings of the Gentiles exercise Lordship over them; and they that exercise authority upon them are called benefactors. 26. But you shall not be so: but he that is greatest among you, let him be as the younger; and he that is chief, as he that does serve. 27. For which is greater, he that sits at meat, or he that serves? is not he that sits at meat? but I am among you as he that serves. 28. You are they which have continued with me in my temptations. 29. And I appoint unto you a Kingdom, as my Father has appointed unto me; 30. That you may eat and drink at my table in my Kingdom, and sit on thrones judging the twelve tribes of Israel.
See Mark 10:42–45. I Peter 5:3. Luke 9:48.

Here we have servant Scriptures again. We are not to be exalted over others even if we're in leadership; however, we are to honor those in authority over us.

177.   Luke 22:35-36

35. And he said unto them, When I sent you without purse, and scrip, and shoes, lacked you anything? And they said, Nothing. 36. Then said he unto them, But now, he that has a purse, let him take it, and likewise his scrip: and he that has no sword, let him sell his garment, and buy one.
Matthew 10:9.

Here we have Yeshua sending the disciples out again. Yeshua/Jesus is teaching the disciples here not to be dependent on other people, but to take provision for themselves this time, and a sword! Doesn't this sound like our day when many are getting conceal and carry licenses or buying guns to protect their homes, family, and churches? Most churches now have trained guards with conceal and carry licenses. This is another "don't be ignorant brothers" Scripture, but don't "assume" that an angel is going to pop down from heaven every time you need rescued, although they do at times! Be prepared spiritually and physically. Also, not everyone on this journey is going to love us and pour out blessings on us. Some messages they don't want to hear!

In our lives, we need to watch for changes in our marching orders from the Lord. We need to always be in touch with the Holy Spirit and follow his guidance. We might have been a youth leader and he's putting a call on our life to pastor. We might have planned to go to college to be an accountant and the Lord calls us to go into ministry. Just be prepared constantly by study, prayer, and service for the Lord and he will guide you, as he did the disciples.

178.   Luke 22:40

And when he was at the place, he said unto them, Pray that you enter not into temptation.
Mark 14:32–42.

The "place" is the Mount of Olives where he frequently went to pray. This is one of his last commandments to his beloved disciples. Daily we should pray this prayer.

Temptation doesn't come up and say, "This is going to be a test." Sometimes we find ourselves heading into a situation and realize "this isn't right." If we know the Scripture, we can recognize that we're facing temptation. No matter what age we are, we're going to face temptations that are testing us; however, what did the Savior say?

Luke 22:32: But I have prayed for you, that your faith fail not: and when you are converted, strengthen your brethren.
John 17:9, 11, 15.

He has prayed for us! How amazing is that! Our friends may or may not understand why we're having to back out of a situation they think is all right, but if they know the Word, they will. If it's an unbeliever, they may look at you badly, but try to explain as well as you can why you cannot do this. And then all of us should be more watchful not to fall into a trap again. Some of the Pharisees tried to trap the Lord, but he recognized what they were doing immediately. We should know the Word so well that we recognize immediately what's going on and back out of situations that are against the Lord, or not get into them in the first place.

See Mark 14:32–42.

179.   Luke 22:46

And said unto them, Why sleep you? Rise and pray, lest you enter into temptation.

Luke 9:32, Luke 22:40.

An admonition to all of us: Rise and pray lest you enter into temptation. First thing in the morning, last thing at night, pray that you do not enter into temptation. This phrase is in the Lord's Prayer. "Lead us not into temptation." God tries us to see how much we love him, but he also warns us here to "pray." Look out for what might tempt you today.

1 Corinthians 10:13: There has no temptation taken you but such as is common to man: but God is faithful, who will not suffer you to be tempted above that you are able; but will with the temptation also make a way to escape, that you may be able to bear it.

Commandments in the Book of John

The Book of John is my favorite book of the New Covenant. As I said in the introduction, the night I got saved in our little Baptist Church in Crescent, Oregon, the lady that prayed with me gave me a little red Book of John. I took that little book home and, up in my room, opening it for the first time at eight years old, standing by my window with the light streaming in from the street light, I started reading it, and it seemed like it was written just to me. And it was. I remember feeling a quietness and stillness, like time had stopped. I was a New Creature in Yeshua HaMashiach, Jesus the Messiah.

God's Word is written to each one of us and he wants us to know that he desires that we come to him as a little child, opening his book to communicate with him. He patiently waits for us day by day, longing to see each one of us come into fellowship with him.

Let's open the Book of John.

The Book of John is different than the other gospels. There are Parallel Bibles that show references in Matthew, Mark, and Luke to the other gospels, but John's Testimony stands apart. Our pastor just started a series on the Book of John as I'm writing this. He brought out that John was very different at the end of the book than he was at the beginning, that Jesus called John and his brother "Sons of Thunder," meaning they had fiery tempers. Remember how James and John wanted to call fire down from heaven one time?

Luke 9:54: And when his disciples, James and John, saw this, they said, Lord, will you that we command fire to come down from heaven, and consume them, even as Elias (Elijah) did?

Ha! Doesn't that sound like some of us? But by the end of the book, John had been transformed. He is thought to be the one leaning on Yeshua's breast at the Passover Seder. He is the only one of the twelve disciples who stayed at the foot of the cross when Yeshua was dying. He is the last one that Yeshua spoke to before he died.

John 19:25–27: 25. Now there stood by the cross of Jesus his mother, and his mother's sister, Mary the wife of Cleophas, and Mary Magdalene. 26. When Jesus therefore saw his mother, and the disciple standing by, whom he loved, he says unto his mother, Woman, behold your son! 27. Then says he to the disciple, Behold your mother! And from that hour that disciple took her unto his own home.

Why? John was so transformed by Yeshua's teachings after some three years that he was well able to take care of Yeshua's most important possession on earth, His mother. Where were Yeshua's brothers and sisters? Sure, James, or Jacob, Yacov in Hebrew, we're told, came to believe in him as the Messiah after his death and resurrection. But to entrust your dear mother to a dear friend, that is the epitome of trust and love.

Then in the Book of Revelation, John finally gets his fire from heaven, but not as he asked Yeshua to do. This is the Antichrist this time.

Revelation 13:13: And he does great wonders, so that he makes fire come down from heaven on the earth in the sight of men.

I'm sure John was remembering what he said to Yeshua as he was writing this.

How changed we all are after we encounter the Living God, Yeshua/Jesus come in the flesh, all God and all man.

The Book of John is the "in the beginning" book of the New Covenant, just as Genesis is the "in the beginning" book of the Torah/Old Testament.

The first verse in John states, "In the beginning was the Word...." The Greek word here for *Word* is *logos*.

From Thayer's Greek Lexicon, *blueletterbible.org*: Word, *Logos*, a two-fold use of the term is to be distinguished: One which relates to speaking, and one which relates to thinking. Strong's Concordance #G3056: In several passages in the writings of John, logos denotes the essential Word of God, i.e. the personal (hypostatic) wisdom and power in union with God, his minister in the creation and government of the universe, the cause of all the world's life, both physical and ethical, which for the procurement of man's salvation put on human nature in the person of Jesus the Messiah and shone forth conspicuously from his words and deeds.

Psalms 33:6: By the word of the Lord were the heavens made; and all the host of them by the breath of his mouth.

John is saying here that the Messiah existed from the beginning. He is saying that the Word existed before all creation and IS God!

John 1:1: In the beginning was the Word, and the Word was with God, and the Word was God.

I don't know how much plainer John could have stated this fact. Yet, there are many people that do not believe this, that Yeshua/Jesus is God, that he is Divine.

If we go back to the beginning:

Genesis 1:1: In the beginning God created the heavens and the earth.

We see in English the facts. Just the facts. If we look at this verse in Hebrew, we see much more:

הָאָרֶץ׃	וְאֵת	הַשָּׁמַיִם	אֵת	אֱלֹהִים	בָּרָא	בְּרֵאשִׁית	1:1
the earth.	and	the Heaven		God	created	In the beginning	
776	853	8064	853	430	1254	7225	
haa'aarets	w°'eet	hashaamayim	'eet	'Elohiym	baaraa'	B°ree'shiyt	

Hebrew reads right to left. We have the first word, Bereishit, The letter bet, or our B. The letter in Hebrew is a prefix meaning "in." Then we have the word "reshit," pronounced reysheit. Beginning. Next is bara, created, God – Elohim, and then the first and last letters of the Hebrew aleph–bet, the aleph and the tav. This word, pronounced "et," is used as a pointer to the direct object, which is created what? The direct object is "the heaven and the earth." So we have, "In the beginning, Elohim created the aleph and the tav, who created the heaven and the earth." In the beginning Elohim created the Word. He then spoke the world, or sung the world, into existence in the Hebrew language. The Word had to be created first. The Jews sing the scriptures in the synagogue. At an early age Jewish children can sing the entire Torah. They learn the cantillation signs that are written right into the Torah. They are like our music notes.

Hebrews 10:7: Then said I, Lo, I come (in the volume of the book it is written of me,) to do your will, O God.

Psalms 40:7–8: 7. Then said I, Lo, I come: in the volume of the book it is written of me, 8. I delight to do your will, O my God: yes, your law is within my heart.

Here in Genesis 1:1 we have Father and Son, and in Genesis 1:2, the Holy Spirit.

And the earth was without form, and void; and darkness was upon the face of the deep. And the Spirit of God moved upon the face of the waters.

Christians call this the Trinity. In Judaism it is Father, Son, and Mother. They say that there are three columns, or foundations, that support the world: Severity, Mildness, and Mercy. Wisdom, Strength, and Beauty.

In Genesis chapter one, only the name Elohim is used. The God of Justice. Not until Genesis chapter 2:4 is the name in Hebrew Yud-Hey-Vav-Hey, Yahweh, God of Mercy, used, along with Elohim. If God had created the world in Mercy, there would be no boundaries. He had to create the world with Justice. Boundaries. These names are written in the King James Version as "LORD God". Yahweh Elohim. Any time you see the name written as *"LORD,"* it is *Yahweh*. When it is written *"God"* it is *Elohim*. These are Strong's Concordance numbers H3068 for Yahweh and H430 for Elohim.

> 1 John 5:7-8: 7. For there are three that bear record in heaven, the Father, the Word, and the Holy Spirit: and these three are one. 8. And there are three that bear witness in earth, the Spirit, and the water, and the blood: and these three agree in one.

The "et" word is used many times in the Torah/Old Testament and never translated because it just points to the direct object, but English speakers/readers have never seen this unless it has been explained by a Hebrew speaker or have discovered it like I did.

We held Bible studies in our home in California for many years. It was after Rosh HaShanah, the Jewish Civil New Year, and our parashah, portion reading, for the next day was from Bereishit, which is Genesis 1:1 through Genesis 6:8. I was up late studying, which I was wont to do often, when I started reading this first verse. I had begun to use the Hebrew and had many resources, as I do today. I used my PC Bible to look this up. There was that word with no translation.

The PC Bible Hebrew interlinear for Genesis 1:1: The word "et", Strong's Concordance #H853: 'eth (ayth). Apparently contracted from OT:226 in the demonstrative sense of entity; properly self, (but generally used to point out more definitely the object of a verb or preposition, even or namely):

Strong's Concordance #H226: 'owth (oth); probably from OT:225 (in the sense of appearing); a signal (literally or figuratively), as a flag, beacon, monument, omen, prodigy, evidence, etc.:

KJV – (used as) mark, miracle, (en–) sign, token.

The *blueletterbible.org* translation of the word "et": Strong's Concordance #H853: Sign of the definite direct object, not translated in English but generally preceding and indicating the accusative.

KJV Translation Count – Total: 22x (total times used as a word)

Used as a mark or a sign or a signal. Okay. I need to pay attention. What is the Lord trying to show me? I prayed. And prayed. What could this mean that the aleph and the tav, the first and last letters of the Hebrew aleph–bet are here as the fourth word in the Bible?

Ah. First and last. It's clicking.

Revelation 1:11,17: 11. Saying, I am Alpha and Omega, the first and the last: and, What you see, write in a book, and send it unto the seven churches which are in Asia; unto Ephesus, and unto Smyrna, and unto Pergamos, and unto Thyatira, and unto Sardis, and unto Philadelphia, and unto Laodicea. 17. And when I saw him, I fell at his feet as dead. And he laid his right hand upon me, saying unto me, Fear not; I am the first and the last:

Revelation 2:8: And unto the angel of the church in Smyrna write; These things says the First and the Last, which was dead, and is alive;

Revelation 22:13: I am Alpha and Omega, the beginning and the end, the first and the last.

Except, Yeshua/Jesus did not speak Greek, he spoke Hebrew, and instead of "the Alpha and Omega" he would have said, "I am the Aleph and the Tav."

As I bowed before him that night, stunned and amazed at His Word, the realization of all we've been missing as English speakers and readers came crashing in on me. "Lord, look at all we've missed. Help me to grasp what you are saying."

He said, "I am the first bet (B) in Genesis 1:1 and the last letter in "amen" in the Book of Revelation."

Psalms 40:7: Then said I, Lo, I come: in the scroll of the book [it is] written of me,

Hebrews 10:7: Then I said, 'Behold, I have come—In the scroll of the book it is written of me—To do your will, O God.'

I sat stunned for what seemed hours as words of the Bible swirled in my head and the enormity of this knowledge. "Lord, I know the whole Bible is about you. I know all the stories that we read are pictures of you. I know you're there on every page, but I never knew how fully and completely."

From that night, my life has never been the same. I realized the necessity of reading the Bible in Hebrew and seeing words in their Hebraic context and seeing words that might be translated a little slanted, and seeing words in the Hebrew that we as English speakers/readers never see. I'm certainly not fluent by any means. My purpose in studying Hebrew is to study His Word in the language in which it was written. That's why I continue to teach Beginning Hebrew and Intermediate Hebrew so that I will not lose what I've learned and I love teaching the Holy Language to people. I use *Blueletterbible.org* and my PC Bible daily to look up verses and the meanings of words. I'm far enough in my study to see a word translated one way and wonder, "Why did they translate it like that, both by Jewish Bible publishers and English Bible publishers. The richness of his word comes alive and it's like you're really walking and talking with him.

I want to make it clear that the WORD "et" is not Yeshua/Jesus. The letters represent him, the aleph and tav, the beginning and the end, the first and the last.

180.   John 1:43,45

43. The day following Jesus would go forth into Galilee, and finds Philip, and says unto him, Follow me. 45. Philip found Nathanael, and said unto him, We have found him, of whom Moses in the law, and the prophets, did write, Jesus of Nazareth, the son of Joseph.
John 6:5, 12:21–22, 14:8–9. Matthew 4:19, 8:22, 9:9, 16:24, 19:21, Mark 1:17, 2:14, 8:34, 10:21, Luke 5:27, 9:23, 9:59, 18:22.

It is thought that Nathaniel is the same man as Bartholomew as he is never mentioned again except in this chapter and chapter 21:2 after this to be amongst the twelve, but Bartholomew is. Nathaniel is thought to be his given name and Bartholomew a title given him from his father. "Bar" in Hebrew is son, then Tolmai, so "son of tolmai."

Nathaniel's name means "gift of God." Natan in Hebrew is "giver." Of course, El is God.

A simple commandment. Follow me. We talked about what this means in Matthew 4:19.

This commandment entails a whole new world for a person that decides to "follow" Yeshua/Jesus. In the first century, there were many "messiahs." In order to "follow" one, you sat at their feet and listened and learned. You imitated him. Yeshua/Jesus chose 12 students, talmidim, or disciples, to join him and learn.

We need to read his Word and try to follow His commandments. That is what this book is all about, becoming a follower of the Jewish Messiah, Yeshua/Jesus, and living as he did. Imitate him.

The first Christians broke off from the branch of Jewish believers after Constantine came in and persecuted the Jews and forbid them to proselytize and made laws against them. The persecuted Jews assimilated into other countries and the Gentile Christians were left to figure things out for themselves. At first, they kept the festivals of the Lord, kept Saturday as the Sabbath, and read the Torah as they had since the Book of Acts, then they began to drift away and assimilate. (They may have had copies of the various books in the New Covenant and letters written by the early Christian believers.)

At the time of Constantine, who lived from 272 to 337, the Bible had not been canonized and was not for several years. Constantine ordered his own "bible" written by Eusebius, a follower of Origen. Constantine wanted this "bible" to be acceptable to Christians, as well as pagans. This book greatly affected the beliefs of the Gentile Christians.

When Constantine came into power and he and his mother "converted" to Christianity, things changed. That change brought about the Christianity we have today. Many believers now are getting back to the beginning and looking at the whole picture of our Jewish roots. We study history and see how Christianity was before and after Constantine and his mother. We are trying to get back to how Yeshua/Jesus and his disciples lived and what they believed. Christianity is a branch of Judaism, Yeshua/Jesus is a Jewish King/Priest, Saturday is still the Sabbath (it is said that the Catholics have admitted changing it), and we are still His talmidim.

"What? We can't go to church on Sunday?" Saturday, the seventh day, is the day set aside to rest. We can go to church and should be worshipping him every day, but Saturday from the creation has been "the rest." This commandment was given to them before they got to Sinai in Exodus 16. It was then given in the Ten Commandments, and Isaiah says it will continue in the World to Come, Isaiah 66:22-23.

In the New Testament, Christians are never commanded to keep Saturday as the Sabbath. The word in Genesis 2:2 for *"rested"* is *Shabbat*. God rested on the seventh day. So should we. The fourth commandment is "remember the Sabbath day, to keep it holy." The commandment about keeping the Sabbath is the only one out of the ten that is not written in the New Covenant; however, Yeshua/Jesus kept it. He was and is a Jew. The commandment concerning the Sabbath was given to the Israelites in the Ten Commandments. It is a "sign" to the world that Yahweh is their God.

If you choose to observe Saturday as a day of rest, the Shabbat, it does bring much joy. To think that the Creator of the universe wants us to actually rest! To my husband and I, it has become a day of study, of reading the portion of the week, listening to teachings by people such as Mark Biltz of El Shaddai Ministries, Rabbi Itzhak Shapira of Ahavat Ministries, or some other Jewish Messianic believer, but not as a legalistic, binding commandment on us. We observe the Festivals of the Lord in the same way, as pictures of the Messiah. The Shabbat is also a picture of the millennium. We also go to church on Sunday.

See the reference to the article *Catholic Confessions on the Sabbath* as one explanation of how it got changed to Sunday.

Remember in the Book of Acts when the Jewish Christians were upset because Gentiles were being saved and none of them knew what to do with them? The conclusion was that there were four "rules" that the Gentiles needed to follow. None of these were to keep the Sabbath. The Jewish believers still kept Saturday as the Sabbath. This obviously tells us that they did not believe we had to keep the 613 commandments as they did not come to this conclusion. Twice in Acts we are told the decision they came to and agreed on. See Acts chapter 15 and chapter 21. It is strange that this same argument goes on today for those in the Messianic movement. If they would only read these two chapters there wouldn't have to be such confusion.

The first believers met on Saturday as they were all Jews, then when the Gentiles started coming in, the Gentiles met with the Jews. They didn't have a separate church on Sunday. When it says "the first day," as in Acts 20:9 when Paul was "long preaching" and Eutychus fell asleep and fell down from "the third loft," it was our Saturday evening as the Jewish day begins at sundown of each day. Notice in the story, "he preached all night."

> Act 20:11: When he therefore was come up again, and had broken bread, and eaten, and talked a long while, even till break of day, so he departed.

Paul was preaching at the service called "havdalah" that the Jews and Messianic believers do every Saturday night after the sun goes down on the Sabbath, or Shabbat, which would be the beginning of their Sunday, our Saturday night. The Jewish day goes from sundown to sundown. So here they were having the havdalah service. We call it Communion. They call it kiddish, which means "holy." They do this on Friday night before sundown, then again on Saturday night after sundown, which separates the holy day from the mundane.

Notice when they got Eutychus back up to them, alive and well, "they were not a little comforted." In other words, they had a great hallelujah time rejoicing! Then they did kiddish, Communion, and talked "a long while" until sunrise! How many of us have done that when we are talking about the Lord and realize we've talked all night! What a joy that is. Then Paul departed on Sunday morning.

Two more verses I like in John are verses 10:27 and 12:26.

> John 10:27: My sheep hear my voice, and I know them, and they follow me, and John 12:26: If anyone serves me, let him follow me; and where I am, there my servant will be also. If anyone serves me, him will my Father honor.

It is our duty to study out what this entails.

> Again: 2 Timothy 2:15: Study to show yourself approved unto God, a workman that needs not to be ashamed, rightly dividing the word of truth.

Paul says in I Corinthians 11:1: Be you followers of me, even as I also am of Christ.

Study out the "follow" verses and learn more about being a follower.

John 2:7: Jesus says unto them, Fill the water pots with water. And they filled them up to the brim.

Here we have a commandment given to Jesus' disciples. A simple commandment: Fill the water pots with water. Does it sometimes seem that we feel like we should do a certain thing, but it seems so meaningless and simple? We think the action might not change anything. But look what happened here when they simply obeyed without a question. The first miracle recorded in the Christian Torah. The water turned into wine!

Shouldn't we think about it next time we feel like we are to do a simple deed, go to a certain place, buy a certain product, or give a $20 bill to someone. We think, "Oh, well, it's probably just me thinking this." We will never know what the outcome of that simple idea would have been. We may have saved a soul that desperately needed someone to just show love to them and that someone cares that day. When those urges strike, stop and consider, "Is this just me, or is the Lord trying to get through to me?"

The first miracle Yeshua/Jesus did brought joy to the wedding party. The Bible speaks a lot about wine. Wine is a picture of the blood of Yeshua/Jesus that he shed at Calvary. It is also a picture of joy. As we partake of this or grape juice during Communion or at Passover, we are reminded of his sacrifice for us and that we are a part of his family now.

The miracle of turning water into wine is also a picture of the outpouring of the Holy Spirit in Acts. They were all filled with the "new wine" and were changed forever.

When he performed this miracle at Cana, he was going against nature. Whoever changed a substance on this earth from one thing to another?

He is showing here that he is the Creator God. He is showing his authority over his creation. He is showing his power. He does it in such a way that it brings joy to people.

181.   John 2:13–16

13. And the Jews' Passover was at hand, and Jesus went up to Jerusalem, 14. And found in the temple those that sold oxen and sheep and doves, and the changers of money sitting: 15. And when he had made a scourge of small cords, he drove them all out of the temple, and the sheep, and the oxen; and poured out the changers' money, and overthrew the tables; 16. And said unto them that sold doves, Take these things hence; make not my Father's house a house of merchandise.

What is the commandment? Verse 16. "Do not make My Father's house a house of merchandise." We have to go back to our teaching on the illegal priesthood and what was going on at the Temple. Caiaphas and Annas bought the priesthood knowing how many millions of dollars would be coming in from the sale of all the livestock and other things needed for the sacrifices/korban, and all the gifts and offerings brought to the temple by the people.

In Josephus, it says that the priesthood went so far as to authorize a daily sacrifice for Caesar! When things got bad right before the destruction of the Temple in 70 BC, the priests stopped making sacrifice for Caesar and this made things worse for the Jewish people. It was considered an act of war!

Here is an article from <u>Thorn Crown Journal</u> by Doug Reed concerning the political situation and what the priesthood had become:

"*In first century Palestine there was no separation between church and state. The priests at the temple in Jerusalem not only officiated over the religious life of the Jews, they were also rulers and judges. Herod, who was himself a pawn of Rome, had his own pawns installed in the Jewish priesthood. By the first century, the election of the High Priest was more political than religious. The Romans wanted the priesthood to support their occupation, and the Herods made sure their desire was carried out. However, it would be unfair to categorize all of the priesthood as sympathetic to Rome. Some did support rebellion against Rome, but those at the highest levels were undoubtedly in Rome's back pocket.*

We see evidence of loyalty to and fear of Rome in the Gospels:

John 11:45–48: "Then many of the Jews who had come to Mary, and had seen the things Jesus did, believed in him. But some of them went away to the Pharisees and told them the things Jesus did.

Then the chief priests and the Pharisees gathered a council and said, "What shall we do? For this man works many miracles. If we let him alone like this, everyone will believe in him, and the Romans will come and take away both our place and nation."

John 19:15: But they cried out, "Away with him, away with him! Crucify him!" Pilate said to them, 'Shall I crucify your King?' The chief priests answered, 'We have no king but Caesar!' Then he delivered him to them to be crucified. Then they took Jesus and led him away."

Josephus recorded that the priesthood went so far as to authorize a daily sacrifice for Caesar in the temple. This was a source of continual angst for the Jews. In the final Roman/Jewish conflict, the cessation of the daily sacrifice for Caesar was considered an act of war that helped lead to the destruction of Jerusalem.

The priesthood lived in luxury well beyond that of the average man. They supported their lavish lifestyles with a temple tax which every Jew was required to pay.

Richard Horsley in his book "The Message and the Kingdom" describes what archeologists have discovered about the living conditions of the priesthood.

"...impressive archeological remains of their Jerusalem residences show how elegant their lifestyle had become. In spacious structures, unhesitatingly dubbed 'mansions" by the archeologists who uncovered them in the 1970's, we can get a glimpse of a lavish life in mosaic floored reception rooms and dining rooms with elaborate painted and carved stucco wall decorations and with a wealth of fine tableware, glassware, carved stone table tops, and other interior furnishings and elegant peristyles.

The priests lived lavish lifestyles while the average Jewish peasant struggled to survive. The temple taxes combined with taxes imposed by Herod and Rome were threatening the existence of the Jewish people. The people of the land were carrying a burden they could scarcely bear or tolerate. Palestine had become a powder keg waiting to ignite.

The priesthood was undoubtedly jealous of Jesus' popularity, but their main motivation for seeking to kill Jesus was fear. When a new king came to power, he would set his version of the priesthood in place. All this talk of Jesus becoming the new king probably unnerved the priests in Jerusalem. If Jesus came to power, they thought they would be out of a job or killed. And the Romans did not take too kindly to unauthorized kings. In their opinion, Jesus was inviting the wrath of Rome. They did not understand that Jesus' Kingdom was not of this world and his priesthood was not according to flesh and blood.

He was stating that he is the Father's, God's, Son. He is showing his authority here. Over and over through the Scriptures he does actions that prove he is God come in the flesh, that he has this authority.

In Psalms 69:9: For the zeal of your house has eaten me up; and the reproaches of them that reproached you are fallen upon me." Here he is acting out this Scripture."

So here we have a bigger picture of what was going on in Israel at that time. Things were heating up. No wonder they feared Yeshua/Jesus. They feared he would try to overthrow them and become king! Well, he will one of these days, but that wasn't his purpose the first time.

In our commandment, we are not to use the church to become rich, as I fear some are. We need to judge each ministry separately and judge whether they are truly trying to spread the gospel or whether they are doing this just for the money. A lot of TV ministries draw people in by what seems to be their sincere message, when behind the scenes they're living better than kings. Beware and don't fall into deception. The local churches can use that money much better to win souls for the Lord and help the local people. We need to truly know the people behind the ministries. Pray a lot before giving to any ministry. Check them out. Check their fruit.

182.   John 3:7

Marvel not that I said unto you, You must be born again.

This is chapter three where Nicodemus comes to Yeshua/Jesus at night. It is thought by some that Nicodemus was the head of the Great Sanhedrin at that time. The Great Sanhedrin was made up of a chief/prince/leader at that time, called a nasi, a vice chief justice, and 69 general members, sometimes called "the 70." He had come at night to not be seen. He shows up two more times in the gospels, once in John 7:45–51 during the Feast of Unleavened Bread where he states the law concerning Yeshua's arrest, then again in John 19:39–42, to help Joseph of Arimathea prepare Yeshua for burial.

"Marvel not" is the commandment here. Certainly we marvel. Such a simple act as asking Yeshua/Jesus into our heart seems so easy. How could saying this prayer help me, change me, make a difference in my life? But then when we pray to receive him and believe in our heart, what a change, what a difference in a soul set free by the Power of God! Our lives are never the same again.

Yeshua/Jesus was speaking here to Nicodemus. The "you" here is plural. Yeshua/Jesus was speaking to all who would listen. Then eight verses further down is our beloved John 3:16. What a change of heart was given to this powerful man of the ruling council Yeshua offered. The chance to know the Jewish Messiah had come.

Are we still marveling today about our salvation? I hope so. Even though he says here, "marvel not," I marvel every day that he chose me.

183.   John 4:35

Say not you, There are yet four months, and then comes the harvest? Behold, I say unto you, Lift up your eyes, and look on the fields; for they are white already to harvest.
Genesis 8:22, Matthew 9:37–38.

What's the commandment here? "Say not there are still four months to harvest." He's saying here, "Look around you! Today is the day of salvation to the world. Look at the throngs that need to be brought in." Here in this verse it is either four months before the festival of First Fruits, the barley harvest, which on the Jewish calendar is Nissan 16, or it is four months before Shavuot, which is the wheat harvest, which is 49 days after First Fruits and falls on the Jewish calendar on Sivan 5. This is the date the Torah was given on Mt. Sinai, which is our Pentecost.

This was said by Yeshua/Jesus after he met the woman at Jacob's well.

John 4:39: And many of the Samaritans of that city believed on him for the saying of the woman, which testified, he told me all that ever I did.

The disciples "marveled" that He was speaking to a Samaritan woman. He talks about "living water" in verse 13. Verse 4:26 is also one place where he says, "I am." He says, "I who speak to you am he."

The woman leaves the well with her water pot and goes back into the city (Sychar, verse 5) and says to the men:

> John 4:29: "Come, see a man, which told me all things that ever I did: is not this the Christ?" Then they went out of the city and came to him. They wind up inviting him to stay and he stayed two nights. Many of them believed on him that he was the Messiah.

> John 4:41-42: 41. And many more believed because of his own word; 42. And said unto the woman, "Now we believe, not because of your saying: for we have heard him ourselves, and know that this is indeed the Christ, the Savior of the world."

Haven't we all experienced this? When we meet him, he knows all about us, yet loves us anyway and saves us because of his mercy and grace, as he did this woman and the people of Samaria.

The Jews wouldn't have anything to do with the Samaritans. See Matthew 10:5.

You can do research yourselves on the history of the Samaritans. It is an interesting study. When we were in Israel in 2004 we got to go to Mt. Gerizim to a town that had a Samaritan synagogue. The Samaritan priest there gave a talk for us and showed us many pictures of past priests and people from many years ago that had lived there. He showed us around the grounds where they sacrifice lambs for Passover and hold the Passover outside. They have their own Torah scrolls, written in their language. They swear they are direct descendants of Aaron through Ithamar.

The Samaritans still to this day believe their temple is the right one, as the Northern Tribes did before being taken into captivity in Assyria.

There is an archeological site on a hill there with the ruins of their temple.

> John 4:21–24: 21. Jesus says unto her, Woman, believe me, the hour comes, when you shall neither in this mountain, nor yet at Jerusalem, worship the Father. 22. You worship you know not what: we know what we worship: for salvation is of the Jews. 23. But the hour comes, and now is, when the true worshippers shall worship the Father in spirit and truth: for the Father seeks such to worship him. 24. God is a Spirit: and they that worship him must worship him in spirit and truth.

In this verse, Yeshua/Jesus goes further than the Great Tribulation, further than the Millennium period of 1000 years. The period this is speaking of is also about the New Heaven and New Earth.

Also, we need to acknowledge that our salvation came from the Jews. Jesus said, "Salvation is of the Jews." John 4:22.

> Romans 1:16: For I am not ashamed of the gospel of Christ: for it is the power of God unto salvation to everyone that believes; to the Jew first, and also to the Greek.

I believe Yeshua/Jesus was opening the door for the disciples to preach the gospel to the whole world; yet, we don't read of any Gentiles being saved until the Book of Acts in Chapter 10 when Cornelius and his family were saved, which was approximately 15 years after Yeshua/Jesus ascended into heaven, although this passage does intimate that a lot of the Samaritans did believe at this time. We have no other information on this. There was no "salvation" until he died on the cross and rose again. Many believed on him, but until his death and resurrection, the price had not been paid.

I believe this was a training period for the disciples to set up the "halacha" (way to walk) for the church. It didn't happen all at once. It took many years and many meetings to decide on a set of rules to follow, a doctrine. That book you hold in your hands has gone through years and years of decisions on what goes in and what stays out. We're more equipped now in this century to look at the writings and see why some were left out and some were included.

184.   John 5:14

Afterward Jesus found him in the temple, and said unto him, Behold, you are made whole: sin no more, lest a worse thing come upon you.
John 8:11.

Yeshua/Jesus is talking to the man that he had healed earlier in this chapter. He reminds us here always to remember the miracles, healings, and blessings he does for us lest he has to take us on another lap around the mountain! Learn it the first time! Be thankful! Give him praise for all he does for us. Be grateful!

John 5:39-40: 39. Search the Scriptures; for in them you think you have eternal life: and they are they which testify of me. 40. And you will not come to me, that you might have life.

I love this verse. What Scriptures? What we call the "Old Testament," and I call the Torah. The Torah can be either the five books of Moses or the entire Tanach, which is a combination of Torah, Nevaim, and Ketuvim; the Torah (teachings, instruction, first five books of the Old Testament), prophets, and writings. He's saying, "I'm in every book of the Bible, Genesis to Revelation. Search for Me."

Hebrews 10:7: Then said I, Lo, I come (in the volume of the book it is written of me,) to do your will, O God.

Psalms 40:7–8: 7. Then said I, Lo, I come: in the volume of the book it is written of me, 8. I delight to do your will, O my God: yes, your law is within my heart.

See the above on the "aleph–tav" in the Book of Genesis.

185.   John 6:27

Labor not for the food which perishes, but for that food which endures unto everlasting life, which the Son of Man shall give unto you: for him has God the Father sealed.

What more can we say? What is your priority? I hope we all labor in our studies, searching deep to learn of him. Sealed? What is that? Where else in Scripture do we find people that are sealed? In Ezekiel 9:4, the angel is told to put a "mark" on the good men. The word for "mark" in the Hebrew aleph-bet is the *tav*, tahv, which is pronounced as our "T" in English.

In the Book of Revelation, Chapter 7, an angel has "the seal of God" to give to the "servants of God." We see another group that receive another mark or seal, the mark of the beast. So what "seal" represents Yeshua? The Father has authorized and authenticated the Son as the Giver of Life. He "seals" us with his mark when we are saved.

The word for "mark" that God told Ezekiel to put on the foreheads of the priests in Ezekiel 9:4 in Hebrew is *Tavah*, or *Tav*. In ancient Hebrew, the letter tav was a cross, see the tav on the chart.

Here is a chart on ancient Hebrew. The one on the left is the ancient tav, or taw as it was called then, and is a cross.

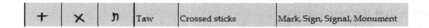

| + | ✕ | ת | Taw | Crossed sticks | Mark, Sign, Signal, Monument |

So, Ezekiel was putting the sign of the cross on their foreheads.

I believe the mark that God will put on the Israelites' foreheads when they flee at the three and a half year period of the tribulation is the tav, or cross.

The Bible says we are marked. I believe we have the sign of the cross on our foreheads, or "seal."

Revelation 7:2-3: 2. And I saw another angel ascending from the east, having the seal of the living God: and he cried with a loud voice to the four angels, to whom it was given to hurt the earth and the sea, 3. Saying, Hurt not the earth, neither the sea, nor the trees, till we have sealed the servants of our God in their foreheads.

So, the servants of God receive a 'seal' in their foreheads.

186.   John 6:41–43

41. The Jews then murmured at him, because he said, I am the bread which came down from heaven. 42. And they said, Is not this Jesus, the son of Joseph, whose father and mother we know? How is it then that he says, I came down from heaven? 43. Jesus therefore answered and said unto them, Murmur not among yourselves.

Youch! Murmur not. Miriam got in dire trouble in the Book of Numbers, chapter 12, when she murmured to Aaron about Moses having another wife. How much more are we to be judged if we murmur against him or against others?

Of course, the "bread" that came down from heaven" is the manna in the wilderness that fed the children of Israel for almost 40 years. He says in another place, "I am the bread of life." There are so many pictures and symbols of the Messiah in the Old Testament. This is one of them. The Word of God is described as bread. This is the bread that feeds our spirit that we need daily.

Read verses 43 through 68. Fascinating insight into the reaction of "the Jews" when he makes this statement. Of course, it wasn't ALL Jews, it was a group of men, just as it wasn't ALL the Pharisees who were always condemning him. His statement again opens a door into the pictures of the Messiah in the Torah. Again, this speaks of "in the volume of the Book it is written of me." There is so much in these Scriptures. I pray you will meditate upon them.

187.   John 7:24

Judge not according to the appearance, but judge righteous judgment.
Proverbs 24:23.

Youch again. Don't be so quick to judge someone unless you know the whole story. Here he is speaking of the fact that he healed a man on the Sabbath. In Jewish law, caring for a sick person takes priority over the Sabbath. It is a mitzvah, a good deed. If a boy is born, he must be circumcised on the eighth day, Sabbath or not. That's the commandment. Of course, now we know that vitamin K peaks on the eighth day, the clotting factor in our blood. If circumcision is done before the eighth day, the surgeon has to give the baby a shot of vitamin K to clot the blood.

It's a wonderful thing to follow how the Jewish people obey because they're told to. They don't ask, "Why?" They just obey. Oh, if we could just follow their example. They obey to please the Father. What a joy to have observed them these last fifteen years or so and see how faithful and obedient they are. Lord, please help us to not question you or your commandments, but just to do them because we want to please you and obey you.

188.   John 12:35-36

35. Then Jesus said unto them, Yet a little while is the light with you. Walk while you have the light, lest darkness come upon you: for he that walks in darkness knows not whither he goes.
36. While you have light, believe in the light, that you may be the children of light. These things spoke Jesus, and departed, and did hide himself from them.
John 1:9, 7:33, 8:12, Ephesians 5:8, I John 2:9–11, Luke 16:8, John 8:59.

Wow. Just think of what he said. "The light is with you." Right here. You know the Book of Revelation tells us:

Revelation 21:23. And the city had no need of the sun, neither of the moon, to shine in it: for the glory of God did lighten it, and the Lamb is the light thereof.

That's because HE will be there, the Lamb of God that takes away the sins of the world. The Light of the World.

John 13:1–12: 1. Now before the Feast of the Passover, when Jesus knew that his hour was come that he should depart out of this world unto the Father, having loved his own which were in the world, he loved them unto the end. 2. And supper being ended, the devil having now put into the heart of Judas Iscariot, Simon's son, to betray him; 3. Jesus knowing that the Father had given all things into his hands, and that he was come from God, and went to God; 4. He rose from supper, and laid aside his garments; and took a towel, and girded himself. 5. After that he poured water into a basin, and began to wash the disciples' feet, and to wipe them with the towel wherewith he was girded. 6. Then comes he to Simon Peter: and Peter says unto him, Lord, do you wash my feet? 7. Jesus answered and said unto him, What I do you know not now; but you shall know hereafter. 8. Peter says unto him, you shall never wash my feet. Jesus answered him, If I wash you not, you have no part with me.

9. Simon Peter says unto him, Lord, not my feet only, but also my hands and my head. 10. Jesus says to him, He that is washed needs not save to wash his feet, but is clean every whit: and you are clean, but not all. 11. For he knew who should betray him; therefore said he, You are not all clean. 12. So after he had washed their feet, and had taken his garments, and was set down again, he said unto them, Know you what I have done to you?

189.   John 13:13–17

13. You call me Master and Lord: and you say well; for so I am. 14. If I then, your Lord and Master, have washed your feet; you

also ought to wash one another's feet. 15. For I have given you an example, that you should do as I have done to you. 16. Verily, verily, I say unto you, the servant is not greater than his Lord; neither he that is sent greater than he that sent him. 17. If you know these things, happy are you if you do them.
Luke 22:27, Romans 12:10, I Peter 2:21–24.

So, let's take a look at the implications here. The second chapter of this book was on the Priesthood of Melchizedek and the Order we as believers in Yeshua/Jesus are under, the Messiah/Priest/King.

Could he be performing a ritual here in this chapter to anoint or inaugurate the disciples into the Order of Melchizedek? A ceremony anointing the priests of the New Covenant? The washing of the priest's feet with the laver in the Torah was a picture of what was to come, their service in the Temple. Now here King, Messiah, High Priest Yeshua/Jesus is inducting us into the Kingdom! He says that we should be doing this, but few these days really do this. If they do they build it up as if it were a new thing and that they are doing something extraordinary. We haven't really understood what this means. It has just been a ceremony to us.

Isn't he saying here we should be doing this regularly? If a person comes to Yeshua/Jesus and asks him into his heart and accepts the covenant, shouldn't we wash his feet? Something to think about and not ignore. You can't say, "This is an Old Testament ritual."

Never did the Levitical priests wash anyone else's feet. They did it themselves at the laver. Abraham did not wash the visitor's feet. He gave them water and they washed their own feet. It was a custom in that day to give visitors water to wash their feet after a long journey.

Genesis 18:4: Abraham says, "Please let a little water be brought, and wash your feet, and rest yourselves under the tree."

I can't find anywhere in the Torah/Old Testament where anyone washed another's feet.

If we do this ceremony for the new believers, we're welcoming and anointing them, inaugurating them into the New Covenant, the Order of Melchizedek. The Messiah/Priest/King covenant with Yeshua/Jesus through the blood. He commands us to do this and most of us don't. We need to bring this back into the churches.

What is the commandment here? Do as he did. Follow his commandments. What do we as parents say and do? Speak as examples, act as examples. The student following the teacher.

There are a couple of references to washing of feet in the Torah/Old Testament in the incident of the angels coming to Lot's house; however, he told them in Genesis 19:2:

> And he said, Behold now, my Lords, turn in, I pray you, into your servant's house, and tarry all night, and wash your feet, and you shall rise up early, and go on your ways. And they said, No; but we will abide in the street all night.

So he invited them to wash their own feet.

The other place in the Torah concerning foot washing is in Exodus 30:17-21. The Levites were to go to the laver and wash their hands and feet before serving in the Temple. This is not a ritual for cleanliness physically, but spiritually. "Lord, I come before you with clean hands and a clean heart." It is symbolic and stands for "dedication."

So what is Our Lord saying here? Is he saying that he is anointing his disciples as priests? Is he doing this symbolically as was done in the Temple? Is he saying, "I wash your feet, now you wash each other's feet in obedience, saying you accept your brother as a priest?

They say that 80% of the Bible is in Temple language. If you've never studied the Tabernacle or Temple you need to in order to learn Temple language.

Now that we've said all that, let's go back and start at verse 34 in Chapter 13.

190.   John 13:34-35:

34. A new commandment I give unto you, That you love one another; as I have loved you, that you also love one another. 35. By this shall all men know that you are my disciples, if you have love one to another.
I Thessalonians 4:9, I John 2:5.

By this! By what? A new commandment! Love one another! Is this one of the ten? No, but "Love your neighbor as yourself" is certainly one.

It is an awesome thing to meet a brother or sister in the Lord. It's an awesome thing to have unity amongst the brethren. When you meet another and the link between you is your love for the Lord Yeshua/Jesus the Mashiach/Messiah, it is a powerful thing. There's no love like it on earth. This love will last for eternity.

Keep in mind that the second temple was destroyed ultimately because of causeless hatred for their brothers.

> From the Talmud, Yoma 9b: Why was the first Sanctuary destroyed? Because of three (evil) things that prevailed there: idolatry, immorality, and bloodshed... But why was the second Sanctuary destroyed, since in that time they were occupying themselves with Torah, (observance of) mitzvos (*good deeds*), and the practice of charity? At that time causeless hatred prevailed. That teaches you that causeless hatred is considered of equal gravity with the three sins of idolatry, immorality, and bloodshed together.

By the way, both Temples were destroyed on Av 9 on the Jewish calendar, which coincides to the day the ten spies brought back the bad report. This day is considered the saddest day in Jewish history. Many other tragedies happened to Israel over the years on this day also.

Let us not enter into any kind of church split or condemnation of a brother without a cause. We need much prayer and fasting in situations like this and going through the proper channels. Let us not be guilty of false accusations and being the cause of someone turning away from the Lord. "Love the brethren."

191.   John 14:1

Let not your heart be troubled: you believe in God, believe also in me.
John 14:27, 6:22, 24.

Commandment: Believe. How can we be "commanded" to believe? The next three verses are the familiar, "In my Father's House are many mansions," or dwelling places. He says in verse 1, "Let not your heart be troubled." He had just predicted Peter's denial. Of course their hearts would be troubled lest they, too, deny him. How do we come to "belief?"

Romans 10:17: Faith comes by hearing, and hearing by the Word of God.

Studying the Bible builds our faith and belief. Faith and belief go hand in hand. If I believe, I have faith. We need to study God's Word, listen to speakers of his Word, pray, and communicate with other believers.

Jude 20-21: 20. But you, beloved, building up yourselves on your most holy faith, praying in the Holy Spirit, 21. keep yourselves in the love of God, looking for the mercy of our Lord Jesus Christ unto eternal life.

Keeping ourselves "in the love of God" is all the above. Staying in communication with the Lord.

192.   John 14:11

Believe me that I am in the Father, and the Father in me: or else believe me for the very works' sake.
John 5:36, 10:38.

Here we have a "believe" verse again. This time he's saying if you believe I'm really the Messiah, then you believe that I am "in" the Father and the Father is "in" me. He's saying, "I and the Father are one." Or, if you can't believe just for that, believe him for the works he did.

193.   John 14:13-14

13. And whatsoever you shall ask in my name, that will I do, that the Father may be glorified in the Son. 14. If you shall ask anything in my name, I will do it.
Matthew 7:7, John 13:31.

This Scripture does not give us the open door to pile upon ourselves riches, but he is giving an example of faith. ASK is the key word here. Not many prayers are answered instantly, but James 5:16 says,

Confess your faults one to another, and pray one for another, that you may be healed. The effectual fervent prayer of a righteous man avails much.

Keep praying and believing.

Remember we talked about Daniel in our study on Luke 18:6 when he was mourning for three full weeks? Finally, "a man" shows up. The description of him is fantastic.

Daniel 10:5-6: Then I lifted up mine eyes, and looked, and behold a certain man clothed in linen, whose loins were girded with fine gold of Uphaz: 6. His body also was like the beryl, and his face as the appearance of lightning, and his eyes as lamps of fire, and his arms and his feet like in color to polished brass, and the voice of his words like the voice of a multitude.

Daniel seems to be thinking, "Where have you been! I've been praying for 21 days!" (Paraphrased) This "man" gives Daniel insight to what has been going on, and so also we get a peek into what goes on when we pray.

> Daniel 10:11–13: 11. And he said unto me, O Daniel, a man greatly beloved, understand the words that I speak unto you, and stand upright: for unto you am I now sent. And when he had spoken this word unto me, I stood trembling. 12. Then said he unto me, Fear not, Daniel: for from the first day that you did set your heart to understand, and to chasten yourself before your God, your words were heard, and I am come for your words. 13. But the prince of the Kingdom of Persia withstood me one and twenty days: but, lo, Michael, one of the chief princes, came to help me; and I remained there with the kings of Persia.

We'd like to go into "who" is this mysterious man, but the point being that even this "man" had to withstand the enemy and get help. If we fervently pray and believe, we're shown here that God will send us "help" in times of need and danger. Never give up and think that he does not hear. Keep the faith and believe.

194.   John 14:15

If you love me, keep my commandments.
1 John 5:3.

> 1 John 5:3–5: 3. For this is the love of God, that we keep his commandments: and his commandments are not burdensome. 4. For whatsoever is born of God overcomes the world: and this is the victory that overcomes the world, even our faith. 5. Who is he that overcomes the world, but he that believes that Jesus is the Son of God?

Whose commandments? His. What are HIS commandments? That is our study. As believers in Yeshua/Jesus, we are to keep HIS commandments and we need to study and learn what he expects of us precisely. What covenant are WE under? What commandments does he expect us to follow? If they were the same, wouldn't he say so? Wouldn't he say, "Keep the Sinaitic Covenants"? Wouldn't he say, "Keep the 613 commandments"? But he didn't. Why did he die on the cross if keeping the 613 commandments given in the Torah would save us? No, he says, "Keep MY commandments."

195. John 14:27

Peace I leave with you, my peace I give unto you: not as the world gives, give I unto you. Let not your heart be troubled, neither let it be afraid.
Philippians 4:7.

Praise the Lord that we do not need to count on this present world to bring us peace. He said in another place: "Think not that I am come to send peace on earth: I came not to send peace, but a sword." Matthew 10:34.

When you become a believer in Yeshua/Jesus, it brings a sword between you and the ruler of this world, but he is saying here, "MY peace I give you." HIS peace is beyond understanding to the world, but when he comes into your heart, your life, and indwells you with HIS spirit, that is the heavenly peace he is speaking about.

The second commandment here is not to let your heart be troubled! That is hard to do when you are going through trials, when you see your family drifting away from the Lord, when you see your grandchildren and great-grandchildren not going to church or being taught about God, when a loved one is sick or in trouble. Very hard.

It's hard for your heart not to be troubled when the doctor has just announced the words, "You have cancer."

It's hard when we go through many circumstances in our lives that we don't understand. But he's standing there saying, "Let not your heart be troubled, neither let it be afraid."

Many believers in Yeshua/Jesus as the Mashiach/Messiah have been martyred for their faith through the ages. Do you think their hearts were troubled? Do you think they were afraid? But he offers to bring peace in any situation. He is always there with us. He never leaves us or forsakes us. Believe.

196. John 15:4-5

4. Abide in me, and I in you. As the branch cannot bear fruit of itself, except it abide in the vine; no more can you, except you abide in me. 5. I am the vine, you are the branches: He that abides in me, and I in him, the same brings forth much fruit: for without me you can do nothing.
Colossians 1:23, Hosea 14:8, 2 Corinthians 3:5.

This chapter is the "vine" chapter. "Abide in me." If I "abide" somewhere, I live there. If we drift away from the root, we're not abiding. We've separated from the foundation. If we abide in HIS house, that includes ALL of him. We accept His Jewishness, His Messiahship, His Kingdom, and His Commandments. We become connected to the foundation, the root of where it all started, the Torah, Genesis 1:1, and on to the end of Revelation, chapter 22:21. He is that root. The entire Bible is our foundation. We can only abide in him if we believe. Then the learning begins. We can only learn if we study, pray, and have fellowship with one another and build one another up in the "Holy Faith."

He says we can't bear fruit unless we're abiding in him. Paul speaks a lot about being "in him."

197.   John 15:9–11

9. As the Father has loved me, so have I loved you: continue you in my love. 10. If you keep my commandments, you shall abide in my love; even as I have kept my Father's commandments, and abide in his love. 11. These things have I spoken unto you, that my joy might remain in you, and that your joy might be full.

My commandments. My Father's commandments. Keep MY commandments. He differentiates HIS commandments from the FATHER'S commandments here.

Continue in MY love. What love is that? A love that has no limits, no boundaries, no racial boundaries, no respecter of person's boundary. HIS love is pure and from above. We cannot have that love completely without him indwelling us by his Holy Spirit.

Many books have been written about this chapter in John. Many hundreds of sermons have been preached. Can we ever conceive in our minds that we ARE in him? Over and over he tells us that. Just believe.

198.   John 15:12

This is my commandment, That you love one another, as I have loved you.
I John 3:11, Romans 12:9.

Every morning and evening the Jews say a prayer called the Shema, as discussed before. "Hear O Israel, the Lord our God is one." Then the v'ahavta, "You shall love your neighbor as yourself, I am the Lord." Reminding us twice a day that we're not alone. We are part of our neighbor. We are to respect and protect and love them.

A commandment to love? We can't just force ourselves to love someone. It has to be by the Holy Spirit. It takes a lot of prayer sometimes for you to love me, but God will help you see things in me or others that you can connect to and love through that. Then the true love will grow from the Holy Spirit.

199.   John 15:17

These things I command you, that you love one another.

This after the verse that says,

> John 15:16: You have not chosen me, but I have chosen you, and ordained you, that you should go and bring forth fruit, and that your fruit should remain: that whatsoever you shall ask of the Father in my name, he may give it you.

So these are the "things" he is commanding us. This is in the same sermon as verse 13.

> John 15:13-15: Greater love has no man than this, that a man lay down his life for his friends. 14. You are my friends, if you do whatsoever I command you. 15. Henceforth I call you not servants; for the servant knows not what his Lord does: but I have called you friends; for all things that I have heard of my Father I have made known unto you.

> John 15:16. You have not chosen me, but I have chosen you, and ordained you, that you should go and bring forth fruit, and that your fruit should remain: that whatsoever you shall ask of the Father in my name, he may give it you.

What is our fruit? For one thing, we first must be attached to the vine. If not, we're living our own way, going our own way. To be attached to the vine means we've accepted Yeshua/Jesus as our Savior and are living for him. John 15:1–16 is Yeshua's/Jesus' sermon on fruit.

We can be secure that we are grafted into the vine. He will never leave us or forsake us. We are legally bought and paid for. He says that we are "in him." How much closer can we get? He calls us "friends." Wow! I'm a friend of God! The creator of the universe! The creator of me! Of course we're bearing fruit if we're connected to the source! Sometimes he has to prune us, but he does this lovingly and gently. We're abiding! We're dwelling with him! One way that others know we belong to him is through our obedience to him, our love for others, and our testimony.

Don't be like those that will be cast out, as in John 15:6:

> If anyone does not abide in me, he is cast out as a branch and is withered; and they gather them and throw [them] into the fire, and they are burned.

Sometimes we don't even realize we're drifting away until it's almost too late. Stay close to him.

John 15:35 says "By this." By this they shall know. Know what? That we are his. I know a lot of us are hard to love. We cannot do this naturally. We need the Holy Spirit to give us that love for one another, a spiritual love the world does not understand.

> John 15:35: By this shall all men know that you are my disciples, if you have love one to another.

200.   John 16:24

> Hitherto have you asked nothing in my name: ask, and you shall receive, that your joy may be full.
> John 17:13, John 15:11.

Again, this is one of my favorite verses. How can we receive if we don't ASK! Here he commands us to ask! Why? That our joy may be full. We go on and on sometimes in our lives in misery, wondering where we went wrong, how did these things happen, etc. He is standing there waiting, telling us to simply ask. And keep asking. Remember Daniel's prayer that seemed to not be answered and the answer came after 21 days. We might have to pray longer than 21 days. We might have to pray for years for a loved one to be saved, but never give up, keep praying fervently.

Again, we see in Daniel that he had to battle through what was going on in the heavenlies. Sometimes we think God doesn't hear our prayers, but if we could see into the invisible realm around us or around that loved one, we would pray harder! Prayer IS our battle weapon! The only one!

2 Corinthians 10:3–6: 3. For though we walk in the flesh, we do not war after the flesh: 4. (For the weapons of our warfare are not carnal, but mighty through God to the pulling down of strongholds;) 5. Casting down imaginations, and every high thing that exalts itself against the knowledge of God, and bringing into captivity every thought to the obedience of Christ; 6. And having in a readiness to revenge all disobedience, when your obedience is fulfilled.

201.   John 16:33

These things I have spoken unto you, that in me you might have peace. In the world you shall have tribulation: but be of good cheer; I have overcome the world.
Ephesians 2:14, 2 Timothy 3:12, Romans 8:37.

Our commandment, "Be of good cheer." What a comforting verse. No matter what we're going through, no matter what the world is going through, no matter what our country is going through, "Be of good cheer." Have confidence that he has everything under his control: Your life, the world, our country. He is in charge. Even though what we physically see seems bleak, "Be of good cheer." That might be a good statement to make to each other!

202.   John 20:22

And when he had said this, he breathed on them, and said unto them, Receive you the Holy Ghost.

John 16:20–22.

This Yeshua/Jesus said after he had been resurrected! He knew that they needed more than their own wit and knowledge. They had no power of their own. He breathed on them here and gave them a taste of what was to come at Shavuot/Pentecost 50 days later, the outpouring of the Holy Spirit on the disciples in the upper room. It is not by ourselves, not by flesh and blood, but by his Spirit that we can be victorious. No one but God the Creator could breathe on us and give us power and life.

203.   John 21:15–17:

15. So when they had dined, Jesus said to Simon Peter, "Simon, son of John, Do you love me more than these?" He said unto him, "Yes, Lord; you know that I love you." He said unto him, "Feed my lambs." 16. He said to him again the second time, "Simon, son of John, do you love me?" He said unto him, "Yes, Lord; you know that I love you." He said unto him, "Feed my sheep." 17. He said unto him the third time, "Simon, son of John, do you love me?" Peter was grieved because he said unto him the third time, "Do you love me?" And he said unto him, "Lord, you know all things; you know that I love you." Jesus said unto him, "Feed my sheep."
Acts 20:28.

"Feed my sheep." Here we have Yeshua/Jesus reminding Peter of his frailty of spirit in denying him before the crucifixion. He asks him three times, the same amount of times that Peter denied him. We also need to be reminded sometimes of our frailty of spirit. We need the Holy Spirit in order to be able to overcome and be victorious. We cannot always stand in our own flesh. We desperately need him to give us strength and power to overcome, then we can feed his sheep.

"Do you love me more than these?" The "these" are the other disciples. Of course we need to love our brothers and sisters in the Lord, but not more than we love the Lord. We need to love our husband or wife, but not more than we love the Lord. If we're not putting him above everything else in our life, we need to do some deep seeking.

204.   John 21:18-19

18. Verily, verily, I say unto you, When you were young, you girded yourself, and walked whither you would: but when you are old, you shall stretch forth your hands, and another shall gird you, and carry you whither you would not. 19. This spoke he, signifying by what death he should glorify God. And when he had spoken this, he says unto him, Follow me.
Acts 12:3–4.

This is such a beautiful verse. The Lord let Peter see a glimpse of his future and how he would be at the end of his life. What love the Master had for him. It is traditionally held that he was crucified upside down at his own request, since he saw himself unworthy to be crucified in the same way as Yeshua/Jesus.

Back to the beginning. He leaves Peter with the same invitation he called him with at the first, "Follow me." I am sure Peter's mind went back to that beautiful time when they met the Messiah for whom that had all been watching. Peter met him while he was just doing his regular job, fishing. Just an ordinary day. But there Yeshua/Jesus stood and turned that day into the beginning of the rest of Peter's life. Peter became the disciple to the Jewish people. He was totally changed and empowered at Shavuot/Pentecost.

Just follow me. Keep it simple. Do what I do. Watch me. See how I minister to people. See how I react to diversity. Watch my life. Learn from me. What a bittersweet time between the Lord and Peter. I'm sure the last three and a half years ran through Peter's mind as he stood there, remembering the wonderful years of following him, hearing his teachings, learning so much from him, loving him, believing in him, and then as his heart dashed to the ground, remembering his betrayal, remembering the shame of being a traitor, now to have the Lord forgive him in such a beautiful way.

Doesn't the Lord do the same with us? Doesn't he remind us of a betrayal to get our attention, then he so lovingly smooths our brow and says, "Follow me."

Peter is my favorite disciple. He had no fear, except at the end before the crucifixion. He walked on water! He cut the ear off the chief priest's servant! I love his fire and zeal, and I love his heart for the Lord. What a day for him to stand there with Yeshua/Jesus and be reminded of his shortcomings, yet be given this simple command, filling him with hope again. He became a changed man when the Holy Spirit was poured out. He was so anointed to preach the good news. He preached a powerful sermon on the day the Holy Spirit was poured out. He was faithful to the end. He refused to go against the Torah and go to the house of a Gentile! But then being obedient to do that because the Lord told him, "It's okay. Go." What a beautiful man. What a beautiful life. Fiery Peter.

All we need to do is be like Peter. Just follow Yeshua/Jesus. Don't run ahead or lag behind. Keep up! And just follow him with everything that's within us. Obey him.

Only in being attached to the source can we follow him. Only by the Holy Spirit can we be strengthened and empowered to take up our cross daily and follow him.

205:   John 21:21–23

21. Peter seeing him (John) says to Jesus, Lord, and what shall this man do? 22. Jesus says unto him, If I will that he tarry till I come, what is that to you? Follow you me. 23. Then went this saying abroad among the brethren, that that disciple should not die: yet Jesus said not unto him, He shall not die; but, If I will that he tarry till I come, what is that to you?

Another "follow me" verse. Jesus was talking to Peter here.

YOU mind your own business, Peter. Yeshua/Jesus wasn't saying John was never going to die, but telling Peter that John's calling and plan was between John and the Lord. We need to mind our own business and not worry about God's plan for others. We have no idea of their calling. It is a one-on-one thing between each one of us and God.

Sure we need to pray for our children, that they will listen to God's calling on their lives. We need to pray for others that they will obey God's call on their lives, but we don't know what that is and it isn't up to us to think we know. Like Peter.

Be obedient to His commandments. And be not troubled.

Epilogue

So now we see that in the gospel books of the New Covenant the key is and the answer to the mystery is that there are at least 205 commandments given to believers in Yeshua/Jesus. You may find more, you may find less, or disagree with me about some, but the gist of the book is that we, as New Believers in Yeshua/Jesus, do have rules to follow. They are not our salvation, but our "works," as James says. They do not save us, but are a sign that we are followers of the Messiah.

I have had great joy in writing this book, delving into the Master's Words, spending a lot of time with him in prayer and gleaning from his Words. I am by no means a Bible Scholar, but I do spend, and have spent, a great deal of time studying the Bible.

I pray that you will be blessed by this book. I pray that you, too, will see that we are not "lawless," but do have a definite set of commandments to follow. The Torah is our moral guidebook to reveal the Heart of God to us. We see by reading it that he loved his people so much and wanted them to be able to commune with him daily.

He feels the same about us. He desires that you know him in an intimate, deep relationship. In order to have that relationship, we need to know what he expects of us, just as a child needs to know what it takes to please his parents.

I pray that this book will open up to you his Heart and draw you ever closer to him. Meditate on his Word daily, "Old" and "New" Testaments, and get to know him, not as a God that is way up there judging us and looking down on us, but as our Father, Yeshua/Jesus, the Creator God, living IN us! Let him speak to your heart and lead you into all understanding on what he expects of us in order for us to have that personal relationship with him.

Don't rush through the Word. When we were in Israel, we went to the excavated town of Chorizim near the Sea of Galilee. The synagogue there had been excavated somewhat. There were some stairs leading into it. We all started to go in, but our guide, Gilla, stopped us. She said, "See how there is one wide step and then two narrower steps? This is how the steps always are that go into the synagogues and the Southern steps going into the Temple. This tells us to never rush into the House of God, to take our time, to meditate on him. You step on the wide step and have to take another step on that one, which slows you down, then you go, step, step onto the other ones. This is also how we need to study God's Word. Never rush through it. Stop and meditate on what you are reading. Study it. Look up words. Study their meanings."

That concept changed the way I study. I could spend a month at least on the first verse in Genesis. Let him speak to you. He can't if you're in a rush. Remember, all these words are his. They are him. John 1:1.

In my next book, we will go through the commandments in The Book of Acts through The Book of Revelation.

My Life Scripture

1 John 3:1–24

1. Behold, what manner of love the Father has bestowed upon us, that we should be called the sons of God: therefore the world knows us not, because it knew him not. 2. Beloved, now are we the sons of God, and it does not yet appear what we shall be: but we know that, when he shall appear, we shall be like him; for we shall see him as he is. 3. And every man that has this hope in him purifies himself, even as he is pure. 4. Whosoever commits sin transgresses also the law: for sin is the transgression of the law. 5. And you know that he was manifested to take away our sins; and in him is no sin. 6. Whosoever abides in him sins not: whosoever sins has not seen him, neither known him. 7. Little children, let no man deceive you: he that does righteousness is righteous, even as he is righteous. 8. He that commits sin is of the devil; for the devil sins from the beginning. For this purpose the Son of God was manifested, that he might destroy the works of the devil. 9. Whosoever is born of God does not commit sin; for his seed remains in him: and he cannot sin, because he is born of God. 10. In this the children of God are manifest, and the children of the devil: whosoever does not righteousness is not of God, neither he that loves not his brother. 11. For this is the message that you heard from the beginning, that we should love one another. 12. Not as Cain, [who] was of that wicked one, and slew his brother. And wherefore slew he him? Because his own works were evil, and his brother's righteous. 13. Marvel not, my brethren, if the world hate you. 14. We know that we have passed from death unto life, because we love the brethren. He that loves not [his] brother abides in

death. 15. Whosoever hates his brother is a murderer: and you know that no murderer has eternal life abiding in him. 16. Hereby perceive we the love [of God], because he laid down his life for us: and we ought to lay down [our] lives for the brethren. 17. But whoso has this world's good, and sees his brother have need, and shuts up his bowels [of compassion] from him, how dwells the love of God in him? 18. My little children, let us not love in word, neither in tongue; but in deed and in truth. 19. And hereby we know that we are of the truth, and shall assure our hearts before him. 20. For if our heart condemn us, God is greater than our heart, and knows all things. 21. Beloved, if our heart condemn us not, [then] have we confidence toward God. 22. And whatsoever we ask, we receive of him, because we keep his commandments, and do those things that are pleasing in his sight. 23. And this is his commandment, That we should believe on the name of his Son Jesus Christ, and love one another, as he gave us commandment. 24. And he that keeps his commandments dwells in him, and he in him. And hereby we know that he abides in us, by the Spirit which he has given us.

Notes and References

INTRODUCTION

p. 4   PC Bible, *Biblesoft.com.*

            Blueletterbible.org.

p. 6   Heart of Wisdom: *http://www.heartofwisdom.com/homeschoollinks/ greek-vs-hebrew-education* (October 31, 2014)

p. 9   Torah Resource: Part one: *http://www.torahresource.com/ EnglishArticles/BigFatGreekMindsetPart1.pdf*

            Torah Resource: *Part two: http://www.torahresource.com/ EnglishArticles/BigFatGreekMindSetPart2.pdf* (October 31, 2014)

PREFACE

p. 22   Dead Sea Scrolls on Melchizedek. *http://en.wikipedia.org/wiki/11Q13.* (October 31, 2014)

p. 23   Arthur Pink, Hebrews. First published as a series of sermons and articles in a magazine he wrote, then put into a book by a publisher after he died. *An Exposition of Hebrews by A.W. Pink.* Now available online free: *http://www.pbministries.org/books/pink/Hebrews/index.htm.* (October 31, 2014)

CHAPTER ONE: MATTHEW

p. 17   *Blueletterbible.org.*

p. 33   *Blueletterbible.org*, Lexicon.

p. 40.   Jacob Neusner's, *The Mishnah, A New Translation.* (Yale University Press, New Haven and London, Copyright 1988 by Yale University) 869.

http://en.wikipedia.org/wiki/Alfred_Edersheim. (October 31, 2014)

Alfred Edersheim: The Temple: Its Ministry and Services: (London, 1874) http://www.piney.com/Edersheim4.html#Temple. (October 31, 2014)

p. 42   Zacharias Presenting Incense in the Temple. *http://www.realtime. net/~wdoud/topics/zachrias.html.* (October 31, 2014)

p. 43   Priestly Divisions: Never Thirsty: *http://www.neverthirsty.org/pp/ series/Life/LH004/LH03.html.* (October 31, 2014)

http://jewishencyclopedia.com/articles/14303-temple-administration-and-service-of. (October 31, 2014)

Mikveh. *http://www.chabad.org/theJewishWoman/article_cdo/ aid/1541/jewish/The-Mikveh.htm.* (October 31, 2014)

Priestly divisions: *http://en.wikipedia.org/wiki/Priestly_divisions.* (October 31, 2014)

p. 44   Allen Ross, February 2, 2009: *https://bible.org/seriespage/priests.* (October 31, 2014)

p. 45   Caiaphas: *http://en.wikipedia.org/wiki/Caiaphas.* (October 31, 2014)

p. 57   Salt covenant: *http://ourcovenantGod.com/pdf/saltcovenant.pdf.* (October 31, 2014)

p. 59   Messiah ben Yosef: *http://www.hebrew4christians.com/Articles/ Mashiach_ben_Yosef/mashiach_ben_yosef.html.* (October 31, 2014)

p. 65   Dr. Masaru Emoto, *Messages from Water.* (Tokyo: Hado, 2000) *http://www.highexistence.com/water-experiment.* (October 31, 2014)

p. 70   Biblical Faith Ministries, *http://bfm101.com.* (October 31, 2014)

p. 71   *Hebrew Gospels, http://vineofdavid.org/resources/dhe/the-delitzsch-hebrew-gospels.* (October 31, 2014)

p. 80   *Blueletterbible.org.*

p. 90   From Jerome's commentary:
         http://www.textexcavation.com/gospelhebrews.html. (October 31, 2014)

         Rabbi Avraham Sutton, Spiritual Technology.
         http://www.avrahamsutton.com. (October 31, 2014)

p. 92   Wearing linen and wool: Quoted from *The Hirsch Chumash* by Rabbi
         Samson Raphael Hirsch with permission of Feldheim Publishers, page
         634 in The Hirsch Chumash on Vayikra/Leviticus.

p. 94   The Lord's Prayer table: *http://yashanet.com/studies/matstudy/mat6d.htm*.
         (October 31, 2014)

p. 95   John Parson, *hebrew4christians.org*. Portion reading for the week of
         July 20, 2013.

p. 96   Joseph Good, Hatikva Ministries. *Hatikva.org.*

p. 103   Carey Kinsolving, *Why Did Jesus say, "Don't Cast Your Pearls Before Swine?"*
         Article Source: *http://EzineArticles.com/313907*. (October 31, 2014)

p. 104   On unity: Yashanet.com: *http://www.yashanet.com/studies/matstudy/*
         mat6e.htm. (October 31, 2014)

p. 107   *The Gospel According To the Hebrews: http://www.textexcavation.*
         com/gospelhebrews.html. (October 31, 2014)

p. 117   NU–Text: Nestle–Aland Greek New Testament (N) and United Bible
         Societies' third edition (U), Hence the acronym "NU–Text." The
         "NU–Text is from the twenty–sixth edition of the Nestle–Aland New
         Testament (N) and in the United Bible Socities' third edition (U);
         hence the acronym "NU–Text."

p. 122   *What is the meaning of Matthew 10:23* by Wayne Jackson.
         https://www.christiancourier.com/
         articles/668-what-is-the-meaning-of-matthew-10:23.

p. 126   *The Yoke of Heaven*, David Stern. Taken from the Complete Jewish Bible
         Commentary by David H. Stern. Copyright © 1998. All rights reserved.
         Used by permission of Messianic Jewish Publishers, 6120 Day Long Lane,
         Clarksville, MD 21029. http://en.wikipedia.org/wiki/David_H._Stern, 44.

p. 137   Wearing tzit–tzit: http://www.jewfaq.org/signs.htm#Tzitzit. (October
         31, 2014)

p. 150   *30 Days To Understanding The Bible, Max Anders.* (Thomas Nelson, Inc., 2011)
        Learn The Bible In 24 Hours, Chuck Missler. (Thomas Nelson, Inc., 2011)

CHAPTER TWO: MARK

p. 154   "Good tidings." Lexicon from *Blueletterbible.org.*

p. 170   Biblical Faith Ministries with Sam Peak, *http://bfm101.com.* (October 31, 2014)

        Delitzsch Hebrew Gospels, http://vineofdavid.org/resources/dhe/the-delitzsch-hebrew-gospels. (October 31, 2014).

CHAPTER THREE: LUKE

p. 199   *"The Sermon on the Plain."* Taken from the Complete Jewish Bible Commentary by David H. Stern. Copyright © 1998. All rights reserved. Used by permission of Messianic Jewish Publishers, 6120 Day Long Lane, Clarksville, MD 21029.

p. 201   The Delitzsch Hebrew Gospels, *http://vineofdavid.org/resources/dhe/the-delitzsch-hebrew-gospels.*

p. 207   The Delitzsch Hebrew Gospels, *http://vineofdavid.org/resources/dhe/the-delitzsch-hebrew-gospels.*

        Siriach 1:29: *http://www.biblestudytools.com/nrsa/ben-sira/1.html.* 11/12/14.
        Siriach 32:15: *http://www.biblestudytools.com/nrsa/ben-sira/32.html.*

p. 209   The Delitzsch Hebrew Gospels, *http://vineofdavid.org/resources/dhe/the-delitzsch-hebrew-gospels.*

p. 213   Story of man who wanted to first bury his father. David Stern on Matthew 8:21–22. Taken from the Complete Jewish Bible Commentary by David H. Stern. Copyright © 1998. All rights reserved. Used by permission of Messianic Jewish Publishers, 6120 Day Long Lane, Clarksville, MD 21029, 35-36.

p. 218   *Names written in heaven.* From David Stern on *Chutzpah.* Taken from the Complete Jewish Bible by David H. Stern. Copyright © 1998. All rights reserved. Used by permission of Messianic Jewish Publishers, 6120 Day Long Lane, Clarksville, MD 21029.

p. 221   Importunity. *Blueletterbible.org.*

p. 222   David Stern on Matthew 6:22 on The Good and Evil Eye. Taken from the Complete Jewish Bible Commentary by David H. Stern. Copyright © 1998. All rights reserved. Used by permission of Messianic Jewish Publishers, 6120 Day Long Lane, Clarksville, MD 21029, 32.

p. 223   From David Stern on Luke 12:15. Taken from the Complete Jewish Bible Commentary by David H. Stern. Copyright © 1998. All rights reserved. Used by permission of Messianic Jewish Publishers, 6120 Day Long Lane, Clarksville, MD 21029, 125.

p. 230   Bible History Online: *http://www.bible-history.com/smiths/W/ Watches+of+night.* (October 31, 2014)

p. 233   *The Jewish Annotated New Testament,* Amy-Jill Levine and Marc Zvi Brettler, New York, Oxford University Press, 2011. 134.

p. 236   From David Stern on Luke 18:6. Taken from the Complete Jewish Bible Commentary by David H. Stern. Copyright © 1998. All rights reserved. Used by permission of Messianic Jewish Publishers, 6120 Day Long Lane, Clarksville, MD 21029, 136.

p. 244   Day of The Lord. *http://en.wikipedia.org/wiki/The_Day_of_the_Lord.* (October 31, 2014)

CHAPTER FOUR: JOHN

p. 251   Thayer's Greek Lexicon "the Word." *Blueletterbible.org.*

p. 252   Copied from PC Study Bible, Bible Soft, Version 4. Hebrew/Greek interlinear.

         The Aleph–Tav. Lexicon. *Blueletterbible.org.*

p. 257   Catholic confessions on the Sabbath. *http://www.biblesabbath.org/ confessions.html.* (October 31, 2014)

p. 261   The Thorn Crown Journal: *http://www.thorncrownjournal.com/ timeofchrist/religiousleaders.html.* (October 31, 2014)

p. 269   The Tav in Ancient Hebrew: Jeff Benner: http://www.ancient-hebrew. org/3_taw.html. (October 31, 2014)

All the Commandments in the New Testament Gospels

King James Version

Scriptures in parentheses are other scriptures used in the main body of the book that make the sentence clearer.

1. Matthew 3:2: (1) 2. And saying, Repent you: for the Kingdom of heaven is at hand.
2. Matthew 3:8: Bring forth therefore fruits meet for repentance:
3. Mathew 3:9–12: 9. And think not to say within yourselves, We have Abraham to [our] father: for I say unto you, that God is able of these stones to raise up children unto Abraham. 10. And now also the axe is laid unto the root of the trees: therefore every tree which brings not forth good fruit is hewn down, and cast into the fire. 11. I indeed baptize you with water unto repentance: but he that comes after me is mightier than I, whose shoes I am not worthy to bear: he shall baptize you with the Holy Ghost, and [with] fire: 12. Whose fan [is] in his hand, and he will thoroughly purge his floor, and gather his wheat into the garner; but he will burn up the chaff with unquenchable fire.
4. Matthew 4:4: But he answered and said, It is written, Man shall not live by bread alone, but by every word that proceeds out of the mouth of God.
5. Matthew 4:7: Jesus said unto him, It is written again, You shall not tempt the Lord your God.

6.   Matthew 4:8–10: 8. Again, the devil took him up into an exceeding high mountain, and showed him all the Kingdoms of the world, and the glory of them; 9. And says unto him, All these things will I give you, if you wilt fall down and worship me. 10. Then says Jesus unto him, Get you hence, Satan: for it is written, You shall worship the Lord your God, and him only shall you serve.

7.   Matthew 4:17: From that time Jesus began to preach, and to say, Repent: for the Kingdom of heaven is at hand.

8.   Matthew 4:19: And he said unto them, Follow me, and I will make you fishers of men.

9.   Matthew 5:12: Rejoice, and be exceeding glad: for great is your reward in heaven: for so persecuted they the prophets which were before you.

10.   Matthew 5:13–16: 13. You are the salt of the earth: but if the salt have lost his savor, wherewith shall it be salted? it is thenceforth good for nothing, but to be cast out, and to be trodden under foot of men. 14. You are the light of the world. A city that is set on an hill cannot be hid. 15. Neither do men light a candle, and put it under a bushel, but on a candlestick; and it gives light unto all that are in the house. 16. Let your light so shine before men, that they may see your good works, and glorify your Father which is in heaven.

11.   Matthew 5:17–19: 17. Think not that I am come to destroy the law, or the prophets: I am not come to destroy, but to fulfill. 18. For verily I say unto you, Till heaven and earth pass, one jot or one tittle shall in no wise pass from the law, till all be fulfilled. 19. Whosoever therefore shall break one of these least commandments, and shall teach men so, he shall be called the least in the Kingdom of heaven: but whosoever shall do and teach them, the same shall be called great in the Kingdom of heaven.

12.   Matthew 5:21-22: 21. You have heard that it was said by them of old time, You shall not kill; and whosoever shall kill shall be in danger of the judgment: 22. But I say unto you, That whosoever is angry with his brother without a cause shall be in danger of the judgment: and whosoever shall say to his brother, Raca, shall be in danger of the council: but whosoever shall say, You fool, shall be in danger of hell fire.

13. Matthew 5:23-24: 23. Therefore if you bring your gift to the altar, and there remember that your brother has ought against you; 24. Leave there your gift before the altar, and go your way; first be reconciled to your brother, and then come and offer your gift.

14. Matthew 5:25-26: 25. Agree with your adversary quickly, while you art in the way with him; lest at any time the adversary deliver you to the judge, and the judge deliver you to the officer, and you be cast into prison. 26. Verily I say unto you, You shall by no means come out thence, till you hast paid the uttermost farthing.

15. Matthew 5:27: You have heard that it was said by them of old time, You shall not commit adultery:

16. Matthew 5:29-30: 29. And if your right eye offend you, pluck it out, and cast it from you: for it is profitable for you that one of your members should perish, and not that your whole body should be cast into hell. 30. And if your right hand offend you, cut it off, and cast it from you: for it is profitable for you that one of your members should perish, and not that your whole body should be cast into hell.

17. Matthew 5:31-32: 31. It has been said, Whosoever shall put away his wife, let him give her a writing of divorcement: 32. But I say unto you, That whosoever shall put away his wife, saving for the cause of fornication, causes her to commit adultery: and whosoever shall marry her that is divorced commits adultery.

18. Matthew 5:33–37: 33. Again, you have heard that it has been said by them of old time, You shall not forswear yourself, but shall perform unto the Lord your oaths: 34. But I say unto you, Swear not at all; neither by heaven; for it is God's throne: 35. Nor by the earth; for it is his footstool: neither by Jerusalem; for it is the city of the great King. 36. Neither shall you swear by your head, because you canst not make one hair white or black. 37. But let your communication be, Yea, yea; Nay, nay: for whatsoever is more than these comes of evil.

19. Matthew 5:39–42: 39. But I say unto you, That you resist not evil: but whosoever shall smite you on your right cheek, turn to him the other also. 40. And if any man will sue you at the law, and take away your coat, let him have your cloak also. 41. And whosoever

shall compel you to go a mile, go with him twain. 42. Give to him who asks you, and from him who wants to borrow from you do not turn away.

20.   Matthew 5:43–48: 43. But I say unto you, Love your enemies, bless them that curse you, do good to them that hate you, and pray for them which despitefully use you, and persecute you; 44. But I say unto you, Love your enemies, bless them that curse you, do good to them that hate you, and pray for them which despitefully use you, and persecute you; 45. That you may be the children of your Father which is in heaven: for he makes his sun to rise on the evil and on the good, and sends rain on the just and on the unjust. 46. For if you love them which love you, what reward have you? do not even the publicans the same? 47. And if you salute your brethren only, what do you more [than others]? do not even the publicans so? 48. Be you therefore perfect, even as your Father which is in heaven is perfect.

21.   Matthew 6:1–4: 1. Take heed that you do not your alms before men, to be seen of them: otherwise you have no reward of your Father which is in heaven. 2. Therefore when you does your alms, do not sound a trumpet before you, as the hypocrites do in the synagogues and in the streets, that they may have glory of men. Verily I say unto you, They have their reward. 3. But when you does alms, let not your left hand know what your right hand does: 4. That your alms may be in secret: and your Father which sees in secret himself shall reward you openly.

22.   Matthew 6:5–8: 5. And when you pray, you shall not be as the hypocrites are: for they love to pray standing in the synagogues and in the corners of the streets, that they may be seen of men. Verily I say unto you, They have their reward. 6. But you, when you pray, enter into your closet, and when you hast shut your door, pray to your Father which is in secret; and your Father which sees in secret shall reward you openly. 7. But when you pray, use not vain repetitions, as the heathen do: for they think that they shall be heard for their much speaking. 8. Be not you therefore like unto them: for your Father knows what things you have need of, before you ask him.

23. Matthew 6:9–13: 9. After this manner therefore pray you: Our Father which art in heaven, Hallowed be your name. 10. Your Kingdom come. Your will be done in earth, as it is in heaven. 11. Give us this day our daily bread. 12. And forgive us our debts, as we forgive our debtors. 13. And lead us not into temptation, but deliver us from evil: For your is the Kingdom, and the power, and the glory, forever. Amen.

24. Matthew 6:14–15: 14. For if you forgive men their trespasses, your heavenly Father will also forgive you: 15. But if you forgive not men their trespasses, neither will your Father forgive your trespasses.

25. Matthew 6:16–18: 16. Moreover when you fast, be not, as the hypocrites, of a sad countenance: for they disfigure their faces, that they may appear unto men to fast. Verily I say unto you, They have their reward. 17. But you, when you fastest, anoint your head, and wash your face; 18. That you appear not unto men to fast, but unto your Father which is in secret: and your Father, which sees in secret, shall reward you openly.

26. Matthew 6:19–24: 19. Lay not up for yourselves treasures upon earth, where moth and rust does corrupt, and where thieves break through and steal: 20. But lay up for yourselves treasures in heaven, where neither moth nor rust does corrupt, and where thieves do not break through nor steal: 21. For where your treasure is, there will your heart be also. 22. The lamp of the body is the eye. If therefore your eye is good, your whole body will be full of light. 23. But if your eye is bad, your whole body will be full of darkness. If therefore the light that is in you is darkness, how great [is] that darkness! 24. No one can serve two masters; for either he will hate the one and love the other, or else he will be loyal to the one and despise the other. You cannot serve God and mammon.

27. Matthew 6:25–27: 25. Therefore I say unto you, Take no thought for your life, what you shall eat, or what you shall drink; nor yet for your body, what you shall put on. Is not the life more than meat, and the body than raiment? 26. Look at the birds of the air, for they neither sow nor reap nor gather into barns; yet your

heavenly Father feeds them. Are you not of more value than they? 27. Which of you by worrying can add one cubit to his stature?

28. Matthew 6:28: And why take you thought for raiment? Consider the lilies of the field, how they grow; they toil not, neither do they spin:

29. Matthew 6:31–34: 31. Therefore take no thought, saying, What shall we eat? or, What shall we drink? or, Wherewithal shall we be clothed? 32. For after all these things do the Gentiles seek: for your heavenly Father knows that you have need of all these things. 33. But seek you first the Kingdom of God, and his righteousness; and all these things shall be added unto you. 34. Take therefore no thought for the morrow: for the morrow shall take thought for the things of itself. Sufficient unto the day is the evil thereof.

30. Matthew 7:1–4: 1. Judge not, that you be not judged. 2. For with what judgment you judge, you shall be judged: and with what measure you mete, it shall be measured to you again. 3. And why behold you the mote that is in your brother's eye, but consider not the beam that is in your own eye? 4. Or how wilt you say to your brother, Let me pull out the mote out of your eye; and, behold, a beam [is] in your own eye?

31. Matthew 7:5: You hypocrite, first cast out the beam out of your own eye; and then shall you see clearly to cast out the mote out of your brother's eye.

32. Matthew 7:6: Give not that which is holy unto the dogs, neither cast you your pearls before swine, lest they trample them under their feet, and turn again and rend you.

33. Matthew 7:7–12: 7. Ask, and it shall be given you; seek, and you shall find; knock, and it shall be opened unto you: 8. For every one that asks receives; and he that seeks finds; and to him that knocks it shall be opened. 9. Or what man is there of you, whom if his son ask bread, will he give him a stone? 10. Or if he ask a fish, will he give him a serpent? 11. If you then, being evil, know how to give good gifts unto your children, how much more shall your Father which is in heaven give good things to them that ask him? 12. Therefore all things whatsoever you would that men should do to you, do you even so to them: for this is the law and the prophets.

34. Matthew 7:13-14: 13. Enter you in at the strait gate: for wide is the gate, and broad is the way, that leads to destruction, and many there be which go in thereat: 14. Because strait [is] the gate, and narrow [is] the way, which leads unto life, and few there be that find it.

35. Matthew 7:15-16: 15. Beware of false prophets, which come to you in sheep's clothing, but inwardly they are ravening wolves. 16. You will know them by their fruits. Do men gather grapes from thorn bushes or figs from thistles?

36. Matthew 8:21–22: 21. And another of his disciples said unto him, Lord, suffer me first to go and bury my father. 22. But Jesus said unto him, Follow me; and let the dead bury their dead.

37. Matthew 9:10–13: 10. And it came to pass, as Jesus sat at meat in the house, behold, many publicans and sinners came and sat down with him and his disciples. 11. And when the Pharisees saw [it], they said unto his disciples, Why eats your Master with publicans and sinners? 12. But when Jesus heard [that], he said unto them, They that be whole need not a physician, but they that are sick. 13. But go you and learn what that means, I will have mercy, and not sacrifice: for I am not come to call the righteous, but sinners to repentance.

38. Matthew 9:36–38: 36. But when he saw the multitudes, he was moved with compassion on them, because they fainted, and were scattered abroad, as sheep having no shepherd. 37. Then says he unto his disciples, The harvest truly [is] plenteous, but the laborers [are] few; 38. Pray you therefore the Lord of the harvest, that he will send forth laborers into his harvest.

39. Matthew 10:5–15: 5. These twelve Jesus sent forth, and commanded them, saying, Go not into the way of the Gentiles, and into [any] city of the Samaritans enter you not: 6. But go rather to the lost sheep of the house of Israel. And as you go, preach, saying, The Kingdom of heaven is at hand. 7. And as you go, preach, saying, "The Kingdom of heaven is at hand." 8. Heal the sick, cleanse the lepers, raise the dead, cast out devils: freely you have received, freely give. 9. Provide neither gold, nor silver, nor brass in your purses, 10. nor scrip for your journey, neither two coats, neither shoes, nor yet staves: for the workman is worthy of his meat.

11. And into whatsoever city or town you shall enter, inquire who in it is worthy; and there abide till you go thence. 12. And when you come into a house, salute it. 13. And if the house be worthy, let your peace come upon it: but if it be not worthy, let your peace return to you. 14. And whosoever shall not receive you, nor hear your words, when you depart out of that house or city, shake off the dust of your feet. 15. Verily I say unto you, It shall be more tolerable for the land of Sodom and Gomorrah in the Day of Judgment, than for that city.

40. Matthew 10:16–20: 16. Behold, I send you forth as sheep in the midst of wolves: be you therefore wise as serpents, and harmless as doves. 17. But beware of men: for they will deliver you up to the councils, and they will scourge you in their synagogues; 18. And you shall be brought before governors and kings for my sake, for a testimony against them and the Gentiles. 19. But when they deliver you up, take no thought how or what you shall speak: for it shall be given you in that same hour what you shall speak. 20. For it is not you that speak, but the Spirit of your Father which speaks in you.

41. Matthew 10:23: But when they persecute you in this city, flee you into another: for verily I say unto you, You shall not have gone over the cities of Israel, till the Son of Man comes.

42. Matthew 10:26–31: 26. Fear them not therefore: for there is nothing covered, that shall not be revealed; and hid, that shall not be known. 27. What I tell you in darkness, that speak you in light: and what you hear in the ear, that preach you upon the housetops. 28. And fear not them which kill the body, but are not able to kill the soul: but rather fear him which is able to destroy both soul and body in hell. 29. Are not two sparrows sold for a farthing? and one of them shall not fall on the ground without your Father. 30. But the very hairs of your head are all numbered. 31. Fear you not therefore, you are of more value than many sparrows.

43. Matthew 10:34: Think not that I am come to send peace on earth: I came not to send peace, but a sword.

44. Matthew 10:41-42: 41. He that receives a prophet in the name of a prophet shall receive a prophet's reward; and he that receives

a righteous man in the name of a righteous man shall receive a righteous man's reward. 42. And whosoever shall give to drink unto one of these little ones a cup of cold [water] only in the name of a disciple, verily I say unto you, he shall in no wise lose his reward.

45.   Matthew 11:11–15: 11. Verily I say unto you, among them that are born of women there has not risen a greater than John the Baptist: notwithstanding he that is least in the Kingdom of heaven is greater than he. 12. And from the days of John the Baptist until now the Kingdom of heaven suffers violence, and the violent take it by force. 13. For all the prophets and the law prophesied until John. 14. And if you will receive [it], this is Elias, which was for to come. 15. He that has ears to hear, let him hear.

46.   Matthew 11:28–30: 28. Come unto me, all you that labor and are heavy laden, and I will give you rest. 29. Take my yoke upon you, and learn of me; for I am meek and lowly in heart: and you shall find rest unto your souls. 30. For my yoke is easy, and my burden is light.

47.   Matthew 12:33: Either make the tree good, and his fruit good; or else make the tree corrupt, and his fruit corrupt: for the tree is known by his fruit.

48.   Matthew 13:9: Who has ears to hear, let him hear.

49.   Matthew 13:18: Hear you therefore the parable of the sower.

50.   Matthew 13:43: Then shall the righteous shine forth as the sun in the Kingdom of their Father. Who has ears to hear, let him hear.

51.   Matthew 15:3–9: 3. But he answered and said unto them, Why do you also transgress the commandment of God by your tradition? 4. For God commanded, saying, Honor your father and mother: and, He that curses father or mother, let him die the death. 5. But you say, Whosoever shall say to [his] father or [his] mother, [It is] a gift, by whatsoever you might be profited by me; 6. And honor not his father or his mother, [he shall be free]. Thus have you made the commandment of God of none effect by your tradition. 7. [You] hypocrites, well did Esaias prophesy of you, saying, 8. This people draw nigh unto me with their mouth, and honor me with [their] lips; but their heart is far from me. 9. But in vain they do worship me, teaching [for] doctrines the commandments of men.

52. Matthew 15:10: And he called the multitude, and said unto them, Hear, and understand:

53. Matthew 15:14: Let them alone: they be blind leaders of the blind. And if the blind lead the blind, both shall fall into the ditch.

54. Matthew 16:6: Then Jesus said unto them, Take heed and beware of the leaven of the Pharisees and of the Sadducees.

55. Matthew 16:24: Then said Jesus unto his disciples, If any man will come after me, let him deny himself, and take up his cross, and follow me.

56. Matthew 17:5: While he yet spoke, behold, a bright cloud overshadowed them: and behold a voice out of the cloud, which said, This is my beloved Son, in whom I am well pleased; hear you him.

57. Matthew 18:8-9: 8. Wherefore if your hand or your foot offend you, cut them off, and cast them from you: it is better for you to enter into life halt or maimed, rather than having two hands or two feet to be cast into everlasting fire. 9. And if your eye offend you, pluck it out, and cast it from you: it is better for you to enter into life with one eye, rather than having two eyes to be cast into hell fire.

58. Matthew 18:10: Take heed that you despise not one of these little ones; for I say unto you, That in heaven their angels do always behold the face of my Father which is in heaven.

59. Matthew 18:15–17: 15. Moreover if your brother shall trespass against you, go and tell him his fault between you and him alone: if he shall hear you, you hast gained your brother. 16. But if he will not hear you, then take with you one or two more, that in the mouth of two or three witnesses every word may be established. 17. And if he shall neglect to hear them, tell it unto the church: but if he neglect to hear the church, let him be unto you as a heathen man and a publican.

60. Matthew 18:22: Jesus says unto him, I say not unto you, Until seven times: but, Until seventy times seven.

61. Matthew 19:6: Wherefore they are no more twain, but one flesh. What therefore God has joined together, let not man put asunder.

62. Matthew 19:14: But Jesus said, Suffer little children, and forbid them not, to come unto me: for of such is the Kingdom of heaven.

63. Matthew 19:16–19: 16. And, behold, one came and said unto him, Good Master, what good thing shall I do, that I may have eternal life? 17. And he said unto him, Why call you me good? there is none good but one, that is, God: but if you wilt enter into life, keep the commandments. 18. He says unto him, Which? Jesus said, You shall do no murder, You shall not commit adultery, You shall not steal, You shall not bear false witness, 19. Honor your father and your mother: and, You shall love your neighbor as yourself.

64. Matthew 19:21: Jesus said unto him, If you will be perfect, go and sell that you hast, and give to the poor, and you shall have treasure in heaven: and come and follow me.

65. Matthew 20:25–28: 25. But Jesus called them unto him, and said, You know that the princes of the Gentiles exercise dominion over them, and they that are great exercise authority upon them. 26. But it shall not be so among you: but whosoever will be great among you, let him be your minister; 27. And whosoever will be chief among you, let him be your servant: 28. Even as the Son of Man came not to be ministered unto, but to minister, and to give his life a ransom for many.

66. Matthew 22:17–21: 17. Tell us therefore, What think you? Is it lawful to give tribute unto Caesar, or not? 18. But Jesus perceived their wickedness, and said, Why tempt you me, [you] hypocrites? 19. Show me the tribute money. And they brought unto him a denarius. 20. And he says unto them, Whose [is] this image and superscription? 21. They said to Him, "Caesar's." And He said to them, "Render therefore to Caesar the things that are Caesar's, and to God the things that are God's."

67. Matthew 22:35–40: 35. Then one of them, [which was] a lawyer, asked [him a question], tempting him, and saying, 36. Master, which [is] the great commandment in the law? 37. Jesus said unto him, You shall love the Lord your God with all your heart, and with all your soul, and with all your mind. 38. This is the first and great commandment. 39. And the second [is] like unto it, You shall love your neighbor as yourself. 40. On these two commandments hang all the law and the prophets.

68.   Matthew 23:1–7: 1. Then spoke Jesus to the multitude, and to his disciples, 2. saying, The scribes and the Pharisees sit in Moses' seat: 3. All therefore whatsoever they bid you observe, that observe and do; but do not you after their works: for they say, and do not. 4. For they bind heavy burdens and grievous to be borne, and lay them on men's shoulders; but they themselves will not move them with one of their fingers. 5. But all their works they do for to be seen of men: they make broad their phylacteries, and enlarge the borders of their garments, 6. And love the uppermost rooms at feasts, and the chief seats in the synagogues, 7. And greetings in the markets, and to be called of men, Rabbi, Rabbi.

69.   Matthew 23:8–10: 8. But be not you called Rabbi: for one is your Master, even Christ; and all you are brethren. 9. And call no man your father upon the earth: for one is your Father, which is in heaven. 10. Neither be you called masters: for one is your Master, even Christ.

70.   Matthew 24:4: And Jesus answered and said unto them, Take heed that no man deceive you.

71.   Matthew 24:6: And you shall hear of wars and rumors of wars: see that you be not troubled: for all these things must come to pass, but the end is not yet.

72.   Matthew 24:15–18: 15. When you therefore shall see the abomination of desolation, spoken of by Daniel the prophet, stand in the holy place, whoso reads, let him understand: 16. Then let them which be in Judea flee into the mountains: 17. Let him which is on the housetop not come down to take anything out of his house: 18. Neither let him which is in the field return back to take his clothes.

73.   Matthew 24:20: But pray you that your flight be not in the winter, neither on the Sabbath day:

74.   Matthew 24:23: Then if any man shall say unto you, Lo, here is Christ, or there; believe it not.

75.   Matthew 24:26: Wherefore if they shall say unto you, Behold, he is in the desert; go not forth: behold, he is in the secret chambers; believe it not.

76.   Matthew 24:42: Watch therefore: for you know not what hour your Lord does come.

77. Matthew 24:44: Therefore be you also ready: for in such an hour as you think not the Son of Man comes.

78. Matthew 25:13: Watch therefore, for you know neither the day nor the hour wherein the Son of Man comes.

79. Matthew 26:26–29: 26. And as they were eating, Jesus took bread, and blessed it, and broke it, and gave it to the disciples, and said, Take, eat; this is my body. 27. And he took the cup, and gave thanks, and gave it to them, saying, Drink you all of it; 28. For this is my blood of the New Testament, which is shed for many for the remission of sins. 29. But I say unto you, I will not drink henceforth of this fruit of the vine, until that day when I drink it new with you in my Father's Kingdom.

80. Matthew 28:18–20: 18. And Jesus came and spoke to them, saying, "All authority has been given to Me in heaven and on earth. 19. Go you therefore, and teach all nations, baptizing them in the name of the Father, and of the Son, and of the Holy Ghost: 20. Teaching them to observe all things whatsoever I have commanded you: and, lo, I am with you always, even unto the end of the world. Amen.

81. Mark 1:15: And saying, The time is fulfilled, and the Kingdom of God is at hand: repent you, and believe the gospel.

82. Mark 1:17: And Jesus said unto them, Come you after me, and I will make you to become fishers of men.

83. Mark 4:9: And he said unto them, He that has ears to hear, let him hear.

84. Mark 4:23-24: 23. If any man have ears to hear, let him hear. 24. And he said unto them, Take heed what you hear: with what measure you mete, it shall be measured to you: and unto you that hear shall more be given..

85. Mark 6:7–11: 7. And he called unto him the twelve, and began to send them forth by two and two; and gave them power over unclean spirits; 8. And commanded them that they should take nothing for their journey, save a staff only; no scrip, no bread, no money in their purse; 9. But be shod with sandals; and not put on two coats. 10. And he said unto them, In what place soever you enter into a house, there abide till you depart from

that place. 11. And whosoever shall not receive you, nor hear you, when you depart thence, shake off the dust under your feet for a testimony against them. Verily I say unto you, It shall be more tolerable for Sodom and Gomorrah in the day of judgment, than for that city.

86. Mark 7:14: And when he had called all the people unto him, he said unto them, Hearken unto me every one of you, and understand:

87. Mark 7:16: If any man have ears to hear, let him hear.

88. Mark 8:15: And he charged them, saying, Take heed, beware of the leaven of the Pharisees, and of the leaven of Herod.

89. Mark 8:34: And when he had called the people unto him with his disciples also, he said unto them, Whosoever will come after me, let him deny himself, and take up his cross, and follow me.

90. Mark 9:35–37: 35. And he sat down, and called the twelve, and says unto them, If any man desire to be first, [the same] shall be last of all, and servant of all. 36. And he took a child, and set him in the midst of them: and when he had taken him in his arms, he said unto them, 37. "Whosoever shall receive one of such children in my name, receives me: and whosoever shall receive me, receives not me, but him that sent me."

91. Mark 9:38–39: (40-41) 38. And John answered him, saying, Master, we saw one casting out devils in your name, and he follows not us: and we forbade him, because he follows not us. 39. But Jesus said, Forbid him not: for there is no man which shall do a miracle in my name, that can lightly speak evil of me.

92. Mark 9:43–48: 43. And if your hand offend you, cut it off: it is better for you to enter into life maimed, than having two hands to go into hell, into the fire that never shall be quenched: 44. Where their worm dies not, and the fire is not quenched. 45. And if your foot offend you, cut it off: it is better for you to enter halt into life, than having two feet to be cast into hell, into the fire that never shall be quenched: 46. Where their worm dies not, and the fire is not quenched. 47. And if your eye offend you, pluck it out: it is better for you to enter into the Kingdom of God with one eye, than having two eyes to be cast into hell fire: 48. Where their worm dies not, and the fire is not quenched.

93. Mark 9:50: Salt is good: but if the salt have lost his saltiness, wherewith will you season it? Have salt in yourselves, and have peace one with another.

94. Mark 10:2–12: 2. And the Pharisees came to him, and asked him, Is it lawful for a man to put away [his] wife? tempting him. 3. And he answered and said unto them, What did Moses command you? 4. And they said, Moses suffered to write a bill of divorcement, and to put [her] away. 5. And Jesus answered and said unto them, For the hardness of your heart he wrote you this precept. 6. But from the beginning of the creation God made them male and female. 7. For this cause shall a man leave his father and mother, and cleave to his wife; 8. And they twain shall be one flesh: so then they are no more twain, but one flesh. 9. What therefore God has joined together, let not man put asunder. 10. And in the house his disciples asked him again of the same [matter]. 11. And he says unto them, Whosoever shall put away his wife, and marry another, commits adultery against her. 12. And if a woman shall put away her husband, and be married to another, she commits adultery.

95. Mark 10:14: But when Jesus saw it, he was much displeased, and said unto them, Suffer the little children to come unto me, and forbid them not: for of such is the Kingdom of God.

96. Mark 10:19: You know the commandments, Do not commit adultery, Do not kill, Do not steal, Do not bear false witness, Defraud not, Honor your father and mother.

97. Mark 10:21: Then Jesus beholding him loved him, and said unto him, One thing you lack: go your way, sell whatsoever you hast, and give to the poor, and you shall have treasure in heaven: and come, take up the cross, and follow me.

98. Mark 11:22: And Jesus answering says unto them, Have faith in God.

99. Mark 11:24-26: 24. Therefore I say unto you, What things soever you desire, when you pray, believe that you receive them, and you shall have them. 25. And when you stand praying, forgive, if you have aught against any: that your Father also which is in heaven may forgive you your trespasses. 26. But if you do not forgive, neither will your Father which is in heaven forgive your trespasses.

100. Mark 12:12–17: 12. And they sought to lay hold on him, but feared the people: for they knew that he had spoken the parable against them: and they left him, and went their way. 13. And they send unto him certain of the Pharisees and of the Herodians, to catch him in [his] words. 14. And when they were come, they say unto him, Master, we know that you art true, and care for no man: for you regard not the person of men, but teach the way of God in truth: Is it lawful to give tribute to Caesar, or not? 15. Shall we give, or shall we not give? But he, knowing their hypocrisy, said unto them, Why tempt you me? bring me a denarius, that I may see [it]. 16. And they brought [it]. And he says unto them, Whose [is] this image and superscription? And they said unto him, Caesar's. 17. And Jesus answering said unto them, Render to Caesar the things that are Caesar's, and to God the things that are God's. And they marveled at him.

101. Mark 12:28–34: 28. Then one of the scribes came, and having heard them reasoning together, perceiving that He had answered them well, asked Him, "Which is the first commandment of all?" 29. And Jesus answered him, "The first of all the commandments is, Hear, O Israel; The Lord our God is one Lord: 30. And you shall love the Lord your God with all your heart, and with all your soul, and with all your mind, and with all your strength: this is the first commandment." 31. And the second is like, namely this, "You shall love your neighbor as yourself. There is none other commandment greater than these." 32. So the scribe said to Him, "Well [said], Teacher. You have spoken the truth, for there is one God, and there is no other but He. 33. And to love Him with all the heart, with all the understanding, with all the soul, and with all the strength, and to love one's neighbor as oneself, is more than all the whole burnt offerings and sacrifices." 34. Now when Jesus saw that he answered wisely, He said to him, "You are not far from the Kingdom of God." But after that no one dared question Him.

102. Mark 12:38–40: 38. And he said unto them in his doctrine, Beware of the scribes, which love to go in long clothing, and love salutations in the marketplaces, 39. And the chief seats in the synagogues, and the uppermost rooms at feasts: 40. Which devour widows' houses, and for a pretense make long prayers: these shall receive greater damnation.

103. Mark 13:5-6: 5. And Jesus answering them began to say, Take heed lest any man deceive you: 6. For many shall come in my name, saying, I am Christ; and shall deceive many.

104. Mark 13:7–23: 7. And when you shall hear of wars and rumors of wars, be you not troubled: for such things must needs be; but the end shall not be yet. 8. For nation shall rise against nation, and kingdom against kingdom: and there shall be earthquakes in divers places, and there shall be famines and troubles: these are the beginnings of sorrows. 9. But take heed to yourselves: for they shall deliver you up to councils; and in the synagogues you shall be beaten: and you shall be brought before rulers and kings for my sake, for a testimony against them. 10. And the gospel must first be published among all nations. 11. But when they shall lead you, and deliver you up, take no thought beforehand what you shall speak, neither do you premeditate: but whatsoever shall be given you in that hour, that speak you: for it is not you that speak, but the Holy Ghost. 12. Now the brother shall betray the brother to death, and the father the son; and children shall rise up against their parents, and shall cause them to be put to death. 13. And you shall be hated of all men for my name's sake: but he that shall endure unto the end, the same shall be saved. 14. But when you shall see the abomination of desolation, spoken of by Daniel the prophet, standing where it ought not, let him that reads understand, then let them that be in Judea flee to the mountains: 15. And let him that is on the housetop not go down into the house, neither enter therein, to take anything out of his house: 16. And let him that is in the field not turn back again for to take up his garment. 17. But woe to them that are with child, and to them that give suck in those days! 18. And pray you that your flight be not in the winter. 19. For in those days shall be affliction, such as was not from the beginning of the creation which God created unto this time, neither shall be. 20. And except that the Lord had shortened those days, no flesh should be saved: but for the elect's sake, whom he has chosen, he has shortened the days. 21. And then if any man shall say to you, Lo, here is Christ; or, lo, he is there; believe him not: 22. For false Christs and false prophets shall rise, and shall show signs and

wonders, to seduce, if it were possible, even the elect. 23. But take you heed: behold, I have foretold you all things.

105. Mark 13:28-29: 28. Now learn a parable of the fig tree; When her branch is yet tender, and puts forth leaves, you know that summer is near: 29. So you in like manner, when you shall see these things come to pass, know that it is nigh, even at the doors.

106. Mark 13:32–33: 32. But of that day and that hour knows no man, no, not the angels which are in heaven, neither the Son, but the Father. 33. Take you heed, watch and pray: for you know not when the time is.

107. Mark 13:35–37: 35. Watch you therefore: for you know not when the master of the house comes, at even, or at midnight, or at the cockcrowing, or in the morning: 36. Lest coming suddenly he find you sleeping. 37. And what I say unto you I say unto all, Watch.

108. Mark 14:22: And as they did eat, Jesus took bread, and blessed, and brake [it], and gave to them, and said, Take, eat: this is my body.

109. Mark 14:38: Watch you and pray, lest you enter into temptation. The spirit truly is ready, but the flesh is weak.

110. Mark 16:15-16: 15. And he said unto them, Go you into all the world, and preach the gospel to every creature. 16. He that believes and is baptized shall be saved; but he that believes not shall be damned.

111. Luke 3:8: Bring forth therefore fruits worthy of repentance, and begin not to say within yourselves, We have Abraham to our father: for I say unto you, That God is able of these stones to raise up children unto Abraham.

112. Luke 3:10–14: 10. And the people asked him, saying, What shall we do then? 11. He answered and says unto them, He that has two coats, let him impart to him that has none; and he that has meat, let him do likewise. 12. Then came also publicans to be baptized, and said unto him, Master, what shall we do? 13. And he said unto them, Exact no more than that which is appointed you. 14. And the soldiers likewise demanded of him, saying, And what shall we do? And he said unto them, Do violence to no man, neither accuse any falsely; and be content with your wages.

113. Luke 4:4: And Jesus answered him, saying, "It is written, That man shall not live by bread alone, but by every word of God."

114. Luke 4:8: And Jesus answered and said unto him, Get you behind me, Satan: for it is written, You shall worship the Lord your God, and him only shall you serve.

115. Luke 4:12: And Jesus answering said unto him, It is said, You shall not tempt the Lord your God.

116. Luke 5:10: And so was also James, and John, the sons of Zebedee, which were partners with Simon. And Jesus said unto Simon, Fear not; from henceforth you shall catch men.

117. Luke 5:27: And after these things he went forth, and saw a publican, named Levi, sitting at the receipt of custom: and he said unto him, Follow me.

118. Luke 6:23: Rejoice you in that day, and leap for joy: for, behold, your reward is great in heaven: for in the like manner did their fathers unto the prophets.

119. Luke 6:27–29: 27. But I say unto you which hear, Love your enemies, do good to them which hate you, 28. Bless them that curse you, and pray for them which despitefully use you. 29. And unto him that smites you on the one cheek offer also the other; and him that took away your cloak forbid not to take your coat also.

120. Luke 6:30-31: 30. Give to every man that asks of you; and of him that took away your goods ask them not again. 31. And just as you want men to do to you, you also do to them likewise.

121. Luke 6:32–36: 32. For if you love them which love you, what thank have you? for sinners also love those that love them. 33. And if you do good to them which do good to you, what thank have you? for sinners also do even the same. 34. And if you lend [to them] of whom you hope to receive, what thank have you? for sinners also lend to sinners, to receive as much again. 35. But love you your enemies, and do good, and lend, hoping for nothing again; and your reward shall be great, and you shall be the children of the Highest: for he is kind unto the unthankful and to the evil. 36. Be you therefore merciful, as your Father also is merciful.

122. Luke 6:37: Judge not, and you shall not be judged: condemn not, and you shall not be condemned: forgive, and you shall be forgiven:

123. Luke 6:38: Give, and it shall be given unto you, good measure, pressed down, and shaken together, and running over, shall men give into your bosom. For with the same measure that you mete withal it shall be measured to you again.

124. Luke 6:41-42: 41. And why behold you the mote that is in your brother's eye, but perceive not the beam that is in your own eye? 42. Either how canst you say to your brother, Brother, let me pull out the mote that is in your eye, when you yourself behold not the beam that is in your own eye? You hypocrite, cast out first the beam out of your own eye, and then shall you see clearly to pull out the mote that is in your brother's eye.

125. Luke 8:8: And other fell on good ground, and sprang up, and bear fruit a hundredfold. And when he had said these things, he cried, He that has ears to hear, let him hear.

126. Luke 8:18: Take heed therefore how you hear: for whosoever has, to him shall be given; and whosoever has not, from him shall be taken even that which he seemed to have.

127. Luke 9:3–5: 3. And he said unto them, Take nothing for your journey, neither staves, nor scrip, neither bread, neither money; neither have two coats apiece. 4. And whatsoever house you enter into, there abide, and thence depart. 5. And whosoever will not receive you, when you go out of that city, shake off the very dust from your feet for a testimony against them.

128. Luke 9:23: (24-27) 23. And he said to them all, If any man will come after me, let him deny himself, and take up his cross daily, and follow me.

129. Luke 9:59-60: 59. And he said unto another, Follow me. But he said, Lord, suffer me first to go and bury my father. 60. Jesus said unto him, Let the dead bury their dead: but go you and preach the Kingdom of God.

130. Luke 10:2: Therefore said he unto them, The harvest truly is great, but the laborers are few: pray you therefore the Lord of the harvest, that he would send forth laborers into his harvest.

131. Luke 10:20: Notwithstanding in this rejoice not, that the spirits are subject unto you; but rather rejoice, because your names are written in heaven.

132. Luke 10:25–28: 25. And, behold, a certain lawyer stood up, and tempted him, saying, Master, what shall I do to inherit eternal life? 26. He said unto him, "What is written in the law? how read you?" 27. And he answering said, "You shall love the Lord your God with all your heart, and with all your soul, and with all your strength, and with all your mind; and your neighbor as yourself." 28. And he said unto him, "You hast answered right: this do, and you shall live."

133. Luke 10:37: And he said, He that showed mercy on him. Then said Jesus unto him, "Go, and do you likewise."

134. Luke 11:2–4: 2. And he said unto them, When you pray, say, Our Father which art in heaven, Hallowed be your name. Your Kingdom come. Your will be done, as in heaven, so in earth. 3. Give us day by day our daily bread. 4. And forgive us our sins; for we also forgive every one that is indebted to us. And lead us not into temptation; but deliver us from evil.

135. Luke 11:9: (10-13) 9. And I say unto you, Ask, and it shall be given you; seek, and you shall find; knock, and it shall be opened unto you.

136. Luke 11:35: (33-36) 35. Take heed therefore that the light which is in you be not darkness.

137. Luke 11:41: But rather give alms of such things as you have; and, behold, all things are clean unto you.

138. Luke 12:1: In the meantime, when there were gathered together an innumerable multitude of people, insomuch that they trod one upon another, he began to say unto his disciples first of all, Beware you of the leaven of the Pharisees, which is hypocrisy.

139. Luke 12:4-5: 4. And I say unto you my friends, Be not afraid of them that kill the body, and after that have no more that they can do. 5. But I will forewarn you whom you shall fear: Fear him, which after he has killed has power to cast into hell; yea, I say unto you, Fear him.

140. Luke 12:7: But even the very hairs of your head are all numbered. Fear not therefore: You are of more value than many sparrows.

141. Luke 12:11-12: 11. And when they bring you unto the synagogues, and unto magistrates, and powers, take you no thought how or what thing you shall answer, or what you shall say: 12. For the Holy Ghost shall teach you in the same hour what you ought to say.

142. Luke 12:15: And he said unto them, Take heed, and beware of covetousness: for a man's life consists not in the abundance of the things which he possesses.

143. Luke 12:22-23: 22. And he said unto his disciples, Therefore I say unto you, Take no thought for your life, what you shall eat; neither for the body, what you shall put on. 23. Life is more than food, and the body [is more] than clothing.

144. Luke 12:24: Consider the ravens: for they neither sow nor reap; which neither have storehouse nor barn; and God feeds them: how much more are you better than the fowls?

145. Luke 12:27: Consider the lilies how they grow: they toil not, they spin not; and yet I say unto you, that Solomon in all his glory was not arrayed like one of these.

146. Luke 12:29: And seek not you what you shall eat, or what you shall drink, neither be you of doubtful mind.

147. Luke 12:31: But rather seek you the Kingdom of God; and all these things shall be added unto you.

148. Luke 12:32: Fear not, little flock; for it is your Father's good pleasure to give you the Kingdom.

149. Luke 12:33-34: 33. Sell that you have, and give alms; provide yourselves bags which wax not old, a treasure in the heavens that fails not, where no thief approaches, neither moth corrupts. 34. For where your treasure is, there will your heart be also.

150. Luke 12:35-36: 35. Let your loins be girded about, and your lights burning; 36. And you yourselves like unto men that wait for their Lord, when he will return from the wedding; that when he comes and knocks, they may open unto him immediately.

151. Luke 12:40: Be you therefore ready also: for the Son of Man comes at an hour when you think not.

152. Luke 12:58-59: 58. When you go with your adversary to the magistrate, as you art in the way, give diligence that you may be delivered from him; lest he hale you to the judge, and the judge deliver you to the officer, and the officer cast you into prison. 59. I tell you, you shall not depart thence, till you hast paid the very last mite.

153. Luke 13:24: Strive to enter in at the strait gate: for many, I say unto you, will seek to enter in, and shall not be able.

154. Luke 14:8–10: 8. When you art bidden of any man to a wedding, sit not down in the highest room; lest a more honorable man than you be bidden of him; 9. And he that bade you and him come and say to you, Give this man place; and you begin with shame to take the lowest room. 10. But when you art bidden, go and sit down in the lowest room; that when he bade you comes, he may say unto you, Friend, go up higher: then shall you have worship in the presence of them that sit at meat with you.

155. Luke 14:12–14: 12. Then said he also to him that bade him, When you makest a dinner or a supper, call not your friends, nor your brethren, neither your kinsmen, nor your rich neighbors; lest they also bid you again, and a recompense be made you. 13. But when you makest a feast, call the poor, the maimed, the lame, the blind: 14. And you shall be blessed; for they cannot recompense you: for you shall be recompensed at the resurrection of the just.

156. Luke 14:34-35: 34. Salt is good: but if the salt have lost his savor, wherewith shall it be seasoned? 35. It is neither fit for the land, nor yet for the dunghill; but men cast it out. He that has ears to hear, let him hear.

157. Luke 16:9: And I say unto you, Make to yourselves friends of the mammon of unrighteousness; that, when you fail, they may receive you into everlasting habitations.

158. Luke 17:3-4: 3. Take heed to yourselves: If your brother trespass against you, rebuke him; and if he repent, forgive him. 4. And if he sins against you seven times in a day, and seven times in a day returns to you, saying, 'I repent,' you shall forgive him."

159. Luke 17:10: So likewise you, when you shall have done all those things which are commanded you, say, We are unprofitable servants: we have done that which was our duty to do.

160. Luke 17:32: Remember Lot's wife.

161. Luke 18:6: And the Lord said, Hear what the unjust judge says.

162. Luke 18:16: But Jesus called them unto him, and said, Suffer little children to come unto me, and forbid them not: for of such is the Kingdom of God.

163. Luke 18:20: (18-20) 20. You know the commandments, Do not commit adultery, Do not kill, Do not steal, Do not bear false witness, Honor your father and your mother.

164. Luke 20:21–25: 21. And they asked him, saying, Master, we know that you say and teach rightly, neither accept you the person of any, but teach the way of God truly: 22. Is it lawful for us to give tribute unto Caesar, or no? 23. But he perceived their craftiness, and said unto them, Why tempt you me? 24. Show me a denarius. Whose image and superscription has it? They answered and said, Caesar's. 25. And he said unto them, Render therefore unto Caesar the things which be Caesar's, and unto God the things which be God's.

165. Luke 20:46: (45-47) 46. Beware of the scribes, which desire to walk in long robes, and love greetings in the markets, and the highest seats in the synagogues, and the chief rooms at feasts;

166. Luke 21:8: And he said, Take heed that you be not deceived: for many shall come in my name, saying, I am Christ; and the time draw near: go you not therefore after them.

167. Luke 21:9: But when you shall hear of wars and commotions, be not terrified: for these things must first come to pass; but the end is not by and by.

168. Luke 21:14: Settle it therefore in your hearts, not to meditate before what you shall answer:

169. Luke 21:19: In your patience possess you your souls.

170. Luke 21:28: And when these things begin to come to pass, then look up, and lift up your heads; for your redemption draw nigh.

171. Luke 21:29–31: 29. And he spoke to them a parable; Behold the fig tree, and all the trees; 30. When they now shoot forth, you see and know of your own selves that summer is now nigh at hand. 31. So likewise you, when you see these things come to pass, know you that the Kingdom of God is nigh at hand.

172. Luke 21:34: And take heed to yourselves, lest at any time your hearts be overcharged with surfeiting, and drunkenness, and cares of this life, and so that day come upon you unawares.

173. Luke 21:36: Watch you therefore, and pray always, that you may be accounted worthy to escape all these things that shall come to pass, and to stand before the Son of Man.

174. Luke 22:17-18: 17. And he took the cup, and gave thanks, and said, Take this, and divide it among yourselves: 18. for I say to you, I will not drink of the fruit of the vine until the Kingdom of God comes."

175. Luke 22:19: And he took bread, and gave thanks, and broke it, and gave unto them, saying, This is my body which is given for you: this do in remembrance of me.

176. Luke 22:25-26: (25-30) 25. And he said unto them, The kings of the Gentiles exercise Lordship over them; and they that exercise authority upon them are called benefactors. 26. But you shall not be so: but he that is greatest among you, let him be as the younger; and he that is chief, as he that does serve.

177. Luke 22:35: (36). 35. Then said he unto them, But now, he that has a purse, let him take it, and likewise his scrip: and he that has no sword, let him sell his garment, and buy one.

178. Luke 22:40: And when he was at the place, he said unto them, Pray that you enter not into temptation.

179. Luke 22:46: And said unto them, Why sleep you? rise and pray, lest you enter into temptation.

180. John 1:43, 45: 43. The day following Jesus would go forth into Galilee, and finds Philip, and says unto him, Follow me. 45. Philip found Nathanael, and said unto him, We have found him, of whom Moses in the law, and the prophets, did write, Jesus of Nazareth, the son of Joseph.

181. John 2:16: (13-16) 16. And said unto them that sold doves, Take these things hence; make not my Father's house a house of merchandise.

182. John 3:7: Marvel not that I said unto you, You must be born again.

183. John 4:35: Say not you, There are yet four months, and then comes harvest? behold, I say unto you, Lift up your eyes, and look on the fields; for they are white already to harvest.

184. John 5:14: Afterward Jesus finds him in the temple, and said unto him, Behold, you art made whole: sin no more, lest a worse thing come unto you.

185. John 6:27: Labor not for the meat which perishes, but for that meat which endures unto everlasting life, which the Son of Man shall give unto you: for him has God the Father sealed.

186. John 6:43: (41-43) 43. Jesus therefore answered and said unto them, Murmur not among yourselves.

187. John 7:24: Judge not according to the appearance, but judge righteous judgment.

188. John 12:35-36: 35. Then Jesus said unto them, Yet a little while is the light with you. Walk while you have the light, lest darkness come upon you: for he that walks in darkness knows not whither he goes. 36. While you have light, believe in the light, that you may be the children of light. These things spoke Jesus, and departed, and did hide himself from them.

189. John 13:13–17: 13. You call me Master and Lord: and you say well; for so I am. 14. If I then, your Lord and Master, have washed your feet; you also ought to wash one another's feet. 15. For I have given you an example, that you should do as I have done to you. 16. Verily, verily, I say unto you, The servant is not greater than his Lord; neither he that is sent greater than he that sent him. 17. If you know these things, happy are you if you do them.

190. John 13:34: (35) A new commandment I give unto you, That you love one another; as I have loved you, that you also love one another.

191. John 14:1: Let not your heart be troubled: you believe in God, believe also in me.

192. John 14:11: Believe me that I am in the Father, and the Father in me: or else believe me for the very works' sake.

193. John 14:13-14: 13. And whatsoever you shall ask in my name, that will I do, that the Father may be glorified in the Son. 14. If you shall ask anything in my name, I will do it.

194. John 14:15: If you love me, keep my commandments.

195. John 14:27: Peace I leave with you, my peace I give unto you: not as the world gives, give I unto you. Let not your heart be troubled, neither let it be afraid.

196. John 15:4: Abide in me, and I in you. As the branch cannot bear fruit of itself, except it abide in the vine; no more can you, except you abide in me.

197. John 15:9: (9-11) 9. As the Father has loved me, so have I loved you: continue you in my love.

198. John 15:12: This is my commandment, That you love one another, as I have loved you.

199. John 15:17: These things I command you, that you love one another.

200. John 16:24: Hitherto have you asked nothing in my name: ask, and you shall receive, that your joy may be full.

201. John 16:33: These things I have spoken unto you, that in me you might have peace. In the world you shall have tribulation, but be of good cheer; I have overcome the world.

202. John 20:22: And when he had said this, he breathed on them, and says unto them, Receive you the Holy Ghost: And when he had

203. John 21:15–17: 15. So when they had dined, Jesus says to Simon Peter, Simon, son of Jonah, love you me more than these? He says unto him, Yea, Lord; you know that I love you. He says unto him, "Feed my lambs." 16. He says to him again the second time, Simon, son of Jonah, love you me? He says unto him, Yea, Lord; you know that I love you. He says unto him, "Feed my sheep". 17. He says unto him the third time, Simon, son of Jonah, love you me? Peter was grieved because he said unto him the third time, Love you me? And he said unto him, Lord, you know all things; you know that I love you. Jesus says unto him, "Feed my sheep."

204. John 21:18-19: 18. Verily, verily, I say unto you, When you were young, you girded yourself, and walked whither you would: but when you shall be old, you shall stretch forth your hands, and another shall gird you, and carry you whither you would not. 19. This spoke he, signifying by what death he should glorify God. And when he had spoken this, he says unto him, Follow me.

205. John 21:21–23: 21. Peter seeing him John says to Jesus, Lord, and what shall this man do? 22. Jesus says unto him, If I will that he tarry till I come, what is that to you? Follow you me. 23. Then went this saying abroad among the brethren, that that disciple should not die: yet Jesus said not unto him, He shall not die; but, If I will that he tarry till I come, what is that to you?

The 613 Commandments the Jewish People Keep

There are 613 commandments that the rabbis say the Jews are to keep. These were not compiled in writing until the third century a.d.

Before we can say, "We're not under the law," we need to know what those laws are. The word "law" that we as Christians use is not "law" in Hebrew. The word we use is Torah in Hebrew. Also there are choqs, and mitsvahs. Torah means "instruction," choq means statute, ordinance, decree, law, portion, bounds, custom, appointed, commandments, etc. The word mitsvah means commandment, precept, commanded, law, ordinances. So, it is more complicated than just being "under the law." Each one of these was commanded by God for different reasons.

So, if we say, "We're not under the law," does that make sense? What law are we not under? Are we lawless? God forbid! I wonder if we've been made so afraid of being "under the law" that we don't realize these "laws," instructions, are Scripture! Commandments! Paul says they are our "school master," or "tutor" to bring us to Christ/Messiah.

Galatians 3:24: Wherefore the law was our schoolmaster to bring us unto Christ, that we might be justified by faith.

The instructions are to show us the heart of God, to teach us morality.

I think a lot of us think about the laws the Jews keep and it's like a big black hole. It's secretive, the unknown. So here you go. Read away. And after reading my book, see if it all comes together for you.

You can study up more on these yourself. They're very interesting. Some of them are just for men, some just for women, some only for the priests, some only if there is a Temple standing, some are only if the people are in the land.

There are different compilations of the same 613. Some are in a different order, some by subject, etc., but I like this one.

1. To know there is a God. Exodus 20:2
2. Not to even think that there are other Gods besides Him. Exodus 20:3
3. To know that He is One. Deuteronomy 6:4
4. To love Him. Deuteronomy 6:5
5. To fear Him. Deuteronomy 10:20
6. To sanctify His Name. Leviticus 22:32
7. Not to profane His Name. Leviticus 22:32
8. Not to destroy objects associated with His Name. Deuteronomy 12:4
9. To listen to the prophet speaking in His Name. Deuteronomy 18:15
10. Not to try the Lord unduly. Deuteronomy 6:16
11. To emulate His ways. Deuteronomy 28:9
12. To cleave to those who know Him. Deuteronomy 10:20
13. To love other Jews. Leviticus 19:18
14. To love converts. Deuteronomy 10:19
15. Not to hate fellow Jews. Leviticus 19:17
16. To reprove a sinner. Leviticus 19:17
17. Not to embarrass others. Leviticus 19:17
18. Not to oppress the weak. Exodus 22:21
19. Not to speak derogatorily of others. Leviticus 19:16
20. Not to take revenge. Leviticus 19:18
21. Not to bear a grudge. Leviticus 19:18
22. To learn Torah. Deuteronomy 6:7
23. To honor those who teach and know Torah. Leviticus 19:32
24. Not to inquire into idolatry. Leviticus 19:4
25. Not to follow the whims of your heart or what your eyes see. Numbers 15:39

26. Not to blaspheme. Exodus 22:27
27. Not to worship idols in the manner they are worshiped. Exodus 20:6
28. Not to worship idols in the four ways we worship God. Exodus 20:6
29. Not to make an idol for yourself. Exodus 20:5
30. Not to make an idol for others. Leviticus 19:4
31. Not to make human forms even for decorative purposes. Exodus 20:21
32. Not to turn a city to idolatry. Deuteronomy 13:14
33. To burn a city that has turned to idol worship. Deuteronomy 13:17
34. Not to rebuild it as a city. Deuteronomy 13:17
35. Not to derive benefit from it. Deuteronomy 13:18
36. Not to missionize an individual to idol worship. Deuteronomy 13:12
37. Not to love the idolater. Deuteronomy 13:9
38. Not to cease hating the idolater. Deuteronomy 13:9
39. Not to save the idolater. Deuteronomy 13:9
40. Not to say anything in the idolater's defense. Deuteronomy 13:9
41. Not to refrain from incriminating the idolater. Deuteronomy 13:9
42. Not to prophesize in the name of idolatry. Deuteronomy 13:14
43. Not to listen to a false prophet. Deuteronomy 13:4
44. Not to prophesize falsely in the name of God. Deuteronomy 18:20
45. Not to be afraid of the false prophet. Deuteronomy 18:22
46. Not to swear in the name of an idol. Exodus 23:13
47. Not to perform ov (medium). Leviticus 19:31
48. Not to perform yidoni ("magical seer"). Leviticus 19:31
49. Not to pass your children through the fire to Molech. Leviticus 18:21
50. Not to erect a pillar in a public place of worship. Deuteronomy 16:22
51. Not to bow down before a smooth stone. Leviticus 26:1
52. Not to plant a tree in the Temple courtyard. Deuteronomy 16:21
53. To destroy idols and their accessories. Deuteronomy 12:2
54. Not to derive benefit from idols and their accessories. Deuteronomy 7:26

55. Not to derive benefit from ornaments of idols. Deuteronomy 7:25
56. Not to make a covenant with idolaters. Deuteronomy 7:2
57. Not to show favor to them. Deuteronomy 7:2
58. Not to let them dwell in the Land of Israel. Exodus 23:33
59. Not to imitate them in customs and clothing. Leviticus 20:23
60. Not to be superstitious. Leviticus 19:26
61. Not to go into a trance to foresee events, etc. Deuteronomy 18:10
62. Not to engage in divination or soothsaying. Leviticus 19:26
63. Not to mutter incantations. Deuteronomy 18:11
64. Not to attempt to contact the dead. Deuteronomy 18:11
65. Not to consult the *ov*. Deuteronomy 18:11
66. Not to consult the *yidoni*. Deuteronomy 18:11
67. Not to perform acts of magic. Deuteronomy 18:10
68. Men must not shave the hair off the sides of their head. Leviticus 19:27
69. Men must not shave their beards with a razor. Leviticus 19:27
70. Men must not wear women's clothing. Deuteronomy 22:5
71. Women must not wear men's clothing. Deuteronomy 22:5
72. Not to tattoo the skin. Leviticus 19:28
73. Not to tear the skin in mourning. Deuteronomy 14:1
74. Not to make a bald spot in mourning. Deuteronomy 14:1
75. To repent and confess wrongdoings. Numbers 5:7
76. To say the Shema twice daily. Deuteronomy 6:7
77. To pray every day. Exodus 23:25
78. The *Kohanim* must bless the Jewish nation daily. Numbers 6:23
79. To wear *tefillin* (phylacteries) on the head. Deuteronomy 6:8
80. To bind *tefillin* on the arm. Deuteronomy 6:8
81. To put a *mezuzah* on the door post. Deuteronomy 6:9
82. Each male must write a Torah scroll. Deuteronomy 31:19
83. The king must have a separate Torah scroll for himself. Deuteronomy 17:18
84. To have *tzitzit* on four–cornered garments. Numbers 15:38
85. To bless the Almighty after eating. Deuteronomy 8:10
86. To circumcise all males on the eighth day after their birth. Genesis 17:10
87. To rest on the seventh day. Exodus 23:12

88. Not to do prohibited labor on the seventh day. Exodus 20:11
89. The court must not inflict punishment on Shabbat. Exodus 35:3
90. Not to walk outside the city boundary on Shabbat. Exodus 16:29
91. To sanctify Shabbat with *Kiddush* and *Havdalah*. Exodus 20:9
92. To rest from prohibited labor on Yom Kippur. Leviticus 23:32
93. Not to do prohibited labor on Yom Kippur. Leviticus 23:32
94. To afflict oneself on Yom Kippur. Leviticus 16:29
95. Not to eat or drink on Yom Kippur. Leviticus 23:29
96. To rest on the first day of Passover. Leviticus 23:7
97. Not to do prohibited labor on the first day of Passover. Leviticus 23:8
98. To rest on the seventh day of Passover. Leviticus 23:8
99. Not to do prohibited labor on the seventh day of Passover. Leviticus 23:8
100. To rest on Shavuot. Leviticus 23:21
101. Not to do prohibited labor on Shavuot. Leviticus 23:21
102. To rest on Rosh HaShanah. Leviticus 23:24
103. Not to do prohibited labor on Rosh HaShanah. Leviticus 23:25
104. To rest on Sukkot. Leviticus 23:35
105. Not to do prohibited labor on Sukkot. Leviticus 23:35
106. To rest on Shemini Atzeret. Leviticus 23:36
107. Not to do prohibited labor on Shemini Atzeret. Leviticus 23:36
108. Not to eat *chametz* on the afternoon of the 14th day of Nissan. Deuteronomy 16:3
109. To destroy all *chametz* on 14th day of Nissan. Exodus 12:15
110. Not to eat chametz all seven days of Passover. Exodus 13:3
111. Not to eat mixtures containing *chametz* all seven days of Passover. Exodus 12:20
112. Not to see *chametz* in your domain seven days. Exodus 13:7
113. Not to find *chametz* in your domain seven days. Exodus 12:19
114. To eat *matzah* on the first night of Passover. Exodus 12:18
115. To relate the Exodus from Egypt on that night. Exodus 13:8
116. To hear the *Shofar* on the first day of Tishrei (Rosh HaShanah). Numbers 9:1
117. To dwell in a *Sukkah* for the seven days of Sukkot. Leviticus 23:42
118. To take up a *Lulav* and *Etrog* all seven days. Leviticus 23:40

119. Each man must give a half shekel annually. Exodus 30:13
120. Courts must calculate to determine when a new month begins. Exodus 12:2
121. To afflict oneself and cry out before God in times of calamity. Numbers 10:9
122. To marry a wife by means of *ketubah* and *kiddushin*. Deuteronomy 22:13
123. Not to have sexual relations with women not thus married. Deuteronomy 23:18
124. Not to withhold food, clothing, and sexual relations from your wife. Exodus 21:10
125. To have children with one's wife. Genesis 1:28
126. To issue a divorce by means of a *Get* document. Deuteronomy 24:1
127. A man must not remarry his ex–wife after she has married someone else. Deuteronomy 24:4
128. To perform *yibbum* (marry the widow of one's childless brother). Deuteronomy 25:5
129. To perform *halizah* (free the widow of one's childless brother from *yibbum*). Deuteronomy 25:9
130. The widow must not remarry until the ties with her brother–in–law are removed (by *halizah*). Deuteronomy 25:5
131. The court must fine one who sexually seduces a maiden. Exodus 22:15–16
132. The rapist must marry his victim if she is unwed. Deuteronomy 22:29
133. He is never allowed to divorce her. Deuteronomy 22:29
134. The slanderer must remain married to his wife. Deuteronomy 22:19
135. He must not divorce her. Deuteronomy 22:19
136. To fulfill the laws of the Sotah. Numbers 5:30
137. Not to put oil on her meal offering (as usual). Numbers 5:15
138. Not to put frankincense on her meal offering (as usual). Numbers 5:15
139. Not to have sexual relations with your mother. Leviticus 18:7
140. Not to have sexual relations with your father's wife. Leviticus 18:8
141. Not to have sexual relations with your sister. Leviticus 18:9

142. Not to have sexual relations with your father's wife's daughter. Leviticus 18:11

143. Not to have sexual relations with your son's daughter. Leviticus 18:10

144. Not to have sexual relations with your daughter. Leviticus 18:10

145. Not to have sexual relations with your daughter's daughter. Leviticus 18:10

146. Not to have sexual relations with a woman and her daughter. Leviticus 18:17

147. Not to have sexual relations with a woman and her son's daughter. Leviticus 18:17

148. Not to have sexual relations with a woman and her daughter's daughter. Leviticus 18:17

149. Not to have sexual relations with your father's sister. Leviticus 18:12

150. Not to have sexual relations with your mother's sister. Leviticus 18:13

151. Not to have sexual relations with your father's brother's wife. Leviticus 18:14

152. Not to have sexual relations with your son's wife. Leviticus 18:15

153. Not to have sexual relations with your brother's wife. Leviticus 18:16

154. Not to have sexual relations with your wife's sister. Leviticus 18:18

155. A man must not have sexual relations with an animal. Leviticus 18:23

156. A woman must not have sexual relations with an animal. Leviticus 18:23

157. A man must not have sexual relations with a man. Leviticus 18:22

158. Not to have sexual relations with your father. Leviticus 18:7

159. Not to have sexual relations with your father's brother. Leviticus 18:14

160. Not to have sexual relations with someone else's wife. Leviticus 18:20

161. Not to have sexual relations with a menstrually impure woman. Leviticus 18:19

162. Not to marry non–Jews. Deuteronomy 7:3

163. Not to let Moabite and Ammonite males marry into the Jewish people. Deuteronomy 23:4
164. Not to *prevent* a third–generation Egyptian convert from marrying into the Jewish people. Deuteronomy 23:8–9
165. Not to refrain from marrying a third generation Edomite convert, or "You shall not abhor (to think of as abominable or to detest) an Edomite; for he is your brother: you shall not abhor an Egyptian; because you were a stranger in his land. (Deuteronomy 23:7). Deuteronomy 23:7–9
166. Not to let a mamzer (a child born due to an illegal relationship) marry into the Jewish people. Deuteronomy 23:3
167. Not to let a eunuch marry into the Jewish people. Deuteronomy 23:2
168. Not to offer to God any castrated male animals. Leviticus 22:24
169. The High Priest must not marry a widow. Leviticus 21:14
170. The High Priest must not have sexual relations with a widow even outside of marriage. Leviticus 21:15
171. The High Priest must marry a virgin maiden. Leviticus 21:13
172. A Kohen (priest) must not marry a divorcee. Leviticus 21:7
173. A Kohen must not marry a *zonah* (a woman who has had a forbidden sexual relationship). Leviticus 21:7
174. A Kohen must not marry a *chalalah* ("a desecrated person") (party to or product of 169–172). Leviticus 21:7
175. Not to make pleasurable (sexual) contact with any forbidden woman. Leviticus 18:6
176. To examine the signs of animals to distinguish between kosher and non–kosher. Leviticus 11:2
177. To examine the signs of fowl to distinguish between kosher and non–kosher. Deuteronomy 14:11
178. To examine the signs of fish to distinguish between kosher and non–kosher. Leviticus 11:9
179. To examine the signs of locusts to distinguish between kosher and non–kosher. Leviticus 11:21
180. Not to eat non–kosher animals. Leviticus 11:4
181. Not to eat non–kosher fowl. Leviticus 11:13
182. Not to eat non–kosher fish. Leviticus 11:11

183. Not to eat non–kosher flying insects. Deuteronomy 14:19
184. Not to eat non–kosher creatures that crawl on land. Leviticus 11:41
185. Not to eat non–kosher maggots. Leviticus 11:44
186. Not to eat worms found in fruit on the ground. Leviticus 11:42
187. Not to eat creatures that live in water other than (kosher) fish. Leviticus 11:43
188. Not to eat the meat of an animal that died without ritual slaughter. Deuteronomy 14:21
189. Not to benefit from an ox condemned to be stoned. Exodus 21:2
190. Not to eat meat of an animal that was mortally wounded. Exodus 22:30
191. Not to eat a limb torn off a living creature. Deuteronomy 12:23
192. Not to eat blood. Leviticus 3:17
193. Not to eat certain fats of clean animals. Leviticus 3:17
194. Not to eat the sinew of the thigh. Genesis 32:33
195. Not to eat mixtures of milk and meat cooked together. Exodus 23:19
196. Not to cook meat and milk together. Exodus 34:26
197. Not to eat bread from new grain before the Omer. Leviticus 23:14
198. Not to eat parched grains from new grain before the Omer. Leviticus 23:14
199. Not to eat ripened grains from new grain before the Omer. Leviticus 23:14
200. Not to eat fruit of a tree during its first three years. Leviticus 19:23
201. Not to eat diverse seeds planted in a vineyard. Deuteronomy 22:9
202. Not to eat untithed fruits. Leviticus 22:15
203. Not to drink wine poured in service to idols. Deuteronomy 32:38
204. To ritually slaughter an animal before eating it. Deuteronomy 12:21
205. Not to slaughter an animal and its offspring on the same day. Leviticus 22:28
206. To cover the blood (of a slaughtered beast or fowl) with earth. Leviticus 17:13
207. To send away the mother bird before taking its children. Deuteronomy 22:6

208. To release the mother bird if she was taken from the nest. Deuteronomy 22:7
209. Not to swear falsely in God's Name. Leviticus 19:12
210. Not to take God's Name in vain. Exodus 20:7
211. Not to deny possession of something entrusted to you. Leviticus 19:11
212. Not to swear in denial of a monetary claim. Leviticus 19:11
213. To swear in God's Name to confirm the truth when deemed necessary by court. Deuteronomy 10:20
214. To fulfill what was uttered and to do what was avowed. Deuteronomy 23:24
215. Not to break oaths or vows. Numbers 30:3
216. For oaths and vows annulled, there are the laws of annulling vows explicit in the Torah. Numbers 30:3
217. The Nazarite must let his hair grow. Numbers 6:5
218. He must not cut his hair. Numbers 6:5
219. He must not drink wine, wine mixtures, or wine vinegar. Numbers 6:3
220. He must not eat fresh grapes. Numbers 6:3
221. He must not eat raisins. Numbers 6:3
222. He must not eat grape seeds. Numbers 6:4
223. He must not eat grape skins. Numbers 6:4
224. He must not be under the same roof as a corpse. Numbers 6:6
225. He must not come into contact with the dead. Numbers 6:7
226. He must shave his head after bringing sacrifices upon completion of his Nazarite period. Numbers 6:9
227. To estimate the value of people as determined by the Torah. Leviticus 27:2
228. To estimate the value of consecrated animals. Leviticus 27:12–13
229. To estimate the value of consecrated houses. Leviticus 27:14
230. To estimate the value of consecrated fields. Leviticus 27:16
231. Carry out the laws of interdicting possessions (*cherem*). Leviticus 27:28
232. Not to sell the *cherem*. Leviticus 27:28
233. Not to redeem the *cherem*. Leviticus 27:28
234. Not to plant diverse seeds together. Leviticus 19:19

235. Not to plant grains or greens in a vineyard. Deuteronomy 22:9
236. Not to crossbreed animals. Leviticus 19:19
237. Not to work different animals together. Deuteronomy 22:10
238. Not to wear *shaatnez*, a cloth woven of wool and linen. Deuteronomy 22:11
239. To leave a corner of the field uncut for the poor. Leviticus 19:10
240. Not to reap that corner. Leviticus 19:9
241. To leave gleanings. Leviticus 19:9
242. Not to gather the gleanings. Leviticus 19:9
243. To leave the unformed clusters of grapes. Leviticus 19:10
244. Not to pick the unformed clusters of grapes. Leviticus 19:10
245. To leave the gleanings of a vineyard. Leviticus 19:10
246. Not to gather the gleanings of a vineyard. Leviticus 19:10
247. To leave the forgotten sheaves in the field. Deuteronomy 24:19
248. Not to retrieve them. Deuteronomy 24:19
249. To separate the "tithe for the poor". Deuteronomy 14:28
250. To give charity. Deuteronomy 15:8
251. Not to withhold charity from the poor. Deuteronomy 15:7
252. To set aside *Terumah* (heave offering) *Gedolah* (gift for the *Kohen*). Deuteronomy 18:4
253. The Levite must set aside a tenth of his tithe. Numbers 18:26
254. Not to preface one tithe to the next, but separate them in their proper order. Exodus 22:28
255. A non–*Kohen* must not eat *Terumah*. Leviticus 22:10
256. A hired worker or a Jewish bondsman of a *Kohen* must not eat *Terumah*. Leviticus 22:10
257. An uncircumcised *Kohen* must not eat *Terumah*. Exodus 12:48
258. An impure *Kohen* must not eat *Terumah*. Leviticus 22:4
259. A *chalalah* (party to #s 169–172 above) must not eat *Terumah*. Leviticus 22:12
260. To set aside *Ma'aser* (tithe) each planting year and give it to a Levite. Numbers 18:24
261. To set aside the second tithe (*Ma'aser Sheni*). Deuteronomy 14:22
262. Not to spend its redemption money on anything but food, drink, or ointment. Deuteronomy 26:14
263. Not to eat *Ma'aser Sheni* while impure. Deuteronomy 26:14

264. A mourner on the first day after death must not eat *Ma'aser Sheni*. Deuteronomy 26:14
265. Not to eat *Ma'aser Sheni* grains outside Jerusalem. Deuteronomy 12:17
266. Not to eat *Ma'aser Sheni* wine products outside Jerusalem. Deuteronomy 12:17
267. Not to eat *Ma'aser Sheni* oil outside Jerusalem. Deuteronomy 12:17
268. The fourth year crops must be totally for holy purposes like *Ma'aser Sheni*. Leviticus 19:24
269. To read the confession of tithes every fourth and seventh year. Deuteronomy 26:13
270. To set aside the first fruits and bring them to the Temple. Exodus 23:19
271. The *Kohanim* must not eat the first fruits outside Jerusalem. Deuteronomy 12:17
272. To read the Torah portion pertaining to their presentation. Deuteronomy 26:5
273. To set aside a portion of dough for a *Kohen*. Numbers 15:20
274. To give the foreleg, two cheeks, and abomasum of slaughtered animals to a *Kohen*. Deuteronomy 18:3
275. To give the first shearing of sheep to a *Kohen*. Deuteronomy 18:4
276. To redeem firstborn sons and give the money to a *Kohen*. Numbers 18:15
277. To redeem the firstborn donkey by giving a lamb to a *Kohen*. Exodus 13:13
278. To break the neck of the donkey if the owner does not intend to redeem it. Exodus 13:13
279. To rest the land during the seventh year by not doing any work which enhances growth. Exodus 34:21
280. Not to work the land during the seventh year. Leviticus 25:4
281. Not to work with trees to produce fruit during that year. Leviticus 25:4
282. Not to reap crops that grow wild that year in the normal manner. Leviticus 25:5

283. Not to gather grapes which grow wild that year in the normal way. Leviticus 25:5

284. To leave free all produce which grew in that year. Exodus 23:11

285. To release all loans during the seventh year. Deuteronomy 15:2

286. Not to pressure or claim from the borrower. Deuteronomy 15:2

287. Not to refrain from lending immediately before the release of the loans for fear of monetary loss. Deuteronomy 15:9

288. The Sanhedrin must count seven groups of seven years. Leviticus 25:8

289. The Sanhedrin must sanctify the fiftieth year. Leviticus 25:10

290. To blow the *Shofar* on the tenth of Tishrei to free the slaves. Leviticus 25:9

291. Not to work the soil during the fiftieth year (Jubilee). Leviticus 25:11

292. Not to reap in the normal manner that which grows wild in the fiftieth year. Leviticus 25:11

293. Not to pick grapes which grew wild in the normal manner in the fiftieth year. Leviticus 25:11

294. Carry out the laws of sold family properties. Leviticus 25:24

295. Not to sell the land in Israel indefinitely. Leviticus 25:23

296. Carry out the laws of houses in walled cities. Leviticus 25:29

297. The Tribe of Levi must not be given a portion of the land in Israel, rather they are given cities to dwell in. Deuteronomy 18:1

298. The Levites must not take a share in the spoils of war. Deuteronomy 18:1

299. To give the Levites cities to inhabit and their surrounding fields. Numbers 35:2

300. Not to sell the fields but they shall remain the Levites' before and after the Jubilee year. Leviticus 25:34

301. To build a Temple. Exodus 25:8

302. Not to build the altar with stones hewn by metal. Exodus 20:24

303. Not to climb steps to the altar. Exodus 20:27

304. To show reverence to the Temple. Leviticus 19:30

305. To guard the Temple area. Numbers 18:2

306. Not to leave the Temple unguarded. Numbers 18:5

307. To prepare the anointing oil. Exodus 30:31

308. Not to reproduce the anointing oil. Exodus 30:32
309. Not to anoint with anointing oil. Exodus 30:32
310. Not to reproduce the incense formula. Exodus 30:37
311. Not to burn anything on the Golden Altar besides incense. Exodus 30:9
312. The Levites must transport the ark on their shoulders. Numbers 7:9
313. Not to remove the staves from the ark. Exodus 25:15
314. The Levites must work in the Temple. Numbers 18:23
315. No Levite must do another's work of either a *Kohen* or a Levite. Numbers 18:3
316. To dedicate the *Kohen* for service. Leviticus 21:8
317. The work of the *Kohanim*'s shifts must be equal during holidays. Deuteronomy 18:6–8
318. The *Kohanim* must wear their priestly garments during service. Exodus 28:2
319. Not to tear the priestly garments. Exodus 28:32
320. The *Kohen Gadol* 's (High Priest) breastplate must not be loosened from the *Efod*. Exodus 28:28
321. A *Kohen* must not enter the Temple intoxicated. Leviticus 10:9
322. A *Kohen* must not enter the Temple with his head uncovered. Leviticus 10:6
323. A *Kohen* must not enter the Temple with torn clothes. Leviticus 10:6
324. A *Kohen* must not enter the Temple indiscriminately. Leviticus 16:2
325. A *Kohen* must not leave the Temple during service. Leviticus 10:7
326. To send the impure from the Temple. Numbers 5:2
327. Impure people must not enter the Temple. Numbers 5:3
328. Impure people must not enter the Temple Mount area. Deuteronomy 23:11
329. Impure *Kohanim* must not do service in the temple. Leviticus 22:2
330. An impure *Kohen*, following immersion, must wait until after sundown before returning to service. Leviticus 22:7
331. A *Kohen* must wash his hands and feet before service. Exodus 30:19
332. A *Kohen* with a physical blemish must not enter the sanctuary or approach the altar. Leviticus 21:23

333. A *Kohen* with a physical blemish must not serve. Leviticus 21:17
334. A *Kohen* with a temporary blemish must not serve. Leviticus 21:17
335. One who is not a *Kohen* must not serve. Numbers 18:4
336. To offer only unblemished animals. Leviticus 22:21
337. Not to dedicate a blemished animal for the altar. Leviticus 22:20
338. Not to slaughter it. Leviticus 22:22
339. Not to sprinkle its blood. Leviticus 22:24
340. Not to burn its fat. Leviticus 22:22
341. Not to offer a temporarily blemished animal. Deuteronomy 17:1
342. Not to sacrifice blemished animals even if offered by non–Jews. Leviticus 22:25
343. Not to inflict wounds upon dedicated animals. Leviticus 22:21
344. To redeem dedicated animals which have become disqualified. Deuteronomy 12:15
345. To offer only animals which are at least eight days old. Leviticus 22:27
346. Not to offer animals bought with the wages of a harlot or the animal exchanged for a dog. Some interpret "exchange for a dog" as referring to wage of a male prostitute.[9][10]. Deuteronomy 23:19
347. Not to burn honey or yeast on the altar. Leviticus 2:11
348. To salt all sacrifices. Leviticus 2:13
349. Not to omit the salt from sacrifices. Leviticus 2:13
350. Carry out the procedure of the burnt offering as prescribed in the Torah. Leviticus 1:3
351. Not to eat its meat. Deuteronomy 12:17
352. Carry out the procedure of the sin offering. Leviticus 6:18
353. Not to eat the meat of the inner sin offering. Leviticus 6:23
354. Not to decapitate a fowl brought as a sin offering. Leviticus 5:8
355. Carry out the procedure of the guilt offering. Leviticus 7:1
356. The *Kohanim* must eat the sacrificial meat in the Temple. Exodus 29:33
357. The *Kohanim* must not eat the meat outside the Temple courtyard. Deuteronomy 12:17
358. A non–*Kohen* must not eat sacrificial meat. Exodus 29:33
359. To follow the procedure of the peace offering. Leviticus 7:11
360. Not to eat the meat of minor sacrifices before sprinkling the blood. Deuteronomy 12:17

361. To bring meal offerings as prescribed in the Torah. Leviticus 2:1
362. Not to put oil on the meal offerings of wrongdoers. Leviticus 5:11
363. Not to put frankincense on the meal offerings of wrongdoers. Leviticus 3:11
364. Not to eat the meal offering of the High Priest. Leviticus 6:16
365. Not to bake a meal offering as leavened bread. Leviticus 6:10
366. The Kohanim must eat the remains of the meal offerings. Leviticus 6:9
367. To bring all avowed and freewill offerings to the Temple on the first subsequent festival. Deuteronomy 12:5–6
368. Not to withhold payment incurred by any vow. Deuteronomy 23:22
369. To offer all sacrifices in the Temple. Deuteronomy 12:11
370. To bring all sacrifices from outside Israel to the Temple. Deuteronomy 12:26
371. Not to slaughter sacrifices outside the courtyard. Leviticus 17:4
372. Not to offer any sacrifices outside the courtyard. Deuteronomy 12:13
373. To offer two lambs every day. Numbers 28:3
374. To light a fire on the altar every day. Leviticus 6:6
375. Not to extinguish this fire. Leviticus 6:6
376. To remove the ashes from the altar every day. Leviticus 6:3
377. To burn incense every day. Exodus 30:7
378. To light the Menorah every day. Exodus 27:21
379. The *Kohen Gadol* must bring a meal offering every day. Leviticus 6:13
380. To bring two additional lambs as burnt offerings on Shabbat. Numbers 28:9
381. To make the show bread. Exodus 25:30
382. To bring additional offerings on Rosh Chodesh ("The New Month"). Numbers 28:11
383. To bring additional offerings on Passover. Numbers 28:19
384. To offer the wave offering from the meal of the new wheat. Leviticus 23:10
385. Each man must count the Omer – seven weeks from the day the new wheat offering was brought. Leviticus 23:15
386. To bring additional offerings on Shavuot. Numbers 28:26
387. To bring two leaves to accompany the above sacrifice. Leviticus 23:17

388. To bring additional offerings on Rosh HaShanah. Numbers 29:2

389. To bring additional offerings on Yom Kippur. Numbers 29:8

390. To bring additional offerings on Sukkot. Numbers 29:13

391. To bring additional offerings on Shemini Atzeret. Numbers 29:35

392. Not to eat sacrifices which have become unfit or blemished. Deuteronomy 14:3

393. Not to eat from sacrifices offered with improper intentions. Leviticus 7:18

394. Not to leave sacrifices past the time allowed for eating them. Leviticus 22:30

395. Not to eat from that which was left over. Leviticus 19:8

396. Not to eat from sacrifices which became impure. Leviticus 7:19

397. An impure person must not eat from sacrifices. Leviticus 7:20

398. To burn the leftover sacrifices. Leviticus 7:17

399. To burn all impure sacrifices. Leviticus 7:19

400. To follow the procedure of Yom Kippur in the sequence prescribed in Parashah *Acharei Mot* ("After the death of Aaron's sons..."). Leviticus 16:3

401. One who profaned property must repay what he profaned plus a fifth and bring a sacrifice. Leviticus 5:16

402. Not to work consecrated animals. Deuteronomy 15:19

403. Not to shear the fleece of consecrated animals. Deuteronomy 15:19

404. To slaughter the paschal sacrifice at the specified time. Exodus 12:6

405. Not to slaughter it while in possession of leaven. Exodus 23:18

406. Not to leave the fat overnight. Exodus 23:18

407. To slaughter the second Paschal Lamb. Numbers 9:11

408. To eat the Paschal Lamb with matzah and maror on the night of the fourteenth of Nissan. Exodus 12:8

409. To eat the second Paschal Lamb on the night of the 15th of Iyar. Numbers 9:11

410. Not to eat the paschal meat raw or boiled. Exodus 12:9

411. Not to take the paschal meat from the confines of the group. Exodus 12:46

412. An apostate must not eat from it. Exodus 12:43

413. A permanent or temporary hired worker must not eat from it. Exodus 12:45

414. An uncircumcised male must not eat from it. Exodus 12:48
415. Not to break any bones from the paschal offering. Exodus 12:46 Ps. 34:20
416. Not to break any bones from the second paschal offering. Numbers 9:12
417. Not to leave any meat from the paschal offering over until morning. Exodus 12:10
418. Not to leave the second paschal meat over until morning. Numbers 9:12
419. Not to leave the meat of the holiday offering of the 14th until the 16th. Deuteronomy 16:4
420. To be seen at the Temple on Passover, Shavuot, and Sukkot. Deuteronomy 16:16
421. To celebrate on these three Festivals (bring a peace offering). Exodus 23:14
422. To rejoice on these three Festivals (bring a peace offering). Deuteronomy 16:14
423. Not to appear at the Temple without offerings. Deuteronomy 16:16
424. Not to refrain from rejoicing with, and giving gifts to, the Levites. Deuteronomy 12:19
425. To assemble all the people on the Sukkot following the seventh year. Deuteronomy 31:12
426. To set aside the firstborn animals. Exodus 13:12
427. The Kohanim must not eat unblemished firstborn animals outside Jerusalem. Deuteronomy 12:17
428. Not to redeem the firstborn. Numbers 18:17
429. Separate the tithe from animals. Leviticus 27:32
430. Not to redeem the tithe. Leviticus 27:33
431. Every person must bring a sin offering (in the temple) for his transgression. Leviticus 4:27
432. Bring an *asham talui* (temple offering) when uncertain of guilt. Leviticus 5:17–18
433. Bring an *asham vadai* (temple offering) when guilt is ascertained. Leviticus 5:25
434. Bring an *oleh v'yored* (temple offering)(if the person is wealthy, an animal; if poor, a bird or meal offering). Leviticus 5:7–11

435. The Sanhedrin must bring an offering (in the Temple) when it rules in error. Leviticus 4:13

436. A woman who had a running (vaginal) issue must bring an offering (in the Temple) after she goes to the Mikveh. Leviticus 15:28–29

437. A woman who gave birth must bring an offering (in the Temple) after she goes to the Mikveh. Leviticus 12:6

438. A man who had a running (unnatural urinary) issue must bring an offering (in the Temple) after he goes to the Mikveh. Leviticus 15:13–14

439. A metzora (one having a skin disease) (this is not leprosy) must bring an offering (in the Temple) after going to the Mikveh. Leviticus 14:10

440. Not to substitute another beast for one set apart for sacrifice. Leviticus 27:10

441. The new animal, in addition to the substituted one, retains consecration. Leviticus 27:10

442. Not to change consecrated animals from one type of offering to another. Leviticus 27:26

443. Carry out the laws of impurity of the dead. Numbers 19:14

444. Carry out the procedure of the Red Heifer (*Para Aduma*). Numbers 19:2

445. Carry out the laws of the sprinkling water. Numbers 19:21

446. Rule the laws of human tzara'at as prescribed in the Torah. Leviticus 13:12

447. The metzora must not remove his signs of impurity. Deuteronomy 24:8

448. The metzora must not shave signs of impurity in his hair. Leviticus 13:33

449. The metzora must publicize his condition by tearing his garments, allowing his hair to grow and covering his lips. Leviticus 13:45

450. Carry out the prescribed rules for purifying the *metzora*. Leviticus 14:2

451. The metzora must shave off all his hair prior to purification. Leviticus 14:9

452. Carry out the laws of tzara'at of clothing. Leviticus 13:47

453. Carry out the laws of *tzara'at* of houses. Leviticus 13:34

454. Observe the laws of menstrual impurity. Leviticus 15:19
455. Observe the laws of impurity caused by childbirth. Leviticus 12:2
456. Observe the laws of impurity caused by a woman's running issue. Leviticus 15:25
457. Observe the laws of impurity caused by a man's running issue (irregular ejaculation of infected semen). Leviticus 15:3
458. Observe the laws of impurity caused by a dead beast. Leviticus 11:39
459. Observe the laws of impurity caused by the eight shratzim (insects). Leviticus 11:29
460. Observe the laws of impurity of a seminal emission (regular ejaculation, with normal semen). Leviticus 15:16
461. Observe the laws of impurity concerning liquid and solid foods. Leviticus 11:34
462. Every impure person must immerse himself in a Mikveh to become pure. Leviticus 15:16
463. The court must judge the damages incurred by a goring ox. Exodus 21:28
464. The court must judge the damages incurred by an animal eating. Exodus 22:4
465. The court must judge the damages incurred by a pit. Exodus 21:33
466. The court must judge the damages incurred by fire. Exodus 22:5
467. Not to steal money stealthily. Leviticus 19:11
468. The court must implement punitive measures against the thief. Exodus 21:37
469. Each individual must ensure that his scales and weights are accurate. Leviticus 19:36
470. Not to commit injustice with scales and weights. Leviticus 19:35
471. Not to possess inaccurate scales and weights even if they are not for use. Deuteronomy 25:13
472. Not to move a boundary marker to steal someone's property. Deuteronomy 19:14
473. Not to kidnap. Exodus 20:14
474. Not to rob openly. Leviticus 19:13
475. Not to withhold wages or fail to repay a debt. Leviticus 19:13
476. Not to covet and scheme to acquire another's possession. Exodus 20:15

477. Not to desire another's possession. Deuteronomy 5:19
478. Return the robbed object or its value. Leviticus 5:23
479. Not to ignore a lost object. Deuteronomy 22:3
480. Return the lost object. Deuteronomy 22:1
481. The court must implement laws against the one who assaults another or damages another's property. Exodus 21:18
482. Not to murder. Exodus 20:13
483. Not to accept monetary restitution to atone for the murderer. Numbers 35:31
484. The court must send the accidental murderer to a city of refuge. Numbers 35:25
485. Not to accept monetary restitution instead of being sent to a city of refuge. Numbers 35:32
486. Not to kill the murderer before he stands trial. Numbers 35:12
487. Save someone being pursued even by taking the life of the pursuer. Deuteronomy 25:12
488. Not to pity the pursuer. Numbers 35:12
489. Not to stand idly by if someone's life is in danger. Leviticus 19:16
490. Designate cities of refuge and prepare routes of access. Deuteronomy 19:3
491. Break the neck of a calf by the river valley following an unsolved murder. Deuteronomy 21:4
492. Not to work nor plant that river valley. Deuteronomy 21:4
493. Not to allow pitfalls and obstacles to remain on your property. Deuteronomy 22:8
494. Make a guard rail around flat roofs. Deuteronomy 22:8
495. Not to put a stumbling-block before a blind man (nor give harmful advice). Leviticus 19:14
496. Help another remove the load from a beast which can no longer carry it. Exodus 23:5
497. Help others load their beast. Deuteronomy 22:4
498. Not to leave others distraught with their burdens (but to help either load or unload). Deuteronomy 22:4
499. Conduct sales according to Torah law. Leviticus 25:14
500. Not to overcharge or underpay for an article. Leviticus 25:14
501. Not to insult or harm anybody with words. Leviticus 25:17

502. Not to cheat a convert monetarily. Exodus 22:20
503. Not to insult or harm a convert with words. Exodus 22:20
504. Purchase a Hebrew slave in accordance with the prescribed laws. Exodus 21:2
505. Not to sell him as a slave is sold. Leviticus 25:42
506. Not to work him oppressively. Leviticus 25:43
507. Not to allow a non–Jew to work him oppressively. Leviticus 25:53
508. Not to have him do menial slave labor. Leviticus 25:39
509. Give him gifts when he goes free. Deuteronomy 15:14
510. Not to send him away empty–handed. Deuteronomy 15:13
511. Redeem Jewish maidservants. Exodus 21:8
512. Betroth the Jewish maidservant. Exodus 21:8
513. The master must not sell his maidservant. Exodus 21:8
514. Canaanite slaves must work forever unless injured in one of their limbs. Leviticus 25:46
515. Not to extradite a slave who fled to (biblical) Israel. Deuteronomy 23:16
516. Not to wrong a slave who has come to Israel for refuge. Deuteronomy 23:16
517. The courts must carry out the laws of a hired worker and hired guard. Exodus 22:9
518. Pay wages on the day they were earned. Deuteronomy 24:15
519. Not to delay payment of wages past the agreed time. Leviticus 19:13
520. The hired worker may eat from the unharvested crops where he works. Deuteronomy 23:25
521. The worker must not eat while on hired time. Deuteronomy 23:26
522. The worker must not take more than he can eat. Deuteronomy 23:25
523. Not to muzzle an ox while plowing. Deuteronomy 25:4
524. The courts must carry out the laws of a borrower. Exodus 22:13
525. The courts must carry out the laws of an unpaid guard. Exodus 22:6
526. Lend to the poor and destitute. Exodus 22:24
527. Not to press them for payment if you know they don't have it. Exodus 22:24

528. Press the idolater for payment. Deuteronomy 15:3
529. The creditor must not forcibly take collateral. Deuteronomy 24:10
530. Return the collateral to the debtor when needed. Deuteronomy 24:13
531. Not to delay its return when needed. Deuteronomy 24:12
532. Not to demand collateral from a widow. Deuteronomy 24:17
533. Not to demand as collateral utensils needed for preparing food. Deuteronomy 24:6
534. Not to lend with interest. Leviticus 25:37
535. Not to borrow with interest. Deuteronomy 23:20
536. Not to intermediate in an interest loan, guarantee, witness, or write the promissory note. Exodus 22:24
537. Lend to and borrow from idolaters with interest. Deuteronomy 23:21
538. The courts must carry out the laws of the plaintiff, admitter, or denier. Exodus 22:8
539. Carry out the laws of the order of inheritance. Numbers 27:8
540. Appoint judges. Deuteronomy 16:18
541. Not to appoint judges who are not familiar with judicial procedure. Deuteronomy 1:17
542. Decide by majority in case of disagreement. Exodus 23:2
543. The court must not execute through a majority of one; at least a majority of two is required. Exodus 23:2
544. A judge who presented an acquittal plea must not present an argument for conviction in capital cases. Deuteronomy 23:2
545. The courts must carry out the death penalty of stoning. Deuteronomy 22:24
546. The courts must carry out the death penalty of burning. Leviticus 20:14
547. The courts must carry out the death penalty of the sword. Exodus 21:20
548. The courts must carry out the death penalty of strangulation. Leviticus 20:10
549. The courts must hang those stoned for blasphemy or idolatry. Deuteronomy 21:22
550. Bury the executed on the day they are killed. Deuteronomy 21:23
551. Not to delay burial overnight. Deuteronomy 21:23

552. The court must not let the sorcerer live. Exodus 22:17
553. The court must give lashes to the wrongdoer. Deuteronomy 25:2
554. The court must not exceed the prescribed number of lashes. Deuteronomy 25:3
555. The court must not kill anybody on circumstantial evidence. Exodus 23:7
556. The court must not punish anybody who was forced to do a crime. Deuteronomy 22:26
557. A judge must not pity the murderer or assaulter at the trial. Deuteronomy 19:13
558. A judge must not have mercy on the poor man at the trial. Leviticus 19:15
559. A judge must not respect the great man at the trial. Leviticus 19:15
560. A judge must not decide unjustly the case of the habitual transgressor. Exodus 23:6
561. A judge must not pervert justice. Leviticus 19:15
562. A judge must not pervert a case involving a convert or orphan. Deuteronomy 24:17
563. Judge righteously. Leviticus 19:15
564. The judge must not fear a violent man in judgment. Deuteronomy 1:17
565. Judges must not accept bribes. Exodus 23:8
566. Judges must not accept testimony unless both parties are present. Exodus 23:1
567. Not to curse judges. Exodus 22:27
568. Not to curse the head of state or leader of the Sanhedrin. Exodus 22:27
569. Not to curse any upstanding Jew. Leviticus 19:14
570. Anybody who knows evidence must testify in court. Leviticus 5:1
571. Carefully interrogate the witness. Deuteronomy 13:15
572. A witness must not serve as a judge in capital crimes. Deuteronomy 19:17
573. Not to accept testimony from a lone witness. Deuteronomy 19:15
574. Transgressors must not testify. Exodus 23:1
575. Relatives of the litigants must not testify. Deuteronomy 24:16
576. Not to testify falsely. Exodus 20:14

577. Punish the false witnesses as they tried to punish the defendant. Deuteronomy 19:19
578. Act according to the ruling of the Sanhedrin. Deuteronomy 17:11
579. Not to deviate from the word of the Sanhedrin. Deuteronomy 17:11
580. Not to add to the Torah commandments or their oral explanations. Deuteronomy 13:1
581. Not to diminish from the Torah any commandments, in whole or in part. Deuteronomy 13:1
582. Not to curse your father and mother. Exodus 21:17
583. Not to strike your father and mother. Exodus 21:15
584. Respect your father or mother. Exodus 20:13
585. Fear your mother or father. Leviticus 19:3
586. Not to be a rebellious son. Deuteronomy 21:18
587. Mourn for relatives. Leviticus 10:19
588. The High Priest must not defile himself for any relative. Leviticus 21:11
589. The High Priest must not enter under the same roof as a corpse. Leviticus 21:11
590. A Kohen must not defile himself (by going to funerals or cemeteries) for anyone except relatives. Leviticus 21:1
591. Appoint a king from Israel. Deuteronomy 17:15
592. Not to appoint a foreigner. Deuteronomy 17:15
593. The king must not have too many wives. Deuteronomy 17:17
594. The king must not have too many horses. Deuteronomy 17:16
595. The king must not have too much silver and gold. Deuteronomy 17:17
596. Destroy the seven Canaanite nations. Deuteronomy 20:17
597. Not to let any of them remain alive. Deuteronomy 20:16
598. Wipe out the descendants of Amalek. Deuteronomy 25:19
599. Remember what Amalek did to the Jewish people. Deuteronomy 25:17
600. Not to forget Amalek's atrocities and ambush on our journey from Egypt in the desert. Deuteronomy 25:19
601. Not to dwell permanently in Egypt. Deuteronomy 17:16
602. Offer peace terms to the inhabitants of a city while holding siege, and treat them according to the Torah if they accept the terms. Deuteronomy 20:10

603. Not to offer peace to Ammon and Moab while besieging them. Deuteronomy 23:7
604. Not to destroy food trees even during the siege. Deuteronomy 20:19
605. Prepare latrines outside the camps. Deuteronomy 23:13
606. Prepare a shovel for each soldier to dig with. Deuteronomy 23:14
607. Appoint a priest to speak with the soldiers during the war. Deuteronomy 20:2
608. He who has taken a wife, built a new home, or planted a vineyard is given a year to rejoice with his possessions. Deuteronomy 24:5
609. Not to demand from the above any involvement, communal or military. Deuteronomy 24:5
610. Not to panic and retreat during battle. Deuteronomy 20:3
611. Keep the laws of the captive woman. Deuteronomy 21:11
612. Not to sell her into slavery. Deuteronomy 21:14
613. Not to retain her for servitude after having sexual relations with her. Deuteronomy 21:14

The Ten Commandments in the Old and New Testaments

Old Testament (Exodus 20)	New Testament
	You shall worship the Lord your God, and Him only you shall serve. (Matthew 4:10)
You shall have no other Gods before Me.	... we know that an idol is nothing in the world, and that there is no other God but one. For even if there are so-called Gods, whether in heaven or on earth (as there are many Gods and many Lords), yet for us there is ONE GOD, THE FATHER... (1 Corinthians 8:4–6)
	Little children, keep yourselves from IDOLS. (1 John 5:21)
You shall not make for yourself a carved image. any likeness of anything that is in heaven above, or that is in the earth beneath, or that is in the water under the earth; you shall not bow down to them nor serve them...	Therefore, since we are the offspring of God, we ought not to think that the Divine Nature is like gold or silver or stone, something shaped by art and man's devising. (Acts 17:29)
	But the cowardly, unbelieving, abominable, murderers, sexually immoral, sorcerers, IDOLATERS, and all liars shall have their part in the lake which burns with fire and brimstone, which is the second death. (Revelation 21:8)

Old Testament	New Testament
(Exodus 20)	

You shall not take the name of the Lord your God in vain, for the Lord will not hold him guiltless who takes His name in vain.

In this manner, therefore, pray: Our Father in heaven, HALLOWED BE YOUR NAME... (Matthew 6:9)

... that the NAME OF GOD and His doctrine may not be blasphemed. (1Timothy 6:1)

... THE SABBATH was made for man, and not man for the Sabbath. Therefore the Son of Man is also Lord of the Sabbath. (Mark 2:27-28)

For He has spoken in a certain place of the seventh day in this way: And God rested on the SEVENTH DAY from all His works... For he who has entered His rest has himself also ceased from his works as God did from His. (Hebrews 4:4,10)

Remember the Sabbath day, to keep it holy. Six days you shall labor and do all your work, but the seventh day is the Sabbath of the Lord your God...

Then Paul, AS HIS CUSTOM WAS, went in to them, and for three SABBATHS reasoned with them from the Scriptures... (Acts 17:2)

Jesus said... Honor your father and your mother (Matthew 19:18-19).

Honor your father and your mother...

Children, obey your parents in the Lord, for this is right. HONOR YOUR FATHER AND MOTHER, which is the first commandment with promise... (Ephesians 6:1)

You shall not murder.

Jesus said, You shall not murder,... (Matthew 5:21, Matthew 19:18)

You shall not murder (Romans 13:9)

Old Testament (Exodus 20)	New Testament
You shall not commit adultery.	Jesus said, You shall not commit adultery. (Matthew 5:27, Matthew 19:18) You shall not commit adultery (Romans 13:9)
You shall not steal.	Jesus said...You shall not steal, (Matthew 19:18) You shall not steal (Romans 13:9)
You shall not bear false witness against your neighbor.	Jesus said... You shall not bear false witness, (Matthew 19:18) You shall not bear false witness (Romans 13:9)
You shall not covet your neighbor's house; you shall not covet your neighbor's wife, nor his male servant, nor his female servant, nor his ox, nor his donkey, nor anything that is your neighbor's.	... For I would not have known covetousness unless the law had said, YOU SHALL NOT COVET. (Romans 7:7) You shall not covet (Romans 13:9)

Written by: Richard Nickels, edited by *BibleStudy.org*

Index

Essenes 42, 44, 45
Eutychus 258, 259
Eve
    Chava 16, 83, 90

F

fences 70, 114, 132, 135, 145

G

Gileadite 76
God-fearers 29, 51, 52

H

H. Clay Trumbull 57
Hasmoneans 44
havdalah 259, 331
hedge 56, 84, 85
Herod 44, 45, 83, 85, 161, 190, 261,
    262, 263, 312
Hillel
    Grandfather of Gamliel, who
    taught Paul 107
humble 38, 67, 164, 171, 179, 180,
    231, 241
hyperbole 70, 136, 167
hyperbolic 76

I

idiom 5, 29, 87, 97, 113, 125, 158, 185,
    186, 197, 229
Idumea 45
Ithamar 44, 266

J

Jacob Neusner 40, 294
John Parson 46, 60, 95, 295
Jonas 181
Joseph Good 96, 295

K

Kinneret
    harp 198

L

Lashon hara 65
lawless 17, 18, 289, 327
lilies 98, 226, 304, 320

M

mahar 90
Marcion 8, 235
Marcion of Sinope 235
Max Anders 150, 296
mingled 91
Minnith 75
mixture 91, 331, 335, 336
Mizpeh 75
Mt. Gerizim 266

N

Nadab and Abihu 93
narrow gate 108, 230
nasi 264
Nathanael 184, 256, 323
Nicodemus 264, 265
non-retaliation 76

O

Onias 44
order 3, 8, 13, 16, 20, 21, 22, 23, 24,
    27, 28, 33, 34, 36, 37, 38, 39, 41,
    43, 46, 63, 70, 71, 95, 97, 109,
    114, 122, 150, 151, 158, 159,
    170, 193, 239, 242, 247, 256,
    273, 274, 285, 289, 290, 328,
    337, 349

P

Persia 120, 237, 278
phylacteries 145, 310, 330
pierced 157, 233
Pirke Avot 151
premeditate 182, 315

Q

Queen of Sheba 226
Qumran 42, 44

R

Rabbi Avraham Sutton 90
Rabbi Tarfon 101
Rahab 35, 127, 215
ravens 225, 226, 320
reconciled 36, 66, 162, 230, 301
remarrying 72, 73
repetitions 88, 302
Reprobates 169

S

Sam Peak 70, 296
shatnez 92
Shem 21, 63, 83
shuva
    teshuva 169
Simon of Cyrene 77
sit sheva 113
skirt 81
s'mikha
    ordination 116, 146
stingy 97, 98, 222
superscription 143, 238, 309, 314, 322
supersubstantial 90
supplications 157, 201
Sychar 266

T

tav 252, 254, 255, 256, 269
tavneet
    pattern 89, 220
Theophilus 39
Thorn Crown Journal 261
Tilapia 199
Tim Hegg 9
Titus 134, 148, 183
tzit–tzit 137

U

Uphaz 277
Uz 84

V

v'ahavta 141, 281
variableness 104
vav 39, 71, 170, 253
vegetative 92, 93, 94
venison 80
vidui 36, 37

W

Wycliffe 9

Y

Yahweh 29, 167, 194, 253, 258

Z

Zadok 44, 45